HAPPENINGS

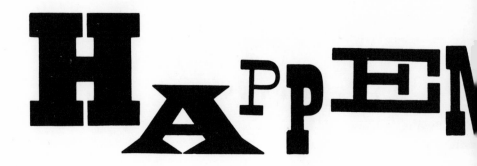

scripts and productions by JIM DINE
RED GROOMS
ALLAN KAPROW
CLAES OLDENBURG
ROBERT WHITMAN

NEW YORK / E. P. Dutton & Co., Inc.
1965

AN ILLUSTRATED ANTHOLOGY

written and edited by MICHAEL KIRBY

INDIVIDUAL COPYRIGHTS

18 Happenings in 6 Parts first appeared in Anthologist © Rutgers, The State University, 1959 / Statement, Coca Cola, Shirley Cannonball?, A Spring Happening, and The Courtyard copyright © 1965 by Allan Kaprow / Statement, and The Burning Building copyright © 1965 by Red Grooms / Statement, The American Moon, Mouth, Flower and Water copyright © 1965 by Robert Whitman / Statement and The Car Crash copyright © 1965 by James Dine / Statement, Injun, World's Fair II, Gayety and Autobodys copyright © 1965 by Claes Oldenburg

PHOTOGRAPH CREDITS

The photographs on pages 3, 45, 89, 91, 96, 99, 100, 102, 103, 111, 116, 135, 141, 144, 146, 147, 151, 153, 154, 155, 156, 157, 162, 163, 166, 168, 170, 171, 185, 194, 195, 196, 197, 198, 201, 224, 227, 228, 229, 232 and 233 are by Robert McElroy; pages 68, 80, 82 by Fred McDarrah; pages 69, 70, 79 by Scott Hyde; pages 115, 117 by Laurence Shustak; page 119 by Dena; pages 126, 129, 130, 131, 132 by Max Baker; pages 174, 181, by Michael Asher; pages 176, 178, 181 by Robert Whitman; pages 211, 212, 213, 219 by Robert Ellison; pages 247, 249, 254, 257, 259 by Steffens Leinwohl; pages 277, 279, 281, 283, 284, 286, 288 by Julian Wasser.

"Suddenly there is a sound in the
distance, as if from the sky—the
sound of a breaking harp-string,
mournfully dying away."

(stage direction from)
ANTON CHEKHOV: *The Cherry Orchard*, Act II

acknowledgments

In addition to the five artists whose work is included in this book, I would like to thank the following for helping to make the descriptions of the Happenings as accurate as possible: Lette Eisenhauer, Lucas Samaras, Pat Oldenburg, Terry Barrell, Marc Ratliff, Simone Whitman, Max Baker, and Anita Baker.

I am also grateful to Lucy Lippard for her suggestions on my Introduction and to my wife, Marj Strider, for her help and encouragement.

contents

Jim Dine

Claes Oldenburg

introduction

THERE IS A prevalent mythology about Happenings. It has been said, for example, that they are theatrical performances in which there is no script and "things just happen." It has been said that there is little or no planning, control, or purpose. It has been said that there are no rehearsals. Titillating to some, the object of easy scorn to others, provocative and mysterious to a few, these myths are widely known and believed. But they are entirely false.

It is not difficult to see why these spurious concepts developed. Myths naturally arise where facts are scarce. Those people who have actually attended even one performance of a Happening and have what might be considered firsthand information are relatively few. Individual audiences have generally been small—they have rarely exceeded one hundred and are usually close to forty or fifty. Productions have been limited to a few performances, and almost all of the artists would reject the idea of "revivals."

Many spectators attended Happenings merely as entertainment. Without concern for the work as art, they noticed only the superficial qualities. In others, the tendency to view everything in terms of traditional categories, making no allowance for significant change, made evaluation difficult. Thus, even among the limited number of people who have been able to see Happenings, a primary distortion has taken place.

Secondary distortion has occurred in the dissemination of information about Happenings. Once people have heard about Happenings, there is the problem of finding one to see. In this atmosphere where facts are scarce, any information takes on much greater significance. The name itself is striking and provocative: it seems to explain so much to someone who knows nothing about the works themselves. And, intentionally or by accident, there have been incorrect and misleading statements in newspapers and magazines. Writing about the Happenings in Oldenburg's store, for example, *The New York Times* stated that, "Mr. Oldenburg and his actors do not follow a script or rehearse." Such a statement naturally has a much wider audience than the works themselves. When a motionless nude appeared on a balcony behind the audience in a Happening at the Edinburgh Drama Festival, all other details of the work were lost in a welter of news items that mentioned only the girl. Although the peculiar, bizarre and titillating may be more worthy of space in the mass media by their own standards than are serious creative works whose originality makes them difficult or even obscure for many people, this commercial emphasis functions as an instrument of distortion.

But if Happenings are not improvisations by a group of people deciding to exhibit themselves at a party; if they are not sophisticated buffoonery designed to give a deceitful impression of profundity nor uncontrolled orgies of audience participation, what are they?

Not all of the fourteen presentations described in this book were called Happenings by their creators. The poster for *The Burning Building* called it "a play"; Whitman refers to his works as "theatre pieces," and Oldenburg uses *Ray Gun Theater.* Even Kaprow's earliest public work, from which the name originated, was not called *a* Happening but *18 Happenings in 6 Parts.* Each has attempted to defend the unique and personal qualities of his work from the destructive, leveling influences of superficial categorization and misleading comparisons, but the word "Happening" has been used long enough by a sufficient number of knowledgeable people to give it a certain validity.

All five of the artists whose Happenings are considered here know each other and each other's work, and all were associated at one time or another with the Reuben Gallery in New York. The germinal development of the Happening was in New York, and, although they have since been presented in other parts of the country and in Europe, this formative propinquity is another reason to treat these works as a formal entity.

Happenings did not develop out of clear-cut, intellectual theory about theatre and what it should or should not be. No commonly held definition of a Happening existed before the creation of these particular works. If a definition is to be arrived at now, it must be inclusive enough to take in all of these works and rigorous enough to exclude works that, although they might have a certain resemblance, are not commonly referred to as Happenings.

Although some of their advocates claim they are not, Happenings, like musicals and plays, are a form of theatre. Happenings are a new form of theatre, just as collage is a new form of visual art, and they can be created in various styles just as collages (and plays) are.

On the surface, the Happenings had certain similarities of stylistic detail in production. As can be seen from the photographs, Happenings have had in common a physical crudeness and roughness that frequently trod an uncomfortable borderline between the genuinely primitive and the merely amateurish. This was partly intentional, due to their relationship with action painting and so-called junk sculpture, and partly the inevitable result of extremely limited finances. All of the Happenings—except, of course, the later ones presented outdoors—were put on in lofts and stores, in limited spaces for limited audiences. But such similarities are not important: they do not define the essence of the work. If more money, larger spaces, or more elaborate equipment had been available, the productions would have been changed somewhat, but the defining characteristics are to be found beneath these superficialities.

All five of the artists included here are (or were) painters or sculptors. Before presenting Happenings, they had exhibited their work in art galleries. Kaprow, a professor of art history, no longer does anything but Environments and Happenings, and Whitman has only recently begun to create again in a more permanent medium. On the other hand, neither Dine, well known for his paintings, drawings and constructions, nor Grooms, who has exhibited short films as well as paintings, have presented a Happening since 1960. Only Oldenburg has worked extensively and exhibited regularly in both areas. The fact that the first Happening in New York and many succeeding ones were presented in the Reuben Gallery—sometimes on the same three- or four-week rotation schedule that is common with art galleries—serves to emphasize the fundamental connection of Happenings with painting and sculpture. Could Happenings be called a *visual* form of theatre?

Certainly they are not *exclusively* visual. Happenings contain auditory material and some have even used odor. To say that they are *primarily* visual, which is true, loses its importance when it is realized that sight has dominated much of traditional theatre. Pantomime and dance are obvious examples, but many individual directors of verbal drama have stressed, like Gordon Craig, "the priority of the eye." Nor, like the Munich Artists' Theatre of 1908 that learned from painters and sculptors how to turn a play into something resembling a bas-relief that moved, can Happenings be called "pictorial." They have rejected the proscenium stage and the conceit that everyone in the auditorium sees the same "picture." In many Happenings there is a great difference, in both amount and quality, in *what* is seen by different spectators.

But Happenings do have a nonverbal character. While words are used, they are not used in the traditional way and are seldom of primary importance. A survey of the fourteen works included here shows verbal material of several types. Actual dialogue—the traditional vocal exchange of ideas and information between performers—occurs in *Mouth*, where it cannot be understood by the audience, and in *The Courtyard*. In both cases, it is ad lib. Spoken directions and requests are part of *Injun* and *Autobodys*. In *18 Happenings in 6 Parts*, *The Burning Building*, *The Car Crash* and *Injun*, stream-of-consciousness monologues in the more-or-less traditional sense are used. Although they are repetitious and discursive, these verbal structures make use of associations and accumulative meaning in addition to affective tone. But some of the monologues in *18 Happening in 6 Parts* are merely random lists of words and phrases, sometimes chosen and arranged completely by chance methods, and an abstract "conversation" occurred in *The Burning Building* when two performers alternately uttered staccato words and phrases. Here the word structure has completely abandoned the power of syntax. It is separated from the usual progressive associations and accumulative meaning and functions as a vocal entity in which pure sound values tend to predominate.

Sound values do predominate in preverbal material—the grunts, laughter and gurglings of the firemen in *The Burning Building*, the stammering vocal fugue in *The Car Crash*, the humming in *The Courtyard*. Used quite frequently, it can most significantly be understood as verbal *effect*. Thus it obviously cannot be said that Happenings do not make any use of language. Although noise and music predominate, they are far from being pantomime. But Happenings are essentially nonverbal, especially when compared to traditional theatre whose substance is vocal exchange between characters.

Of even greater importance is the fact that Happenings have abandoned the plot or story structure that is the foundation of our traditional theatre. Gone are the clichés of exposition, development, climax and conclusion, of love and ambition, the conflicts of personality, the revelatory monologue of character. Gone are all elements needed for the presentation of a cause-and-effect plot or even the simple sequence of events that would tell a story. In their place, Happenings employ a structure that could be called insular or *compartmented*.

Traditional theatre makes use of an *information structure*. There we need information in order to understand the situation, to know who the people are, to know what is happening, or what might happen; we need information to "follow" the play, to apprehend it at all. Much of this information is visual, conveyed by the set, the lights, the expressions and movements of the actors, and much of it is contained in spoken words. This information is essentially cumulative. Although "exposition" conventionally is placed early in the play, additional information is provided by each element. But information structure also functions reflexively, explaining and clarifying material that has already been presented.

Compartmented structure is based on the arrangement and contiguity of theatrical units that are completely self-contained and hermetic. No information is passed from one discrete theatrical unit—or "compartment"—to another. The compartments may be arranged sequentially, as in *Water*, for example, or simultaneously, as in the "combinations" of *Gayety*. *18 Happenings in 6 Parts* is a clear example of both simultaneous and sequential compartmentalization: the physical structure of the three separate rooms emphasizing the isolation of units functioning at the same moment, and the six separate "parts" underline the disjunction in continuity.

This does not mean that Happenings have no structure. A three-ring circus, using both simultaneous and sequential "compartmentalization," exists as an experiential entity with its own character and overall quality. A well-arranged variety show has a unity of style and a cohesiveness that makes it *a* show. But beyond this it has been demonstrated in other fields of art that a work does not require information structure. Although each of the photographs and objects in a Rauschenberg "combine," for example, conveys information, they do not relate to each other in any logical way: they exist in simultaneous compartments. Ignoring "program music" and intellectual "explanations," a unity exists in the separate movements of a symphony even though the formal differences between them may be large.

Degree and type of compartmentalization naturally vary with different works. In *The American Moon,* the "walls" of the unit compartments may be penetrated by sensory repetitions or similarities. The use of recurrent images such as the various balls or mounds loosely covered with various layers of cloth "connect" with each other beyond the limits of the compartments in which they occur and provide their own isomorphic structuring. Although Claes Oldenburg used a primarily compartmented structure in *Injun,* for example, the elements and images within each of the compartments are poetic and evocative; their implications and allusions tend to escape the confines of the unit to interrelate on an ideational and emotional level.

It should be noted that the terms "scene," or even "hermetic scene," and "compartment" are not the same. "Scene" has primary reference to people and to place. A scene is "played" between actors and by an actor. A "French scene" begins and ends with the entrance or exit of a major character. But many units in Happenings contain only sounds or physical elements, and not performers. Frequently, although performers are in physical proximity, there is no interplay between them, and an imaginary place (such as in *Mouth*) is seldom established.

It is when we look within the compartments in this manner and study the various theatrical elements—principally the behavior of the performers themselves—that another essential characteristic of Happenings becomes clear. In traditional theatre, the performer always functions within (and creates) a matrix of time, place and character. Indeed, a brief definition of acting as we have traditionally known it might be the creation of, and operation within, this artificial, imaginary, interlocking structure. When an actor steps onstage, he brings with him an intentionally created and consciously possessed world, or matrix, and it is precisely the disparities between this manufactured reality and the spectators' reality that make the play potentially significant to the audience. This is not a question of style. Time-place-character matrices exist equally in Shakespeare, Molière and Chekhov. Nor is it equivalent to the classic "suspension of disbelief," although the matrix becomes obvious when pressure is applied to it. (This pressure can be intentional, as in *Six Characters in Search of an Author*, where we seem to be asked to *believe* that these new people onstage are not actors inside of characters but characters without actors; or unintentional, as when Bert Lahr loses his place in the confusingly similar lines of *Waiting for Godot* and, starkly out of character, confides to the audience, "I said that before.") Presentational acting and devices designed to establish the reality of the stage-as-a-stage and the play-as-a-play do not eliminate matrix. Nor do certain characters who function in the same time and place as the audience rather than that of the other roles: the Stage Manager in *Our Town*, Tom in *The Glass Menagerie*, Quentin in *After the Fall*. Even in musical comedies, which interrupt the story line with little logical justification for a song or dance in which the personality of the performer himself predominates, the relationship of mood and atmosphere to situation and plot is retained, and the emotions and ideas expressed are obviously not those of the singer or dancer himself.

Time-place matrices are frequently external to the performer. They are given tangible representation by the sets and lighting. They are described to the audience in words. Character matrices can also be external. For example, the stagehands rearranging the set of *Six Characters in Search of an Author* may be dressed like real stagehands and function like real stagehands (they may even *be* real stagehands), and yet, because of the nature of the play that provides their context, they are seen as "characters." As part of the place-time continuum of the play, which happens to include a stage and the actual time, they "play roles" without needing to "act." They cannot escape the matrix provided by the work. Even when one of the actors in *The Connection* approaches you during the intermission to ask for a handout (as he has promised to do from the stage during the first act), he is still matrixed by character. He is no longer in the physical setting of the play, and he is wearing ordinary clothes that seem disreputable but not unreal in the lobby, but neither these facts nor any amount of improvised conversation will remove him from the character-matrix that has been produced.

Since time and place may be ambiguous or eliminated completely without eliminating character (i.e., time and place both as external, physical, "environmental" factors and as elements that may be subjectively acted by a performer), role-playing becomes primary in determining matrix. By returning from the lobby too soon or sitting through the intermission of a production performed on a platform stage with no curtain to conceal the set changes, one can see the stagehands rearranging props and furniture. Although some productions might rehearse mimes or costumed bit players for these changes, most would just expect you to realize that this was not part of the play. The matrices are neither acted nor imposed by the context: the stagehands are "nonmatrixed." This is exactly what much of the "acting" in Happenings is like. It is *nonmatrixed* performing.

A great variety of nonmatrixed performances take place outside of theatre. In the classroom, at sporting events, at any number of private gatherings and public presentations there is a "performer-audience" relationship. The public speaker can function in front of an audience without creating and projecting an artificial context of personality. The athlete is functioning as himself in the same time-place as the spectators. Obviously, meaning and significance are not absent from these situations, and even symbolism can exist without a matrix—as exemplified in relogous or traditional ritual or a "ceremony" such as a bullfight. In circuses and rodeos, however, the picture becomes more complex. Here clowns who are strongly matrixed by character and situation function alternately with the nonmatrixed performances of the acrobat and the broncobuster. The distinction between matrixed and nonmatrixed behavior becomes blurred in nightclubs, among other places. The stand-up comedian, for example, may briefly assume a character for a short monologue and at other times present his real offstage personality. From the clearly nonmatrixed public speaker to the absolutely matrixed performer delivering a "routine," there is a complete continuum. Yet the concept of the nonmatrixed performer is still valid, as in the case of the football player making a tackle, the train conductor calling out stops, even the construction worker with his audience of sidewalk supervisors. A difference of opinion has traditionally existed between the "monists" such as Stanislavski, who felt that the performer should be unseen within his character, and "dualists" such as Vakhtanghov and Brecht, who felt that the performer should be perceived simultaneously with the character so that the one could comment on the other. Now a new category exists in drama, making no use of time, place, or character and no use of the performer's comments.

Let us compare a performer sweeping in a Happening and a performer sweeping in traditional theatre. The performer in the Happening merely carries out a task. The actor in the traditional play or musical might add character detail: lethargy, vigor, precision, carelessness. He might act "place": a freezing garret, the deck of a rolling ship, a windy patio. He might convey aspects of the imaginary time situation: how long the character has been sweeping, whether it is early or late. (Even if the traditional performer had only a bit part and was not required to be concerned with these things, he would be externally matrixed by the set and lights and by the information structure.)

If a nonmatrixed performer in a Happening does not have to function in an imaginary time and place created primarily in his own mind, if he does not have to respond to often-imaginary stimuli in terms of an alien and artificial personality, if he is not expected either to project the subrational and unconscious elements in the character he is playing or to inflect and color the ideas implicit in his words and actions, what is required of him? Only the execution of a generally simple and undemanding act. He walks with boxes on his feet, rides a bicycle, empties a suspended bucket of milk on his head. If the action is to sweep, it does not matter whether the performer begins over there and sweeps around here or begins here and works over there. Variations and differences simply do not matter—within, of course, the limits of the particular action and omitting additional action. The choices are up to him, but he does not work to create anything. The creation was done by the artist when he formulated the idea of the action. The performer merely embodies and makes concrete the idea.

Nonmatrixed performing does not eliminate the factor of ability, however. Although the walking section of *Autobodys*, for example, could be performed by almost anyone, the prone hopping of *The American Moon* would be difficult or impossible for many people to do well.

Nor is all performing in Happenings nonmatrixed. Character and interpretation have sometimes been important and traditional acting ability has been required. This was especially true in Oldenburg's productions at his store when he employed a "stock company" of himself, his wife Pat, and Lucas Samaras in every performance. On the other hand, Whitman, in an attempt to prevent "interpretation," prefers not to explain "meanings" to his performers.

Although entrances and exits may occasionally be closely cued, the performer's activities are very seldom controlled as precisely as they are in the traditional theatre, and he generally has a comparatively high degree of freedom. It is this freedom that has given Happenings the reputation of being improvised. "Improvised" means "composed or performed on the spur of the moment without preparation," and it should be obvious that this definition would not fit the Happening as an artistic whole. Its composition and performance are always prepared. The few Happenings that had no rehearsal were intentionally composed of such simple elements that individual performers would have no difficulty in carrying them out, and in many of the works the creators themselves took the major roles.

Nor would it be accurate or precise to say that even the small units or details of Happenings are improvised. For one thing, the word already has specific references—primarily to the *Commedia dell'Arte,* various actor-training techniques connected with the Stanislavski method, and certain "improvisational theatres" (such as Second City and The Premise)—which have no significant relationship to the freedom of the performer in Happenings. All of these uses of improvisation are concerned with accurate and successful functioning within the traditional matrices. In both *Commedia dell'Arte* and improvisational theatre, character, time and place are given: details within, and in terms of, the matrix are invented. Although Stanislavski's techniques are diverse enough to find use in ordinary nonmatrixed behavior, the actual application in countless acting classes and study groups is on the specific control of various aspects of personality and of imaginary time-place orientation. Secondly, in improvisational theatre and in jazz improvisation, one performer reacts to and adjusts his own work to that of another. There is a constant qualitative crisis of choice. But in Happenings, there is no momentary challenge. One performer reacts only functionally, and not esthetically or creatively, to the actions of another. If involved in a movement pattern, for example, he may get out of another's way or fall down if bumped by him, but he does not consciously adjust the qualities of his movement in order to fuse it visually with that of the other performers. The action in Happenings is often *indeterminate* but not improvised.

Even the most rigid acting technique will show variation from performance to performance if measured carefully, but these small differences are overlooked as presenting no artistic problem. Because of indeterminacy, the differences in detail are greater between two successive performances of a Happening than between two successive performances of a traditional play, but, again, these variations are not significant. (This does not mean that one performance of a Happening cannot be much better than another, but, just as in traditional theatre, this entails discussion of essential performance qualities rather than technique and method.)

Thus in many Happenings the "acting" tends to exist on the same level as the physical aspects of the production. While allowing for his unique qualities, the performer frequently is treated in the same fashion as a prop or a stage effect. When there is no need for continuity of character or statement of personality, the same performer will appear many times, carrying out a variety of tasks. As the individual creativity and technical subtlety of the human operation decreases, the importance of the inanimate "actor" increases. Occasional compartments in Happenings contain nothing but performers; more frequently they work with props, and the balance between the human and the mechanical varies with each work and each artist. But there are numerous examples of entire compartments dominated by physical effects: the balloon in *The American Moon*, the sound passages in A *Spring Happening*, the cars and concrete mixer in *Autobodys*. Performers become things and things become performers. The frequently used shadow sequence perfectly symbolizes this blending of person into thing, this animation and vitalization of the object. From this point of view, Happenings might simply be called a "theatre of effect."

Functioning in terms of an information structure, the elements in traditional theatre are used in either logical or, as in the

Theatre of the Absurd, illogical ways. It can be seen that the elements of a Happening have an *alogical* function. This does not mean that either structure or detail does not have an intellectual clarity to the artist, but rather that any private idea structure used in creation is not transformed into a public information structure.

Abstract significance would be one possible alternative for alogical theatre. Particular colors, shapes and movements might be used in a pure manner with no relevance beyond their own special qualities and physical characteristics. Although sensory qualities are always fundamental to Happenings, there is rarely any tendency toward idealization or pure abstraction. Green is not just an optical sensation, or a circle a form without any implications or associations. The materials of Happenings—performer, physical element or mechanical effect—tend to be *concrete*. That is, they are taken from and related to the experiential world of everyday life. Within the overall context and structure, the details in Happenings relate to things (or classes of things: note the already conventional one-word titles) and function as direct experience.

This does not mean that the concrete details may not also function as symbols. They often do. But the symbols are of a private, nonrational, polyvalent character rather than intellectual. The black "mountains" in *The Courtyard*, the transvestite "cars" in *The Car Crash*, the "ball girls" in *Flower*, for example, do not have any one rational public meaning as symbols. Although they may, like everything else, be interpreted, they are intended to stir the observer on an unconscious, alogical level. These unconscious symbols compare with rational symbols only in their aura of "importance": we are aware of a significance and a "meaning," but our minds cannot discover it through the usual channels. Logical associations and unambiguous details that would help to establish a rational context are not available. There is no relevant framework of reason to which impressions may be referred.

There are two contemporary forms of theatre that might become confused with Happenings and must be considered before arriving at a definition. Chance theatre is any theatre work whose elements are derived or assembled by chance methods. For example, in *Motor Vehicle Sundown* (*Event*) (1960) by George Brecht an unspecified number of performers each uses, but does not drive, a motor vehicle; the performance directions ("Sound horn," "Strike a window with knuckles," "Pause," etc.), written on cards, are shuffled and distributed equally to each performer. Although chance structure may exist within the compartments of a Happening, the relationship of the compartments is intentional rather than fortuitous.

Events are short, uncomplicated theatre pieces with the same alogical qualities as details of Happenings. For example, Brecht places three glasses on the floor of the "playing area" and then fills them with water from a pitcher: it is his *Three Aqueous Events*. An Event is not compartmented. Formally, if not expressively, it is equivalent to a single compartment of a Happening.

Based upon the general characteristics and the specific terms that have been mentioned above, a definition can now be formulated. Happenings might be described as *a purposefully composed form of theatre in which diverse alogical elements, including nonmatrixed performing, are organized in a compartmented structure.*

This definition successfully differentiates Happenings from all other forms of theatre, but, unfortunately, it eliminates one of the works used as examples. *The Burning Building* does not fulfill the requirements of nonmatrixed performing or compartmented structure. Although the alternation of quasi-realistic movement and dance gives the superficial impression of compartmentalization, any hermetic tendency is destroyed by the fact that the same characters exist in contiguous units. Character and place are important: the "dance" of the firemen, for example, establishes their characters which in turn will heighten the sense of danger and suspense during "The Pasty Man's" search and flight. In order to be absolutely correct, it would be best to consider *The Burning Building*, as Grooms himself did, a play.

It should also be pointed out that a large portion of *The Courtyard* does not fit the definition. With the entrance of the girl, compartmentalization disappears. Character and situation exist, and even the swinging tire, extinguished light, and descending mountains become actors in a symbolic story. The earlier sections of *The Courtyard* are clearly compartmentalized, however.

Every work of art is formed in a historical context of attitudes and influences that make the work possible. No new art form springs fully grown into existence. By investigating the historical sources of Happenings it may be possible to fit Happenings into proper perspective in terms of artistic and cultural development and to clarify further the nature of Happenings themselves.

Writing in 1961, soon after the presentation of the first Happening in New York, William Seitz stated that, "Although the connection is far too dispersive to make precise, the productions known as 'happenings' . . . had their origin in painting and collage" [1] and placed the works within a detailed and authoritative analysis of "juxtaposition" in the arts. The following year Rudi Blesh and Harriet Janis also traced a historical progression from painting to Happenings.[2]

Although the latter treatment of Happenings is frequently inaccurate and generally superficial, the development documented by these writers has a certain significance.

In 1911 Boccioni used part of a wooden window frame in a piece of Futurist sculpture, and ever since 1911 or 1912 when Braque or Picasso, depending on which authority you follow, glued the first piece of real material to the canvas and originated collage, actual elements have been incorporated into painting.

The picture—transformed into "combines," assemblages or constructions which hang on the wall—moved out into the real space of the room. As an Environment the painting took over the room itself, and finally, as sort of an Environment-with-action, became a Happening. The simplicity of this theory is one of its strong points, and, if it does not completely explain Happenings, at least it does relate them intellectually to some of their most important precedents.

Kurt Schwitters, the great master of collage, almost completed the whole cycle in his own work. In about 1924, he transformed his house in Hanover, Germany, into a *Merzbau*—into an Environment or series of Environments. Called *Column* or *Cathedral of Erotic Misery*, its walls and ceilings were covered solidly with angled and protruding abstract shapes. There were recessed lights, secret sliding panels, and, in one of the cave rooms, the "blood"-splattered figure of a nude female mannequin. The house was destroyed by bombs in 1943, and the partly completed *Merzbarn* in Ambleside, England, is the only existing example of Schwitters' work on Environments, but he did not stop there.

[1] William G. Seitz, *The Art of Assemblage* (New York: The Museum of Modern Art, 1961), p. 91.

[2] Harriet Janis and Rudi Blesh, *Collage* (Philadelphia and New York: Chilton Co., 1962).

Schwitters himself was a writer and a performer. He had read his own poetry with great success (one "poem" was only the letter *W* shown to the audience on a large card and recited with continuously varied vocal dynamics). It seems natural that he thought of theatre. *Merz,* a word derived from a fragment of the word *Kommerz* which Schwitters had used in a collage, was applied by its originator to all his art, and he wrote of the "Merz composite work of art" or the Merz theatre:

In contrast to the drama or the opera, all parts of the Merz stage-work are inseparably bound up together; it cannot be written, read or listened to, it can only be produced in the theatre. Up until now, a distinction was made between stage-set, text, and score in theatrical performances. Each factor was separately enjoyed. The Merz stage knows only the fusing of all factors into a composite work. Materials for the stage-set are all solid, liquid and gaseous bodies, such as white wall, man, barbed wire entanglement, blue distance . .
. . . .
The stage-set can be conceived in approximately the same terms as a Merz picture . . . .
. . . .
Take the dentist's drill, a meat grinder, a car-truck scraper, take buses and pleasure cars, bicycles, tandems and their tires, also war-time ersatz tires and deform them. Take lights and deform them as brutally as you can. Make locomotives crash into one another, curtains and portieres make threads of spider webs dance with window frames and break whimpering glass. Explode steam boilers to make railroad mist. Take petticoats and other kindred articles, shoes and false hair, also ice skates and throw them into place where they belong, and always at the right time. For all I care, take man-traps, automatic pistols, infernal machines, the tinfish and the funnel, all of course in an artistically deformed condition. Inner tubes are highly recommended. Take in short everything from the hairnet of the high class lady to the propeller of the S.S. Leviathan, always bearing in mind the dimensions required by the work.
Even people can be used.
People can even be tied to backdrops.
People can even appear actively, even in their everyday position . . .[3]

[3] *The Dada Painters and Poets* (New York: Wittenborn, Schultz, Inc., 1951), pp. 62-63. First appeared in *Der Ararat* (Munich, 1921). By permission of Ernst Schwitters.

Schwitters might have been describing certain aspects of Happenings, and, although he never actually produced an example of Merz theatre, he apparently documents the progression from painting to collage to Environment to Happening. Since he was primarily an artist and only secondarily a poet, this would also support the relationship between Happenings and their artist-creators on the most obvious level. It is not that simple, however.

In the first place, it is based on a misunderstanding of the actual development of Happenings and of their environmental aspect. In the second place, there is a historical progression to Happenings that is basically unrelated to painting, collage or assemblage. And in the third place, the diversity of the "composite work of art," which Happenings as well as almost all theatre represent, is, by its nature, susceptible to a much wider range of influences than the collage theory allows, and the only complete explanation of Happenings lies in a total picture of all developmental factors.

Any collage theory of the development of Happenings must include a clear definition of an Environment. As applied to non-theatrical art, an Environment is usually considered to be a work of art or creation that surrounds or encloses the viewer on all sides. Thus a "found environment," such as *The Courtyard* or the house and shed in *Injun,* cannot be considered artistically equivalent to the Environment that apparently developed out of collage. The "found environment" has its own history and has even been used in traditional theatre. Eisenstein, for example, produced *Gas Masks* (1923-24), a play about a gas factory, in an actual gas factory. If the definition of Environment is strictly applied to Happenings, it can be seen that many Happenings do not make use of an Environment.

Nor are the spectators *within* an environment in all cases. Although Oldenburg's first presentation, *Snapshots from the City,* was performed in a work of art that had its own independent life as an Environment, the spectators watched it from a doorway. This is not significantly different from the viewing experience of a realistic play with an "environmental" set enclosing it on three sides. The Happenings in Oldenburg's store did not make use of expressive elements that surrounded the audience. Except for the fact that the spectators had to stand, *World's Fair II* used the same arrangement as the traditional theatre-in-the-round. A modified version of theatre-in-the-round was employed in *Coca*

Cola, Shirley Cannonball? where the two relatively small and widely separated walls created by Kaprow made no attempt to enclose the audience.

Actually the environmental factor is one aspect of an attempt in almost all Happenings to alter the audience-presentation relationship, as we have generally known it, and to use this relationship artistically. This manipulation of the physical relationship between the spectator and the theatre elements that he perceives is broader than, and includes, environmental considerations. *World's Fair II*, for example, which is not environmental, presses the spectators with cardboard panels, pokes them and hides performers behind cloth walls. It is the factor of a drive-in performance (rather than a drive-in movie) that makes *Autobodys* unique.

Whether or not the works include environmental factors, the intimacy of the audience-presentation relationship has been exploited to increase the immediacy of the theatrical material. The painters in *18 Happenings in 6 Parts* could have walked in from the control room rather than getting up from their places among the audience; the final chase in *The Burning Building* could have occurred behind the proscenium rather than almost in the laps of the spectators. These fairly conventional attempts to "get through" to the audience by "breaking the fourth wall" are certainly not from the collage tradition, and later Happenings developed more inventive and insistent methods of forcing themselves into the awareness of the spectator in ways that could not be avoided or dismissed. The roaring lawnmower pushing at the people in *A Spring Happening* and the girl crawling on the floor in *World's Fair II*, untying a spectator's shoelaces, are obvious examples.

The tendency to change the audience-presentation relationship by entirely re-creating the overall physical context of the performance is most apparent in *The American Moon* and *A Spring Happening* in which the manner of perception is controlled. At first glance these unique transformations of the viewing experience might not seem incompatible with traditional theatre. Spectators inside a tunnel similar to that of *A Spring Happening*, for example, might look out the slots to watch a play by Shakespeare or Genet. Although this might not hurt the play—theatregoers have been forced to use awkward viewing positions and angles before—it certainly would not add anything significant. But once a presentation becomes concrete, the direction of the presented elements and its distance become integral expressive elements in their own right. The content of *A Spring Happening* lies in the comparisons and contrasts that are made between right and left, loud and soft, immediate and remote. Without this particular and exact physical arrangement, the work could not exist. It would be utterly impossible to transfer it to any other physical setup. The viewing situation has become an organic part of the work itself.

These dynamic characteristics of the audience-presentation space have no necessary connection with the passive atmospheric qualities that are exploited in some works. The white decor surrounding the spectators and the action of *The Car Crash* functioned only as a constant thematic presence and did not (excluding the "help machine") operate actively in terms of the dramatic structure. Norman Bel Geddes did the same thing when he turned an entire Broadway theatre into an early Gothic cathedral for Max Reinhardt's production of *The Miracle* (which, being entirely in pantomime, was less verbal than many Happenings). The atmosphere obtained by presenting *The Courtyard* in the Greenwich Hotel or the intellectual reference of the space in *Mouth* are no more significant than the enveloping "setting" of Christopher Fry's *A Sleep of Prisoners* when, as was Fry's explicit intent, it is performed in an actual church.

Environmental factors and other attempts to expressively alter the audience-presentation relationship are so common in Happenings that they might easily be mistaken for part of the form itself. Each of the examples included here manipulates the relationship in one way or another. But Happenings presented on a stage with the traditional audience-presentation relationship (and with no environmental aspects) are still Happenings. It must be concluded that spatial arrangement and control and active contact with the spectators are matters of style rather than form.

The collage theory parallels, but does not explain, the psychological reasons why New York artists began working in theatre.

Although Kaprow himself progressed from painting and sculpture to assemblages, to Environment, and, finally, to Happenings, the esthetic possibility for Happenings had existed at least since Schwitters' time. Additional factors outside of the collage-Environment esthetic apparently were necessary.

In the late 1940's and early 1950's in New York, certain artists began to shift the emphasis in painting upon the act itself. Influenced by Surrealist theories and experiments in automatic creation, Jackson Pollock produced his famous "drip" paintings. The unpremeditated slashing brushstrokes of Willem de Kooning became the ideal of many younger artists. The painter's hand was directed by intuition and emotion, and the "happy accident" was treasured. Swirls and spatters of paint were dynamic traces of the significant gesture. Paintings became records of movement rather than merely visual compositions. "Action painting" was born. Although critical judgment operated after the fact, it could not make a painting, and the crucial moments were those when the painter was "acting" in front of the canvas.

With the success of action painting (better known as Abstract Expressionism), New York artists received attention that they did not expect and that they were not experienced at handling. America finally had an art it could brag a little about, and the artists became internationally known. Not only did their work bring increasingly higher prices, but the mass media devoted more and more time and space to art and to the men who made it. The traditional "opening" of an exhibition changed from a gathering of artists and friends into a cosmopolitan party. Within little more than a decade the artist was thrown from the relative anonymity of WPA arts projects into the celebrity spotlight. All of these internal and external factors focused attention on the artist himself and helped to create a performance mentality.

In March of 1959 *Art News* quoted "Woks," an ex-Russian abstract painter, as saying:

I believe that we are living a critical moment in the history of painting. Since Cézanne, it has become evident that, for the painter, what counts is no longer the painting but the process of creation. Tachism, or whatever you call it, has drawn the lesson. Whether you regard painting as a means of penetrating the self or the world, it is creation. When Pollock painted, his situation, his inner behavior as an artist, were certainly more complex than the painting, for he was living the process. Why should this creation be pinned down, shut up in a rectangle, hung on the wall? I believe that when an "automatist" paints, there are actually two painters in him: the one who wants to act, the other who wants to create an object. That is why the most precious goal of painting cannot be attained completely. Henceforth, the essential aim of painting must be the process of creation; the viewer must no longer be made to look at the painting alone, but the very process of making it.[4]

He went on to describe one way of achieving this goal—a hall in which spectators would watch two painters working simultaneously on opposite sides of a screen lit by spotlights. Each painter "imagines that everything is going on on his side of the screen." (Except for the limited number and type of brushstrokes in the Happening, this is almost exactly the procedure followed in *18 Happenings in 6 Parts.*)

Mathieu, the French action painter, dramatized the painting of a picture until the creation reached theatrical proportions. When he re-enacted the thirteenth-century Battle of Bouvines on canvas, he wore a costume made up of black trousers, a black silk jacket, white cross-leggings, and a white helmet that tied under his chin. Friends represented the opposing Counts of Flanders and Toulouse. The creation of the painting, which was based upon detailed historical research and executed during the same hours of the day that the battle itself was fought, was filmed. When Mathieu was invited to Japan, he appeared on television, rushing furiously up various ladders in costume to paint a huge mural. He was a tremendous popular success.

When Jim Dine exhibited constructions at the Reuben Gallery, he attended his opening in costume. Red Groom's first theatrical work was to paint a painting in front of an audience at the Sun Gallery in Provincetown in 1958. Announced as "a play" called *Fire,* the action lasted about twenty-five minutes. The finished work, in free brushstrokes, included the helmeted heads of several firemen.

The Gutai is a group of Japanese artists in Osaka under the leadership of Jiro Yoshihara. Influenced by painters such as Mathieu and well aware of contemporary directions in Western art, they expanded the means used in the action of painting. One artist tied a paintbrush to a toy tank and exhibited the marks it left on the canvas; others painted with their feet, with boxing gloves made of rags and dipped in paint, or by throwing bottles filled with paint at a canvas with rocks under it.

In 1957 the Gutai presented more formal theatre works for an audience. A large plastic bag filled with red smoke was pushed

[4] Reprinted from *Art News,* March, 1959, p. 62.

through a hole at the back of the stage and inflated. Smoke puffed out through holes in the side. Another presentation employed a large box with three transparent plastic walls and one opaque white wall. Performers inside the box dipped balls of paper into buckets of paint and threw them against the white wall, coloring the surface. Then colored water was thrown against the plastic walls that separated the spectators from the performers. (The activities of the Gutai were described in an article on the front page of the art section of *The New York Times* on Sunday, December 8, 1957, and might, therefore, have had some influence on the origins of Happenings.)

Thus it would seem that performances by artists are more closely related to the tradition of action painting than to collage-Environment. Secondly, all of the defining characteristics (and many of the stylistic ones) were in existence by 1924 when Schwitters and the collage progression produced an Environment.

It is in Dada that we find the origins of the nonmatrixed performing and compartmented structure that are so basic to Happenings. Dada was officially born with the 1916 performances at the Cabaret Voltaire in Zurich. In a small room that could seat thirty-five to fifty guests at fifteen or twenty tables, there were lectures, concerts, readings, sound poems and dances in bizarre costumes. Diverse activities were presented at the same time, and simultaneous poems were common. (Simultaneity, a concept that went back to the Futurist, Marinetti, was part of Dada theory.) Everyday life was brought onto the stage. Announcing the title of a poem, Tzara read an article from the newspaper. Although many of the performers were artists, the actual confrontation of the public was the vital focus of Dada at that time, and, in addition to the café, theatre stages in Zurich were utilized.

Under the pressure of absolute theories that applied to life rather than to a specific art, the distinction between performing and not performing began to break down for the Dadaists. Schwitters not only read his poetry to audiences, but visitors to his home in Hanover found him seated in a tree in his front yard speaking a "bird language" of pure sounds that he and Raoul Hausmann had invented.

The "found environment" was used in many Dada activities. In April, 1920, an exhibition of works by Arp, Baargeld, and Ernst was held in a small court behind a café in Cologne. It could be reached only through the public urinal. At the opening a young girl in a communion dress recited obscene poetry. (Ernst exploited spectator-presentation relationship by exhibiting a wooden object to which a hatchet was chained.)

The inclination toward the "found environment" was given impetus in April, 1921, when Breton suggested that the Dadaists meet the public in the streets rather than in the theatres and exhibition halls, and a series of "excursions and visits" was planned. Breton and Tzara lectured in the garden of the church of St. Julien-le-Pauvre, and Ribemont-Dessaignes conducted a tour, now and then reading random definitions from a dictionary, but the succeeding visits and walks—to the Louvre, the Saint-Lazare station, and the Canal de l'Ourcq, among other places—were abandoned.

In May, 1921, the Dadaists turned an exhibition of collages by Max Ernst at the Galerie Au Sans Pareil into a theatrical performance. Wearing white gloves but without ties, they walked among the visitors. Benjamin Péret and Charchoune shook hands repeatedly. Aragon miaowed. Breton chewed matches. Soupault and Tzara played hide-and-seek. A voice from the closet called out insults. Over and over, Ribemont-Dessaignes yelled, "It's raining on a skull!" while Jacques Rigaut stood at the door, loudly counting the arriving cars and the pearls of the ladies who entered the exhibition. Simultaneous presentation of nonmatrixed performances was typical of the Dadaists, but in this case they not only altered the usual spectator-presentation relationship by mixing with the guests but made use of a space not intended for theatre.

Relâche by Picabia with a score by Satie, performed at the Théâtre des Champs-Élysées in 1924, was apparently nothing more than a ballet with Dada additions. Spotlights were beamed directly into the eyes of the spectators, making it difficult to see what was taking place on the stage. Upstage, the dancers went through their movements. A naked man and woman, standing motionless in the poses of Cranach's *Adam and Eve,* were intermittently illuminated, while downstage, a man dressed as a fireman constantly poured water from one bucket to another. Man Ray, also unrelated to the dancers or the other performers, was sitting on a chair near the edge of the stage, and occasionally he would stand and walk back and forth. Not only were indeterminacy, nonmatrixed performing, and simultaneously compartmented structure used in a theatrical presentation, but the motion picture *Entr'acte*, shown between the two parts of the program, increased the traditional range of functional elements.

Unique and expressive physical relationship between the spectators and the presentation was not attempted by *Relâche*, but the composer, Erik Satie, who had also composed the partially *bruitist* score for *Parade*, had already made a striking investigation of that area in his own work. In 1920 a play by Max Jacob, a concert of music by *les Six*, and songs by Stravinsky were presented at the Barbazange gallery in Paris. An exhibition of children's paintings was held at the same time. During the intermission of the play, a trombone in the balcony and a piano and three clarinets, one in each corner of the room, played a piece by Satie. This was the introduction of *musique d'ameublement* or "furniture music," but the important point regarding the development of Happenings was the purposeful investigation of audience-performance relationship by a man who was later to be held in high regard by John Cage.

John Cage, the composer, integrated various dominant strains in the Futurist-Dada tradition into his own work. Speaking along with tape recordings of his own voice, Cage was able to give "simultaneous lectures" reminiscent of the activities in the Cabaret Voltaire. He proposed the "simultaneous presentation of unrelated events"—a theoretical position clearly derived from Dada activities. And in a single presentation at Black Mountain College in the summer of 1952 (the authoritative anthology on Dada which included, among other things, Kurt Schwitters' description of Merz theatre had been published the preceding year), he was able to combine a variety of expressive elements including indeterminate nonmatrixed performing in a compartmented structure that made use of an expressive spectator-performance relationship.

The chairs, all facing the center, were arranged in the middle of the dining hall, leaving open space between the audience and the walls of the room. Timed to the second as in a musical composition, the various performances took place in and around the audience. Cage, dressed in a black suit and tie, read a lecture on Meister Eckhart from a raised lectern at one side. (The Dadaists, similarly dressed, had solemnly declaimed from Jakob Böhme and Lao-tzu.) M. C. Richards recited from a ladder. Charles Olsen and other performers "planted" in the audience each stood up when their time came and said a line or two. David Tudor played the piano. Movies were projected on the ceiling: at first they showed the school cook, then the sun, and, as the image moved from the ceiling down the wall, the sun sank. Robert Rauschenberg operated old records on a hand-wound phonograph, and Merce Cunningham improvised a dance around the audience. A dog began to follow Cunningham and was accepted into the presentation.

John Cage's ideas have had a profound influence on all the arts. Perhaps his greatest contribution has been through his teaching, both formal and informal. From 1956 to 1958 Allan Kaprow studied with Cage at the New School in New York. The subject was music composition, but Cage saw no reason why the limits could not be stretched to include visual material as well. Kaprow composed short pieces that, in addition to using concrete sounds, contained movements and purely visual images. There is no question that much of the material and structure of *18 Happenings in 6 Parts* resulted directly from this work.

Thus a clear progression which has little to do with collage-Environment esthetics can be traced from Dada activities to the first New York Happening. But another group of artists, quite different from the Dadaists in inclination, also developed performances that were formally identical with Happenings although stylistically quite different. The German Bauhaus of the 1920's was involved with actual and theoretical work in every field of art, including theatre.[5] The artists of the Bauhaus were well aware of the Dada theatre and of Schwitters' Merz theories, but, although they endorsed the rejection of logical and "literary encumbrance," they considered these earlier approaches to be structurally and stylistically arbitrary. Their theatre was based on rationally determined "laws."

At its practical core the theatre of the Bauhaus, directed by Oskar Schlemmer, who had enlarged the scope of his sculpture workshop to include the stage, was a dance theatre. Space, form and gesture (emotional expression) were studied separately, and independent dances of each type were composed. But Schlemmer merely saw Man as Dancer (*Tänzermensch*) as the focus for

[5] See: O. Schlemmer, L. Moholy-Nagy, F. Molnar, *The Theatre of the Bauhaus* (Middletown, Conn.: Wesleyan University Press, 1961).

transition to the absolute visual stage (*Schaubühne*), and in both theory and accomplishment the theatre of the Bauhaus progressed far beyond dance.

In accordance with the basic principles of abstraction and mechanization, the Bauhaus tended to dehumanize its human performers, frequently hiding them under elaborate costumes and masks. This led, on one hand, to marionette plays such as *The Adventures of the Little Hunchback*, where the wooden "actors" were matrixed by character and place, and, on the other, to productions in which physical effects dominated the action or took it over completely. "Light plays" combined human forms, shadow effects and projection. Heinz Loew built a model for a totally mechanical stage in which various circles, columns, panels, volumes and geometric shapes could be spun, turned, raised, lowered and moved across a proscenium stage by machinery that was visible to the audience.

Laszlo Moholy-Nagy made a colorful sketch for a "score" for a "Mechanized Eccentric," a "synthesis of form, motion, sound, light (color) and odor." [6] Three stages were to be arranged more or less above each other and used simultaneously. The effects on the upper and lower stages included moving arrows, spinning discs, shifting grids, "gigantic apparatus," odors, and "mechanized men" (apparently wrestlers). Rear projection of films and moving, variable, colored lights played an important part. On the middle stage, mechanical instruments, sound effects and noisemakers would play in view of the audience.

The stage designed in 1926 by Walter Gropius for the Dessau Bauhaus was a platform located between the assembly hall and the dining room. It could be used as a proscenium stage, as it almost always was, or opened so that spectators faced it from both sides. But again theory went far beyond practice, and the artists of the Bauhaus proposed to change the spectator-presentation relationship by changing the design of the theatre itself. Gropius designed a "Total Theater" in which projection screens completely surrounded the audience. (Its construction in Berlin for Erwin Piscator was halted in 1926 by the Nazi rise to power.) Andreas Weininger designed a "Spherical Theatre" in which the audience would sit against the walls of a huge sphere and watch mechanical presentations in the central space.

[6] *Op. cit.*, p. 48.

Although the theatre of the Bauhaus had no direct influence on Happenings, and only *Coca Cola, Shirley Cannonball?* bears any resemblance to their work, a very important formative factor deriving from theatre was the publication in 1958 of an English translation of *The Theater and Its Double* by Antonin Artaud. The single spectacle that is described (*The Conquest of Mexico*) is not a Happening, but the general theory propounded in the book is almost a text for Happenings. For example, Artaud writes in *The Theater of Cruelty (First Manifesto)*:

> . . . instead of continuing to rely upon texts considered definitive and sacred, it is essential to put an end to the subjugation of the theatre to the text, and to recover the notion of a kind of unique language half-way between gesture and thought.
>
> This language cannot be defined except by its possibilities for dynamic expression in space as opposed to the expressive possibilities of spoken dialogue. And what the theater can still take over from speech are its possibilities for extension beyond words, for development in space, for dissociative and vibratory action upon the sensibility. This is the hour of intonations, of a word's particular pronunciation. Here too intervenes (besides the auditory language of sounds) the visual language of objects, movements, attitudes and gestures, but on condition that their meanings, their physiognomies, their combinations be carried to the point of becoming signs, making a kind of alphabet out of these signs. Once aware of this language in space, language of sounds, cries, lights, onomatopoeia, the theater must organize it into veritable hieroglyphs, with the help of characters and objects, and make use of their symbolism and interconnections in relation to all organs and on all levels.
>
> . . . .
> . . . .
>
> It would be meaningless to say that [this language] includes music, dance, pantomime, or mimicry. Obviously it uses movement, harmonies, rhythms, but only to the point that they can concur in a sort of central expression without advantage for any one particular art.[7]

In addition to proposing the rejection of the "supremacy of speech" and the creation of a pure theatrical language based on the *mise en scène* in which representation would be secondary to the sensory knowledge of the elements, Artaud wished to change

[7] Antonin Artaud, *The Theater and Its Double* (New York: Grove Press, Inc., 1958), pp. 89-90.

the traditional spectator-presentation relationship by placing the audience within the spectacle, and he asked for the elimination of the "duality between author and director" and the combination of both functions in a single "Creator."

Artaud, an actor-director-playwright-poet, was essentially a man of the theatre. Although his scripts make use of Surrealist dream matrices and, like Schwitters, he was never able to realize his theories in production, the impact of his thought was entirely independent from collage and construction considerations. Some Happenings are the best examples of Artaud's Theater of Cruelty that have yet been produced.

Of course there are stylistic similarities between particular Happenings and certain constructions, assemblages and Environments. Since the men who originated Happenings in New York all worked in other art forms, resemblance between their work in various forms is to be expected, but stylistic detail must not be mistaken for defining characteristics which predated the arrival of the Happening in New York.

With the consideration of the style of the New York Happenings we are faced with the relevance of many different art forms. Since theatre has duration—it exists in time—it is susceptible to influence from arts such as literature and music which have duration. Since it may make use of both visual and auditory material, it is open to influence from all other arts. If the development of Happenings is approached exclusively from the point of view of painting and sculpture, the basic relationship of theatre to all other arts is overlooked and the possibility of influence from other areas is ignored.

Several of the stylistic tendencies in Happenings can also be related to Dada and to John Cage. Methodical use of Chance method began with Dada. According to one version of the story, the movement's name itself was chosen by chance from a German-French dictionary. In 1916-17 Jean Arp made a collage of colored squares of paper arranged according to "the law of chance." (He also repeated exactly the same drawing each morning in order to illustrate the significant differences resulting from the human, technical factor in art, and, although this is not Chance method, it helps to illustrate the type of thought and is certainly pertinent to the performance techniques used in Happenings.) Marcel Duchamp dropped three threads, each exactly one meter long, onto three sheets of glass from a height of one meter. Fastening them down, he used the sinuous lines arrived at by chance (that is, gravity, etc.) to make three measuring sticks, the varying curved edges of which are each exactly one meter in length. The six pieces are called *Trois Stoppages-Etalon* or *Three Standard Needle Weavings* (1913-14). Picabia, Man Ray and others were preoccupied by chance in various forms. Tristan Tzara recited poems "composed" from the individual words on slips of paper drawn at random from a hat.

Bruitisme (or "Noise Music") was originated by Russolo, the great Italian Futurist, and explained in his 1913 manifesto *The Art of Noises*. In keeping with general Futurist beliefs, he called for a music of noise, of machines, of the industrial and commercial city, and he conducted noise concerts in Milan and London in 1914 on *Intonarumori* (or "Noise Organs") that he had constructed. The new approach to music was adopted by the Dadaists: noise by bells, rattles, cans, keys, sirens, falling objects, etc., would often accompany, and perhaps drown out, "poetry" readings in the Cabaret Voltaire. Hugo Ball, who opened the cabaret in 1916, composed a complete "concert Bruitisme" which was performed behind a white screen.

According to the theory, traditional music with its discrete notes, scales and harmonies is *abstract*. Noise, on the other hand, since it is part of everyday life and experience, is *concrete*. Sirens, motors, typewriters and other concrete elements were blended with both popular tunes and music of a more classical feeling in Erik Satie's score for *Parade*, a ballet performed in 1917 in Paris.

John Cage has accepted, enriched and promulgated both of these relatively young traditions. He has made extensive use of "noise" (and silence) in his work. He has systematically investigated and employed Chance methods—dice, the flipping of coins, random number tables, the use of imperfections in the paper to determine notes—in his compositions. Some of his pieces are indeterminate, limiting but not setting the number and type of instruments, for example, while any part or the whole may be performed. Indeterminacy and "bruitisme" are both very commonly used in Happenings.

One of the most direct influences on Happenings has been from the dance. Classical ballet was, of course, entirely matrixed in character and place. It told stories. But since its origins in Germany before the First World War, modern dance has tended to eliminate matrix. Although the *Tanzgymnastik,* or gymnastic exercises, apparently were used only for conditioning, they influenced a certain kind of thought that began to consider movement for its own sake rather than as a means of artistically conveying character information. A Hungarian, Rudolf von Laban, attempted to set down laws of movement based on everyday life. In order to study movement, he built a glass-faced icosahedron within which a person could stand and move. In Zurich during World War I the Laban-Wigman troupe, of which Sophie Taeuber was a member, danced during Dada performances.

Mary Wigman, once a pupil of Von Laban, was perhaps the most influential figure in modern dance during the early 1920's. Although she often told stories in her dances and almost always concentrated on an emotional core that turned her works into character studies, she did away with music and even rhythm as necessities in dance.

The emphasis in modern dance in general has been away from the two-dimensional picture-frame approach of classical dancing and into a dynamic three-dimensional use of space that might be related to the dominant tendency in Happenings to reject the traditional stage, but most modern dance retained a matrix. The plot turned inward and dance became a representation of subjective emotional states and stories.

Merce Cunningham, who was a soloist with Martha Graham's company from 1940 until 1945, felt that such emotional continuity was unimportant. Forming his own group in 1950 with John Cage as musical director, he created works with neither story nor consistent characters. Sometimes he organized the dance movements by chance methods in order to ensure objectivity of development. It was Cunningham who danced in Cage's "Happening" (the name would not be coined for several years yet) in 1952 at Black Mountain College.

Paul Taylor moved away even farther from accepted views of dance. One of the numbers on a program given at Rutgers University in 1957-58, for example, consisted of Taylor, alone onstage, making movements to ten-second time signals such as those heard on the telephone. A girl's voice would announce the actual time, and at each time tone Taylor, standing erect and facing the audience, would move—turn his head, raise his arm, crouch or twist, etc.—and return to the "neutral" position. The dance itself was compartmented, and a series of such relatively brief dances (in another "dance" on the program, the curtain opened and closed on motionless figures) would give the effect, if not the overall esthetic unity, of sequential compartmentalization. Kaprow and Whitman both saw this performance, and Kaprow has stated that Taylor, as well as Cage, influenced his work on *18 Happenings in 6 Parts.* James Waring and Ann Halprin, who found stimulation in many of Cage's concepts, also influenced the style of Happenings. Although Happenings as complete works cannot be confused with dances, many of them contain compartments that are basically dances or indeterminate systems of movement.

In spite of their formal indebtedness, Happenings on the whole cannot be considered to be Dadaist works. In the New York performances with which we are concerned here, Dada lost its stylistic dominance after *18 Happenings in 6 Parts.* With *The Burning Building* Surrealism, in the broadest use of the term, became the most obvious precedent. Just as there have been Surrealist paintings, sculpture, poems, novels and plays, *Injun,* for example, could be called a Surrealist Happening.

Of course the parallel may be drawn between the Surrealist device for joining disparate images in order to create a new reality (Lautréamont's famous ". . . possibility of a sewing machine and an umbrella meeting on a dissecting table") and the relationship of logically unrelated compartments in Happenings, but often the material within the compartments has also been in the Surrealist tradition.

Surrealism was concerned with dreams and the products of the unconscious. *The Burning Building* with its passage of unnaturally slow movement, its grotesque characters, its distorted shadows and frequently dim illumination had a kinship to dream. All of Oldenburg's works have contained nightmare images: it is not surprising, since for years he diligently recorded all his dreams. In dreams the scale of things may change—as it did in *Mouth,* for example. The revelation of repressed sexual material, often in symbolical ways, is a common characteristic of dreams; the symbolical or oblique treatment of sexual material, a frequent Surrealist concern, is central to many Happenings.

(Similarity in the type of images only helps to make obvious the difference between Happenings and plays, however. Dada,

Surrealist and Expressionist plays by Tzara, Ribemont-Dessaignes, Aragon, Artaud, Lorca and Kokoschka are similar in many details to some Happenings, but in the plays the dream elements and distortions always exist in a matrix. They follow a distorted continuity: time, place and character change with the fluidity of thought, but they are always present, and a continuous information structure exists. They cling to story chronology. *The Burning Building* and Oldenburg's *Injun I* (almost entirely different from the *Injun* included here) very closely resemble the dream story of Expressionist-Surrealist theatre and this sets them apart from true Happenings.)

In Happenings as in Surrealism we find a frequent blending, metamorphosis and interpenetration of the animate and the inanimate. Ernst's plants assume the forms of birds and men. Dali fuses man and object. Arp gives stone and wood vitality of organisms. The "ball girls" in Whitman's *Flower* have been transferred from the human to the botanical. A cardboard box comes alive in Kaprow's *A Spring Happening*. The men encased in burlap sacks who wrestle in Oldenburg's *Gayety* are vital but impersonal.

The Environmental aspect of Happenings also relates most directly to the Surrealist tradition. Since at least 1938, major Surrealist exhibitions have tended to become single or multiple Environments. Marcel Duchamp, who was the "generator-referee" of the 1938 exhibition at the Galerie Beaux Arts in Paris, designed a great central hall with a pool surrounded by real grass. Four large comfortable beds stood among the greenery. Twelve hundred sacks of coal hung from the ceiling. In order to illuminate the paintings which hung on the walls, Duchamp planned to use electric eyes that would switch on lights for the individual works when a beam was broken. Because of technical difficulties this project was abandoned, and flashlights were loaned to the visitors (they were all stolen, and more traditional lighting was finally employed). At the opening of the exhibition, the odor of roasting coffee filled the hall. A recording of a German army marching song was broadcast, and a girl performed a dance around the pool.

Duchamp transformed the 1942 Surrealist Exhibition, held in New York, into an Environment by crisscrossing the space with a complicated network of twine. The 1947 exhibition, which was again held in Paris, included a room where rain constantly fell onto artificial grass, and another attempt to involve the visitors failed when all of the balls were stolen from a billiard table in the room.

When a Surrealist exhibition was held in early 1960 in Paris, it was made up of several connected Environments. The first room, which had oval doorways, was lined with pink velvet. The velvet ceiling moved, and recorded sighs and murmurs could be heard. Another room was covered with green padding and there was the suggestion of stalactites and stalagmites. At the end of a narrow corridor lined with black was a black Fetish Chamber. During the opening, Surrealists enacted a homage to De Sade there, using a naked girl as a banquet table. Later, wax figures replaced the real ones.

Finally the Surrealist tradition is stylistically related to Happenings through Abstract Expressionist painting and the "combines" of Robert Rauschenberg. Abstract Expressionism was, theoretically, the purist form of Surrealist painting, although its practitioners did not consider themselves Surrealists. Influenced by Surrealist thought and practice, it was in essence the "pure psychic automatism" demanded by Breton in the *Surrealist Manifesto* of 1924. The emotional energy and spontaneous use of materials of Abstract Expressionism have been echoed in many Happenings.

Rauschenberg has been closely associated with John Cage. He designed lighting and sets for dance concerts by Merce Cunningham and Paul Taylor. Although his handling of paint in his assemblages of the late 1950's was roughly Abstract Expressionist, he also incorporated a wide variety of objects and images from everyday life into his work, creating pieces that seem to be personal journals filled with emotionally weighted statements that are not intended to have an explicit meaning or a logical clarity to the observer. This balance between private and public has also been struck in many Happenings.

Motion pictures have also had a broad and diffuse influence on Happenings. Surrealist films and those making use of hallucinatory images are more readily available than productions of Surrealist plays: *Entr'acte* by Picabia and René Clair (1924: first screened during the intermission of *Relâche*), *An Andalusian Dog* (1929) by Louis Buñuel and Salvador Dali, *The Blood of a Poet* (with its four distinct parts tending toward compartmentalization), *Beauty and the Beast* and *Orpheus* by Cocteau, *Dreams That Money Can*

Buy (1944) by Hans Richter (in six parts). But beyond questions of form, use of symbols and the character of images, some of these works had a homemade, unsophisticated technical quality. *The Cabinet of Dr. Caligari* (1919) with its crudely painted sets and grotesque makeup and *8 X 8* (1956-57) by Richter with its back-yard locations, ingenuous costumes, and cast of nonactor friends are good examples. (Arp, Ernst, Duchamp, Calder, Cocteau, Tanguy and Hülsenbeck appeared in the latter film in which eight parts continued the minor convention of dividing a Sur-realist film into sections.) This "nonprofessional" approach has often been apparent in Happenings.

The primitive quality of early films was also provocative. Red Grooms was so impressed by Georges Méliès' 1902 film, *A Trip to the Moon*, that he and Rudy Burckhardt made their own version called *Shoot the Moon* (1962). *A Trip to the Moon* handled fan-tastic material—the inhabitants of the moon, for example, are part bird, part man, and part lobster—in a style which now seems very naïve, childlike and homemade. As in his other works, Méliès wrote, designed, directed and acted in the film.

Many of the people who produced Happenings found stimula-tion in American comedy films: Chaplin, W. C. Fields, the Marx Brothers (for whom the Surrealists showed so much enthusiasm) with their deadpan fantasy, sequences of frantic activity, and emphasis on the visual. Although Oldenburg never saw the stage version of *Hellzapoppin'*, he did see the Olsen and Johnson movie.

Certain types of literature, especially poetry, also must be rec-ognized for their formative influence on Happenings. Certainly the general tendency in much modern poetry to base structure on association and implication rather than on traditional formal pat-terns and sequential logic is a precedent for Happenings. Kaprow's published script which later became the partial basis for *18 Hap-penings in 6 Parts* bears a resemblance to Mallarmé's *A Throw of the Dice Never Will Abolish Chance* (1897) in its use of various type faces and the special composition of words and word groups on the page. Oldenburg published three poems in *Exodus* (spring-summer 1960), a small review. (Behind a cover photograph of Jim Dine the issue also included correspondence between Antonin Artaud and Jacques Rivière, drawings by Red Grooms of *The Burning Building*, and drawings by Oldenburg.) In the script to *Autobodys*, the major formal sections are referred to as "poems."

Mention might also be made of the stream-of-consciousness monologue that has been used in several Happenings and of its literary tradition. But detailed analysis of stylistic detail on this level is not of primary importance. It is enough to emphasize the fact that every field of art (not just painting and sculpture) has had some formative influence on Happenings. Since the Happenings with which we are concerned here were produced by educated and perceptive men living in what, at the moment, is the greatest cultural center in the world, the use of diverse stimuli should not be surprising.

Nor is discussion of historical influence intended to minimize the important accomplishments of the men who created Happenings. For a good number of years many people have felt that theatre was not functioning at the profound esthetic level of the other arts. Over half a century ago, in 1905, Konstantin Stanislavski wrote:

> . . . realism, and (depicting) the way of life have outlived their age. The time has come to stage the unreal. Not life itself, as it occurs in reality, must be depicted, but rather life as it is vaguely perceived in fantasies and visions at moments of lofty emotion. This is the spiritual situation that must be transmitted scenically, in the way that painters of the new school use cloth, musicians of the new trend write music, and the new poets, poetry. The works of these painters, musicians, and poets have no clear outlines, definite and finished melodies, or precisely expressed ideas. The power of the new art lies in its combinations of colors, lines, musical notes, and the rhyming of words. They create general moods that carry over to the public unconsciously. They create hints that make the most unobservant person create with his own imagination.[8]

At the time he wrote, the first collage had not yet been made and the arts were beginning to move in unprecedented new directions. Stanislavski could not have guessed that painters, musicians and poets would have to make their own theatre before theatre began to approach the level of the other arts.

---

[8] Konstantin Stanislavski, *Moia zhizn' v iskusstve*, p. 501, as quoted in Nikolai A. Gerchakov, *The Theatre in Soviet Russia*, trans. by Edgar Lehrman (New York: Columbia University Press, 1957), p. 44.

HAPPENINGS

ALLAN KAPROW

a statement

(Rewritten from a recorded interview.)

IN MY SHOW AT THE Hansa Gallery in 1952 were paintings in a variety of styles, but the variety was expressive of different kinds of interests. I now realize that I was not just casting around for a way to paint, but was casting around for a way to include all the levels of meaning that I was intending. For, in addition to paintings, there were also constructions, or what we would call today "assemblages." Some were suspended on the wall, others from the ceiling.

I had begun to clarify what I felt, even then, was a multileveled attitude toward painting. When I painted pictures, they were not "pure paintings"; they were toy soldiers at war, my girl friend in one corner and myself in the other; or they were musical structures, or they were literary stories—they were everything under the sun. Hence my seemingly "abstract" pictures were anything but abstract!

Soon afterward I developed a kind of action-collage technique, following my interest in Pollock. These action-collages, unlike my constructions, were done as rapidly as possible by grasping up

44

great hunks of varied matter: tinfoil, straw, canvas, photos, newspaper, etc. I also cut up pictures which I had made previously, and these counted as autobiographical fragments, as much as they were an intended formal arrangement. The straw, the tinfoil, occasional food, whatever it was, each of these had, increasingly, a meaning that was better embodied in the various nonpainterly materials than in paint. Their placement in the ritual of my own rapid action was an acting-out of the dramas of tin soldiers, stories, and musical structures, that I once had tried to embody in paint alone.

The action-collage then became bigger, and I introduced flashing lights and thicker hunks of matter. These parts projected farther and farther from the wall and into the room, and included more and more audible elements: sounds of ringing buzzers, bells, toys, etc., until I had accumulated nearly all the sensory elements I was to work for during the following years.

The next exhibition was an extension of these single works. Now I just simply filled the whole gallery up, starting from one wall and ending with the other. When you opened the door, you found yourself in the midst of an entire Environment. I made its parts in my studio in New Jersey according to a floor plan of the gallery, and what I thought would be able to fill it properly. I then hung the parts in an overlapping planar arrangement along the dominant axis of the room. The materials were varied: sheets of plastic, crumpled-up cellophane, tangles of Scotch tape, sections of slashed and daubed enamel and pieces of colored cloth hung in bands that looked like Jewish prayer shawls or other ceremonial adornments. From any position, you could see the lights hung in the space but dimly through various layers of the materials, and every person entering the place was immediately cast in a suspended atmosphere because no one could clearly see another. The lanes, the passageways, the breaks in the planes were all small, so that you tended to move in a waving, billowing, cloud world slowly and with some difficulty. Once every hour for about fifteen minutes, five tape machines spread around the space played electronic sounds which I had composed.

But I complained immediately about the fact that there was a sense of mystery until your eye reached a wall. Then there was a dead end. At that point my disagreement with the gallery space began. I thought how much better it would be if you could just go out of doors and float an Environment into the rest of life so that such a caesura would not be there. I tried camouflaging the walls one way or another. I tried destroying the sense of bounded space with more sound than ever, played continuously. Hidden up in the lights were all kinds of toys that I had gimmicked up so that it was impossible to tell their identity: bells, tinkles, rattles, grinders, marbles in tin cans that turned over, and so on. But this was no solution, it only increased the growing discord between my work and the art gallery's space and connotations. I immediately saw that every visitor to the Environment was part of it. I had not really thought of it before. And so I gave him occupations like moving something, turning switches on—just a few things. Increasingly during 1957 and 1958, this suggested a more "scored" responsibility for that visitor. I offered him more and more to do, until there developed the Happening. My first Happenings were performed elsewhere, in lofts, stores, classrooms, gymnasiums, a friend's farm and so forth. The integration of all elements—environment, constructed sections, time, space, and people—has been my main technical problem ever since. Only now am I beginning to see results.

The name "Happening" is unfortunate. It was not intended to stand for an art form, originally. It was merely a neutral word that was part of a title of one of my projected ideas in 1958-59. It was the word which I thought would get me out of the trouble of calling it a "theatre piece," a "performance," a "game," a "total art," or whatever, that would evoke associations with known sports, theatre, and so on. But then it was taken up by other artists and the press to the point where now all over the world it is used in conversation by people unaware of me, and who do not know what a Happening is. Used in an offhand fashion, the word suggests something rather spontaneous that "just happens to happen." For example, walking down the street people will say, humorously, when they see a little dog relieving himself at a hydrant, "Oh, isn't that a Happening?" Now there is a certain natural poetry in such instances. But there is also the question of whether people are not just relating them to show that they suspect every authored Happening of being no more than a casual and indifferent event, or that, at best, it is a "performance" to release inhibitions. It is one thing to look acutely at moments that just happen in one's life. It is quite another to pay no attention to these moments ordinarily but then invoke them as evidence of the foolishness of the Happening as an art form. This hostile sense of the "Happening" is unfortunate.

In another sense it is unfortunate because the word still has those implications of light indifference which such people pick up on. It conveys not only a neutral meaning of "event" or "occurrence," but it implies something unforeseen, something casual, perhaps—unintended, undirected. And if I try to impress everyone with the fact that I really direct a Happening inside out, as most of us do, they do not believe it. They say, "It's not spontaneous? We don't do what we want to do?" I say, "No, not at all," and they say, "Well, why do you call it a Happening?" It is hard to give an answer to such questions. At one time, perhaps, I did think of something spontaneous, and I did think that maybe the spontaneous could be achieved by the greatest discipline and control—which is, ideally, the best spontaneity. This, however, is asking too much of people and so I gave up the problem. I am not interested in the spontaneous, at this moment, at all. Thus, just as Cubism may at first have caused one to look for "cubes" which weren't to be seen, so for a while we shall be stuck with the implication of Happening-as-happenstance.

In first doing Happenings, I looked for friends to perform, anybody who would help me out, and they tended to be the artists, poets, musicians that I knew. Since I knew very few actors, I did not go to them except when Julian Beck recommended a few, who immediately turned out to be useless to me because they wanted to act. They wanted to have stellar roles. They wanted to *speak* for the most part, and I utilized little verbiage in my work. And all the things which I suggested were quite contrary to their background. Even with the best of intentions, they were very self-conscious and awkward. But my other friends, who were unaccustomed to acting, were quite capable because they sensed the origins of what they were doing in painting and felt that they were almost acting out planes, spacings and images in an art form they knew. They did not have to worry about their "projectability," their verbal ability, their "onstageness," and so forth. Even the public which came to my first performance largely consisted of such people interested in the plastic arts who went along with it because in some remote way they recognized my sources, my background, and, therefore, my intentions.

After that, very quickly, it developed that I could not depend upon even those original friends, because they either went their own way and were too busy, or they decided they did not like what I was doing. The problem was, then, "How to get performers?" So, unlike Oldenburg, who very soon attracted a troop of standbys upon whom he could depend—who, like a *Commedia dell'Arte* troop, could do better and better as they went along—I, changing my work very often in different directions, and having no such troop, had to depend upon new people each time.

I found an alternative. This was to make deliberate use, simply, of what was available—the people as well as the environment. At the time, commissions from various universities, museums, and civic groups began to come my way. Traveling schedules severely limited my preparations which formerly had been done at a leisurely pace. Rehearsal time was cut by about 90 percent or more. Instead of having two or three weeks, I had maybe two hours. I thought, This is ridiculous. It's getting too hectic, and I'll never be able to go on this way. The work depends so much upon the unique site, the unique group and the unique moment that conventional preparations are self-defeating. So the next thing was to find a method to do a performance without rehearsal —to make use of available people on the spot as quickly as possible. Which meant the development of new techniques, new forms, and new thoughts about my whole purpose. Especially since I wanted people involved rather than as spectators, I had to find a practical way to do this. So I thought of the simplest situations, the simplest images—the ones having the least complicated mechanics or implications on the surface. Written down on a sheet of paper sent in advance, these actions could be learned by anyone. Those who wished to participate could decide for themselves. Thus, when I arrived shortly before the scheduled event, I already had a committed group, and I could then discuss the deeper implications of the Happening with them as well as the details of performance. This has proven to be an efficient and workable method. Innovations can be introduced almost painlessly this way. The more "unartistic" they are, the more natural and easy to do and the less they seem inhibiting to performers. Activities scattered over diverse spaces and time units (dismantling a car, building a tower, eating in a luncheonette) are so "ordinary" they disguise the radical nature of the art form evolving.

My works are conceived on, generally, four levels. One is the direct "suchness" of every action, whether with others, or by themselves, with no more meaning than the sheer immediacy of what is going on. This physical, sensible, tangible being is to me very important. The second is that they are performed fantasies not exactly like life, though derived from it. The third is that they are an organized structure of events. And the fourth level, no less important, is their "meaning" in a symbolical or suggestive sense.

For example, regarding this last, if I call for a single female in a work, whether it be a twist dancer or the dream girl in *The Courtyard*, she is usually the embodiment of a number of old, archetypal symbols. She is the nature goddess (Mother Nature). She is either benign, yielding nature or devouring, cruel nature (she usually has those two sides to her) just as nonhuman nature yields up and takes back upon death what she has yielded up.

When the girl in *Courtyard* walked amongst the people, lost in herself, she was Aphrodite (Miss America) as well—a goddess of Beauty, which is another subdivision of the large, benign nature image: a further refinement of it into the realm of love, the realm of beauty and art. Her listening to the rock-and-roll music on the radio—although it was a contemporary image, as her gown was a contemporary gown—was, nevertheless, the beautification of her own internal rhythms; in other words, the rhythms of nature which, in a crude fashion, had been presaged earlier in the Happening by the eruption of the mountain when the rhythms were much more forcible, more abrupt, explosive, and harsh. By the time the girl came out into the crowd—all female, all beautiful, listening to the music—those rhythms (now in the music) had become "art." Then when she climbed the mountain, she was once more assuming her connection with what the mountain meant in the first place—an eruption of herself, Mother Nature yielding forth. However high now, or close to the bosom or womb of nature (the simultaneous conception of that mountain was internal and external), she, nevertheless, posed for the press photographers again, recalling her Aphrodite self. And, finally, when the mountain above came down and joined the mountain below, she was enveloped in the tips of the two and disappeared once more into nature and became abstract and nonhuman, nonbeautiful—the pure operation of the earth. I thought of it in a more poetic way— that the tip of one mountain kissed the tip of another mountain. (I frequently use this element of the kiss in many ways—sometimes more abstractly than at other times when it is literally a kiss.)

I think that very, very few of the visitors got these implications out of *The Courtyard*, although they sensed, as I found out by talking to a dozen or more people, that there was something like that going on, but exactly how and in what depth, they did not know.

It is not that such symbols are esoteric: they are not. They are so general and so archetypical that actually almost everyone knows vaguely about these things. This is just the opposite from what I call "private" symbols—the sort where a teacup stands for Grandma's house; as, for example, the cookie in Proust. . . . In my case I try to keep the symbols universal, simple, and basic. However, the language, the medium itself, of a Happening, is of such an unusual nature to most people, that they have not got time to see how commonplace the symbolism is, where in another context they probably would.

None of the works included in this book is my most recent. Now I send a scenario in the mail to potential participants and discuss the various levels of meaning in my works beforehand, and my performance tends to be, as a result, much better because, unquestionably, understanding is greater.

The structure of my recent Happenings (the earlier ones were somewhat different) is that which I find typical of most classical arts. They tend to be simple in outline, very often threefold and circular; that is to say, the conclusion is very often an inversion of, a variation of, or a continuation of, the beginning—a kind of resolution, if you want. And so the work tends to have an introductory statement of the thematic possibilities. It amplifies, builds up—often with strong implications of climax in it—and then, in one way or another, either rapidly or slowly, diminishes, and returns upon itself. However, if this is classical, it is not because I have derived the structure from the classical arts, but rather because I have seen these movements in nature, such as in the seasons, the circling of the stars, and in the cycle of a man's life.

Obviously things are done variously and flexibly in the actual performance. There are the contributions of each person, the accidents of weather, the slips in timing, etc., which nobody can figure on. Sometimes they are marvelous, sometimes not. I allow for this. I try to plan for different degrees of flexibility within parameters of an otherwise strictly controlled imagery. For example, a part may consist of sweeping thirty square yards of paper in a "slow, unhurried way." One could sweep it this way or that way, with a brown broom or a pink broom—in any fashion that one wishes, if it is generally done in that slow, ritualized way. Or: a riot is called for. Everybody exchanges clothes; a complete orgy is taking place. Who exchanges clothes with whom makes no difference at that point as long as one just keeps on exchanging clothes. In these cases I will permit almost any flexibility. But there are other, stricter, limits of variability which may go like this: at a certain time the performer may either throw a barrel, on which he's been pounding out a beat, as far as he can, letting it bounce in any fashion until it stops; or he can tip it end over end in counts of ten; or he can drag it on the ground, or roll it; but these actions prescribe the *manner* of involvement with the barrel, not merely the basic *fact* of involvement. The choice is restricted as well to only that time, and it remains up to the performer to decide what the *action* demands then (as opposed to what he would *like* to do). However, such parameters of planned variation are relatively few at the present. The majority of them are scored for no alternatives, and the overall theme is followed to the letter. In the future I shall loosen up the structure when all concerned know more.

I find it practically necessary to appear in my own works because my presence amongst the other participants is extremely important as an example. If I stayed apart and watched, especially now when I insist on there being no spectators, they would say, "What kind of a man is this?" Furthermore, I need to be part of it to find out what it is like myself. Imagining a Happening and being in one are two different things.

Ideally it should be possible to do a mail-order Happening. But responsibility for its proper execution still remains. Someone has to be in charge. And thus far there is no one besides myself who can speak to the participants (as a football coach speaks to his players beforehand) and, by such a talk, convey something of the levels of meaning and the cohesiveness of the whole. I intend to continue this since it has had good results. But on the other hand, I like the idea of letting others execute a scenario according to their own directorship. I have already done this with some of my Environments, such as *Words* and *Push and Pull*. But with the Happening a longer tradition has to develop; then some man from Oshkosh, ordering a Happening through a Sears, Roebuck catalog, could set the whole thing into motion and play a part too, just as I now do. I am working on ways to make this possible.

18 HAPPENINGS IN 6 PARTS / *the script*

NOTE: *Behind a cover by Lucas Samaras, a 1959 issue of the* Anthologist, *a literary review published at Rutgers University, included photographs of constructions by Allan Kaprow and Robert Whitman, sculpture by George Segal and paintings by Samaras. There were poems by Francis Fergusson and John Ciardi and translations of three short plays by Federico García Lorca, including* Buster Keaton's Ride. *The first article was a piece by Kaprow, then teaching art history at the university, which was called* The Demiurge. *Toward the end of a brief essay on the need for an artist to create something entirely new ("I have always dreamed of a new art, a really new art."), what might have appeared at first glance to be a long poem had been inserted. The heading read, "Something to take place: a happening," and it was the "script" for a rather unusual performance. This was probably the first time that the word "happening" was publicly applied to a form of theatre. Although it was never presented in the manner described in the article script, many of the elements from it were used in 18* Happenings in 6 Parts. *Certain elements from the essay itself also found their way into the Happening when it was performed. However, it was not until later works that some of the images, or forms of them, were realized.*

53

Something to take place: a happening [1]

VAST SPACE—FIVE HUNDRED FEET DEEP AND THREE
     HUNDRED AND FIFTY WIDE AND AT LEAST
     TWENTY HIGH

Fourteen groups of chairs — random — in rows circles rectangles
and singly — spotted here and there over floor of this area

Long bands on floor diagonal to the axes of room
PURPLE BLACK WHITE (paint roughly flung daubed — here
and there spreading over the edges of the bands onto the floor-
boards or other bands)

(Chairs colored silver and yellow also at random freely leaving
wood showing forgetting a chair here or there)

People will sit in the chairs whose arrangement causes them to
face in different directions

Some are dressed in WINTER COATS — others NUDE — others
quite EVERYDAYISH (Visitors will be given numbers of seats
where they will go upon entry — They will find themselves seated
next to nudes coats and bums who will be placed amongst the
seats)

[1] *Anthologist* (publication of Rutgers, The State University of New Jersey) vol.
30, no. 4, 1959, pp. 5-16.

OLD MAN SITTING IN A FRONT ROW SEAT SOMEWHERE
GETS UP AND DOWN CONSTANTLY and plays with tin
cans variously colored moving them from one band of
the floor to the other

Elsewhere in the space a
large, cubic framework
covered with transparent
plastic film

An artist dressed in white
duck sneakers and dress
shirt sits on a red stool in
the center of the enclosure
and lights NINETEEN WOODEN
MATCHES blowing them out in
turn slowly without great
movement

He walks to each filmy wall
of the framework where there
is a pot of black or white
paint and brushes

SOLEMNLY HE PAINTS

At another point a young
boy goes to a striped pole
of black and white hung with
red lights and grasping it
SHAKES for a while like a
victim of palsy returning to
his seat when he wishes

OUT EACH WALL until he is

visible no longer from the

outside, thus ENTOMBED

The light throughout becomes BLUE

A nude girl painted all white emerges from some doorway and walks
GREEN
to a long white and red bench (This may be in the section where the
GREEN and BLUE
old man is moving tin cans) She lies down on it as an odalisque
to WHITE
raises her eyebrows shoulders drawn up mouth slightly set but apart
(very stiffly and blankly) breath indrawn gets up after a few moments
and walks back to the doorway and out

EVERYTHING STOPS

PEOPLE CHANGE

SEATS ACCORDING

TO NUMBERS

ARRANGED ON

THEIR ENTRY TICKETS

PROCEEDING TO AN

ENTIRELY

DIFFERENT

SECTION OF

THE SPACE

OLD MAN SCREAMS

furiously turning wildly

in all directions and is

joined by impossible high-

frequency sounds that come

over loudspeakers from each

corner of the room one

after the other

(light becomes more intensely white)

SCREEN

Still photo of nude girl

shown wherever she is not

actually visible — When

she is seen the slide is

changed to a picture of a

large black and white circled

affair with just a touch of

violet on one circle

SCREEN

Two persons standing in front

of the screen receive the image

of several slides shown on them

and the screen: stripes in red

stripes in black stripes in pink:

all different

SCREEN

Movie of large rows of

splotches pass slowly

(or rapidly) across screen

in white — One flash of

dirty green dots in uneven

rows — Interrupted by

quick stills of artist at

work in cubicle

SCREEN

Slides change from all purple

with white dot in center to all

black with purple dot in center

to word "OFTEN"

(light fades imperceptibly over a long period of time but does
not go out — comes up suddenly after this)

NUDE ENTERS repeats former action

A raised platform with yellow lights strung over it like a
used-car lot at night — A couple garishly made up standing
stiffly facing each other — At the next sound they suddenly
do a frenzied Charleston for about thirty seconds immediately
returning to their standing positions afterward

LOUDSPEAKER

High sounds rapidly changing
nervous agitated light barely
remaining long enough to be
heard clearly

LOUDSPEAKER

High sounds rapidly changing
nervous agitated light barely
remaining long enough to be
heard clearly

Old man plays TIN CANS young boy SHAKES at pole
LECTURES BEGIN

(from three places amongst seats persons
give a lecture without rising broken by
silences unbearingly long pauses between
uncompleted sentences or by inaudible
whispering)

LOUDSPEAKER

High sounds rapidly changing
nervous agitated light barely
remaining long enough to be
heard clearly

LOUDSPEAKER

High sounds rapidly changing
nervous agitated light barely
remaining long enough to be
heard clearly

ONCE during this activity

a three-minute steady complex

of sounds is heard feeling

as it should absolutely boring

changing only subtly as it

stretches on

On one side of the space the entire wall is a collage of vibrating patches of red black silver yellow and white cloth torn and shredded pasted in as great an ordered disorder as possible edges hanging free — All over this sea of confusion will be scrawled broken words in all sizes and colors such as HEY! HI! RAH! HOO! BARROOM! YAY! BARROOM! BOO! OH! HO! WHOOM! AH! — readable sometimes and sometimes not — Fellow in sloppy clothes daubed with white polka dots stands in front of the wall raises his hands to it every time he hears a very low noise as if in hypnotic response to the adulation of a roaring crowd in a stadium above him — When this happens

ANOTHER ARTIST

(also in white like the first one)

(noise like exhaled breaths)   (noises heaving

       pastes colored papers on a   heavy rolling)

       four-sided standing panel shaped

       in its floor plan like a plus sign

When the CHEERLEADER lowers his arms the artist sits down wherever he happens to be and picks up a colored box and contemplates it
until the next low sound (pulsing at about seventeen cycles floor shaking) when he resumes pasting

        EVERYTHING STOPS

        SEATS ARE CHANGED

        YELLOW LIGHT

At the other end of the large space a high affair of hanging thin
purple banners detached about ten feet from the wall — On either
side of these hangings are six persons who utter words (reading
them from placards which they hold) words which should convey
a ritualistic yet nonsensical feeling

When these persons stop a girl gets up from a chair against one of the side walls where she has been sitting and walks up and down one of the aisles on the floor bouncing a ball for ONE HUNDRED AND THIRTY SEVEN SLOW BEATS

LAUGHTER BRIEF QUIET IRREPRESSIBLE FROM INSIDE TOMB

WILD ENDURING NOISE

BOY SHAKES AT POLE NUDE LIES DOWN ON BENCH OLD MAN MOVES TIN CANS COUPLE ON PLATFORM LEAN FORWARD HANDS ON KNEES AND LAUGH MADLY FOR AS LONG AS THEY CAN ROCKING BACK AND FORTH ON THEIR HEELS RETURNING AGAIN TO THEIR STANDING

At the end of this time she suddenly throws the ball to a person in one of the groups of chairs who catches it appearing afterwards as though nothing happened — The girl sits down as before

On the wall
opposite the girl
with the ball
and behind her
(the long axis   **BRIGHT**
of the vast space) **WHITE**
are painted   **LIGHT**
in rapid almost
spurtlike fashion
red stripes of
all sizes —
They often change   **RED**
direction and
continuity and
are interrupted by
silver screens of
cutout doily-like
canvas (handmade
in appearance)
whose perforations
should seem
delicate by
contrast

Next to some
of these quieter
parts possibly
embedded in them
or hung behind
them will be
some full-length
mirrors — The
cheerleader will
turn away from
the stadium and
will face three   **BRIGHT WHITE**
suspended mirrors
of the same
kind as the
others — He   **PURPLE**
walks to one
quickly and looks
at himself
scrutinizing but
without grimacing

At the next one
he spreads his
eyelids apart as
though looking
for specks of
foreign matter   **PURPLE**
but slowly in-
terestedly —
At the third to
which he proceeds
also rapidly he
moves very close
to it perhaps
touching it and
smiles maniacally —
He then suddenly
wheels about still
smiling stands body
poised for some
action never ful-
filled — and then
walks smiling
hideously as before
to his place in
front of the stadium
and raises his arms
at the next low sound

The girl with
the ball will
look at herself
in one of the
mirrors nearest   **NO LIGHT**
her chair as
she approaches
when bouncing
in that direc-
tion — She will
stand pensively
for a moment
bouncing more   **RED**
slowly than
before smile
secretly and
then turn around
bouncing the ball
with resumed
careful steps
along the aisle
as before

When the cheerleader smiles six groups of two three five eight,
nine and ten persons each rise up in front-row seats and while
standing unfurl their purple black red and white banners to the
floor (which they had secreted in their upraised hands) — Complete darkness silence

Five red bulbs
on and off slowly
for six times   One large spot-
            light revolving
            flashing regularly
            twenty seconds

Sixteen blue bulbs
in two rows of nine
and seven pulsing with
dimmer slowly insidiously

Green bulb
White bulb
Green bulb
on and off
quickly

Three black and three
white bulbs on for one
minute — off and on
for another minute

SLIDE OF NUDE

MOVIE OF DOTS

LAUGHTER FROM TOMB

MAN IN BLACK

out of a side doorway

> Walks to a red table and chair on which there are
> a knife a juice squeezer and lines of several dozen
> glasses — Each will have an orange in its mouth
>
> He cuts ceremoniously an orange and squeezes it
> into its glass
>
> PALSIED BOY SHAKES AT POLE
>
> CROWD ROARS
>
> He cuts all the oranges in the same way and the
> air becomes suffused with the smell of the fruit —
> (brief sound of breathing over loudspeakers
> changing to crackling almost pitchless rhythms)

(The actual presentation of *18 Happenings in 6 Parts* had a large amount of detailed script material. In volume, it is probably still greater than that for any other Happening. There were scripts for the recordings that were used in the production, the technician had a complete schedule to follow, and each performer was given [or made copies of] written instructions, diagrams, and speeches for each of the segments that he would perform. For example, the directions for "Person 1" in "Room 1 Set 1" read:

> walks slowly along corridor (ahead of those going to Room 2), stops at entrance 5", walks slowly, in a straight line, eyes ahead, to within 3 feet of the person seated opposite, stops here for 7", turns around for 2", takes one step to the left and proceeds as follows:

Then there were twenty different stick drawings of a figure—a circle for the head and straight lines for arms, legs, torso, etc.—in various positions. Beside each figure was a verbal description and a notation of the number of seconds the pose should be held. The first explanation read "hands on hips," and the drawing represented an erect figure in that pose. The given duration was sixteen seconds. The description beside the second drawing read "elbows up, hands touching chest, waist bent at an angle"; the pose was to be held for five seconds. There were similar drawings and instructions for each performer who was to carry out a movement sequence, and there were equally detailed instructions for every section of the presentation.)

18 HAPPENINGS

IN 6 PARTS / *the production*

IN THE EARLY FALL of 1959, a form letter was sent by "Reuben-Kaprow Associates" to many people in the New York metropolitan area. "Eighteen happenings will take place . . . ," it began and, after listing the dates and time, invited the reader ". . . to collaborate with the artist, Mr. Allan Kaprow, in making these events take place . . . As one of the seventy-five persons present, you will become a part of the happenings; you will simultaneously experience them." The letter then quoted Kaprow: "In this different art, the artist takes off from life. Think of a buying spree at Macy's; how to grow geraniums in New York. Do not look for paintings, sculpture, the dance, or music. The artist disclaims any intention to provide them. He does believe that he provides some engaging situations . . ." After listing Kaprow's exhibition credits, the letter continued: "The present event is created in a medium which Mr. Kaprow finds refreshing to leave untitled." It was partially as a result of this letter—certainly as a result of this event—that the name "Happening" came into being.

Later, following the usual procedure of art galleries, formal announcements were sent out. They were of two types, and on them the presentation now bore the title, *18 Happenings in 6 Parts*. Only a limited number of the first type were sent: each was different, consisting of a basic plastic envelope filled with collaged bits of paper, photographs, wood, painted fragments and cutout figures, and a small irregularly edged notice (torn from the other announcement) of the dates, time and place. Because of its plastic container, the arrangement—which perhaps had some freely moving elements—could be looked at from either side. The other announcement was more routine, with the crucial information of date, place and time repeated over and over in a red-ink wallpaper pattern. On one panel of the large folded sheet was a description of what the potential spectator could expect. "There are

Construction of the dividing walls. View is from the control room toward the outer door of the gallery. Note plastic covering the partitions on the left which make a passage with entrances into each of the three rooms.

three rooms for this work," it began, "each different in size and feeling," and it went on to list the various elements—the lighting, the wall collages, the slides, etc.—that would make up the work. "Some guests will also act," it said. "The actions will mean nothing clearly formulable so far as the artist is concerned. It is intended, however, that the whole work is to be intimate, austere, and of somewhat brief duration. These eighteen happenings will take place on October 4, 6, 7, 8, 9, and 10 at 8:30 P.M." The announcement closed with a plea for contributions and said that admission would be only by advance reservation.

The Reuben Gallery, which was sponsoring the new type of presentation, was then located at 61 Fourth Avenue in New York—only a block from the Cooper Union hall where Abraham Lincoln had delivered a famous address almost one hundred years earlier. The gallery was in a loft two flights above the row of old stores with their tightly packed display windows and sidewalk browsing-racks that helped to make the area the regional center of the used-book trade.

As mentioned in the announcement, three smaller rooms had been created within the long space of the loft gallery, their walls made of a framework of wood covered with semitransparent plastic. About nine feet high, the inner walls did not, except for necessary supports, extend to the patterned tin ceiling, so that the artificiality of the rooms was emphasized. Along one of the walls of the gallery, the skeletal framework stood about three feet from the real wall, making a passageway that ran the length of the space. Open doorways in the wood-and-plastic walls connected the series of rooms and joined each room to the corridor that had been created at one side. If a visitor walked from the door of the gallery toward the far end of the long room, he began in the largest of the three rooms, passed into the smallest, and finally into a room slightly narrower than the others but relatively deep.

In each room, different numbers of folding chairs had been arranged, and the lighting in each room was different. The first room had 30 or 35 seats, placed to face toward the other rooms (which were vaguely visible through the plastic dividers), and it was illuminated by a continuous series of 25-watt bulbs—alternately red and white—mounted in fixtures a foot apart, lining the top of the three outer walls of the framed space.

In the second room, two groups of chairs faced each other. There were perhaps twelve chairs in each section. By turning to either side, their occupants would be able to see into the flanking rooms. A single blue light globe hung from a cord in the center of the space, and the plastic wall fronting the corridor (directly

View of Room 2 from Room 1.

behind one group of chairs) was covered with a random arrangement of strings of multicolored Christmas-tree lights.

The third room, at the far end from the outside door, was bordered on the top of its three outer walls, like the first room, with alternately colored lights. Here the colors were white and blue. Large circles of colored, transparent theatrical gelatin—amber, violet, orange, and red—had been glued to the plastic wall between the second and third rooms. About fifteen or twenty folding chairs were arranged in the third room so that those seated in them would be looking back toward the other two rooms. The temporary wall behind this seating group was not transparent but a large, bold, ragged collage of roughly torn canvas: the lower portion primarily contained crudely lettered words of various sizes ("was," "Ha," "BIRD," etc.); the upper, a band of diagonal stripes and a slatted construction that jutted out over the chairs. Unseen behind this collage wall was the control room from which the performers would enter and to which they would exit. A wall of the first room—the side opposite the outer corridor—was also a large collage: one panel held rows of artificial apples; the other was essentially a wooden framework built out from a ground of newspaper and painted cloth. Two full-length mirrors in the first

Detail of the wall assemblage in Room 1 (electric cord hangs in foreground).

room and one in the second reflected their reversed images of the complex Environment and any action that took place within it.

When those who had made reservations arrived, they were given a program sheet and three small cards stapled together. Under the title heading of the program were two columns: "Cast of Participants," on the left and "Instructions" on the right. "The performance is divided into six parts," the instructions began. "Each part contains three happenings which occur at once. The beginning and end of each will be signaled by a bell. At the end of the performance two strokes of the bell will be heard." Large hand-lettering on the cards read, for example, "Part 1 and 2—take a seat in room 2," "Part 3 and 4—take a seat in room 3," "Part 5 and 6—take a seat in room 1." The program admonished the spectator to be sure to follow the individual directions he had been given and to change his seat at the specified times. (Since each arrival was given a combination of cards at random, this would mean that couples and groups who came together would probably not always, if ever, sit in the same room. Because of the unequal number of seats in the rooms, some people only went to two of the rooms rather than all three, returning for the last "set" of two "parts" to the room in which they watched set 1, but everyone changed rooms twice during the evening.) The instructions explained that there would be two-minute intervals between parts and two fifteen-minute intermissions between sets—during which time the spectator would change rooms—and they ended with the statement: "There will be *no applause after each set*. You may applaud after the sixth set if you wish, although there will be no 'curtain call.'"

Six participants—three men and three women—were listed alphabetically beginning with "Allan Kaprow—who speaks and plays a musical instrument" and ending with "Robert Whitman—who moves, speaks and plays a game." Sam Francis, Alfred Leslie, and George Segal were listed among a group of eight names "each of whom paints." The final entry under "Cast of Participants" was: "The visitors—who sit in various chairs."

The spectators found seats in the rooms they had been assigned and waited. The light—pink in the first room, blue in the second, and pale blue in the third—was bright, flat and unchanging. The single reverberating note of a bell was heard; loud nonharmonic sounds came from four loudspeakers, one mounted high in each corner of the gallery. (The four tapes that were being broadcast over these speakers were similar but not identical; that is, they were made from the same sound producers, and they had the same structure, intensity, duration, etc., of major parts. Since no attempt was made to synchronize the machines, one tape might begin a few seconds before or after another. Throughout Kaprow's compositions, silence played an important part, and when one loudspeaker went quiet those at a greater distance suddenly became more audible: the sound was antiphonal, the dominant source changing frequently.) The blue and white lights that surrounded the third room were switched off. Walking slowly in single file, two men and three women started along the corridor between the temporary plastic walls of the rooms and the real wall of the loft. Dressed in ordinary street clothes (a Negro girl wore a black leotard), their blurred images could be seen from the moment they stepped out of the control room. The girls turned into the middle room, while the men continued on to the first. No one entered the darkened third room.

The movements of the performers—as they would consistently be throughout the presentation—were clear, simple and unspontaneous. Their faces never expressed feeling or emotion. They walked slowly, carefully, almost stiffly, and always in straight lines parallel to one of the walls: all turns, as if marching, would be at right angles (or an about-face), and they would never cross the space diagonally. Each performer paused silently for a few seconds in the doorway of the room he entered. Then he walked straight in, perhaps turned or stepped a few feet to the side, stood still, and finally—seldom moving from the spot to which this alternate pacing, turning and waiting had brought him—began to perform a sequence of simple, quasi-gymnastic movements.

In the first room, one of the two men stood with his hands on his hips for sixteen seconds, then bent forward with his elbows extended like wings for five seconds. Perhaps one of the girls in the next room was standing erect for ten seconds with her left arm raised, the forearm pointing toward the floor, while another was touching her left hand to her right forearm, stepping three or four paces along one of the axes of the room, and then raising one hand to her forehead for four seconds. The electronic sounds were still heard from the four speakers. In the semidarkness of the third room, slides were being shown.

As one entered the third room from the second, he was faced with a plastic-covered partition, parallel to the doorway and braced into it at the top, which forced him to turn either to the right or left. Soon after the lights in the room were turned out, a projector in the control room behind the audience group—only its lens visible as an element in the wall collage—began to throw a series of abstract, colored slides on the plastic. (They were collaged pieces of children's art and Kaprow's own work.) When the girls entered the second room, one of them—still following the precise simplicity and angularity of the movement patterns—walked into the third room and pulled down a window shade affixed to the top of the frame. Until the shade was lowered, spectators in the second room could also see the reversed image of the slides on the transparent plastic; now the opaque shade became the screen. (Projection was not synchronized with the movements of the girl. Perhaps the screen was lowered before the slides began. Perhaps the colors were momentarily projected on her as she lowered the shade.) Thus the spectators in the third room sat watching the rapid flashing of sixteen colored slides, while on either side of the screen, through the semitransparent wall dividing the rooms, they could see to some extent the silent, ritualistic movements of the three girls.

Within a few seconds of each other, all of the loudspeakers went silent. Then, after exactly five minutes and twenty seconds, the bell rang for the second time; the performers, one or two of whom were standing motionless, turned and walked slowly out of their respective rooms.

The lights in the third room were turned on. For two minutes nothing happened. Spectators talked with each other, studied the programs, and waited. Then the bell rang again. The lights around the walls of the third room were again turned off.

Two men in suits appeared, walking slowly and formally down the side corridor. Each carried a placard on a small stick vertically in front of him. The second man paused a moment in the doorway of the third room; the first man reached the first room and turned into it. They walked into the respective rooms and turned to face the audiences. No one had entered the second (center) room, but the two audience groups that were facing each other in it could turn to either side to see with a certain clarity what was going on.

When the second man entered the semidark room, another

series of slides was being projected rapidly on the window-shade screen. These were recognizable images: paintings by Old Masters, nude photographs, Kaprow's own paintings of figures, and collages made from portions of pictures of both male and female nudes. (All groups of slides had a set order of presentation, but the projector operator could, rather than follow the sequence, show them in reverse order or merely reverse the order of the second half. In addition, he had the option of making his own arrangement—during one performance, a stranger, asked to serve as projectionist, used what Kaprow considered extremely inventive sequences.)

Standing stiffly, both of the men began to read from the placards they held. "It is said that time is essence . . . we have known time . . . spiritually . . . as expectation, remembrance, revelation and projection, abstracting the moment from its very self . . . ," the bearded man began in the room where the slides were being projected. He spoke carefully and clearly, with calculated rather than spontaneous inflection. In the enclosure at the opposite end of the gallery, the other man was also reading: "I was about to speak yesterday on a subject most dear to you all—art. I wanted to speak then about art, but I was unable to begin—" Occasionally the speaker would lower his placard to his side, continuing to talk. In the center room, both speeches were equally loud. ". . . we remark—that is, after all, simple to tell time. We have designed the clock . . . yes . . . ," was heard from one side, ". . . and reflected, knowing full well how cannily the mistress of our heart's flower can elude . . ." from the other. When one of the speakers paused, which was quite frequent, the voice of the other could be heard in all the rooms: "A . . . word . . . about . . . clocks . . ." "there are those, who, with facile word and mocking eye, . . ." When the bell rang, both men, apparently finished with their reading, were standing silently, and the slides had stopped. As the men walked slowly back down the corridor to the control room, the various audience groups were beginning to stir, knowing from the program that a fifteen-minute intermission was scheduled.

During the intermission, the spectators followed the directions on the second small card they had each been given and found new seats. As they wandered about, two chairs, a small table, and a record player were placed in the second room. When the bell rang to announce the beginning of part three, everyone was in a different room than he had been in for the first two parts.

This time two girls led the procession down the corridor, followed at long intervals by two men and then another girl. Thin, high-pitched wailing or buzzing tones came from the four loudspeakers. (Again the recorded material was similar but not identical, and the lack of exact correlation tended to produce discordant warbles.) The two girls entered the first room, each pausing at the door, and one began to perform a series of movements similar to those seen in the first part. The other girl, also moving slowly and methodically, paced and bounced a small rubber ball, using little wrist movement.

(All of the movements in 18 *Happenings in 6 Parts* were very carefully rehearsed. The pages of annotated stick drawings that Kaprow had made were memorized. If the performers seemed to be counting steps, it was because they were. Steps, the number of counts between movements, the duration of positions—everything was controlled. Rehearsals began at least two weeks before the first performance and, during the second week, were held every day. First Kaprow explained what he wanted and gave each performer copies of the script material. He rehearsed each person separately until he was satisfied, then had all actions in the same part performed simultaneously while he took notes. When the chairs were delivered, last-minute adjustments in the performers' spacing were necessary because no realistic allowance had been made for the areas the audience would occupy.)

The first man had entered the middle room and sat down at the table, when the second man, carrying a board loaded with wooden blocks, stood briefly in the doorway to the third room, sat down, and began arranging an equal number of blocks on opposite sides of the board. The first man walked to a record player, turned it on, and placed the needle on the record. "Are the gentlemen ready?" it asked. (Kaprow had read in the third room during the last part, and some of the spectators might have recognized the voice on the record as being his.) The man walked back to the table and sat down. The two silent, expressionless performers faced each other across the blocks.

At the same time, a girl had entered the third room, walked behind the screen on which the slides had been shown, and turned at the other side of the room to face the audience. For over a minute, she was silent and motionless. The high, piercing whine of the loudspeakers could be heard.

In the first room, one girl was bouncing the ball while the other was going through a series of formal movements: she stood with one hand on her head, the other arm straight in front of herself and one leg raised to the side; she bent the raised leg back at the knee; she reached back with the arm that had been extended and grasped the lifted ankle.

The record in the middle room continued to speak with long pauses between phrases. "They shall ready themselves . . . ," it said. "The time is near . . . Now is the time. Number 1, his move . . ." The first man picked up one of the four-inch wooden cubes which were painted white with single red letters on the sides and placed it down on the center of the table. "Number two shall move," the voice on the record intoned. The other man picked up a block and thumped it down. "Now one . . . Again two . . ." The expressionless men each moved a block when directed to do so.

In the next room, the single standing girl had begun to recite. "Fine cocked-feathered moon, me friend," she began in a soft, lilting style, "over an' up in the moon—" When the brief speech ended, perhaps forty-five seconds later (". . . Lissen, shy Jim, jus' look, jus' look, jus' look . . ."), the blue and white lights edging the room were turned out, and another group of slides was projected rapidly. This time the new spectators—none of whom had seen the slides during the first two parts—looked at photographs of objects: a clock reflected in a mirror, a cornflakes box, smoke rising from a pipe, smoke reflected in a mirror as it rose from a cigarette.

At the opposite end of the gallery, one of the two girls was still carefully bouncing the ball, while the other, with the disinterested blankness of someone who is hypnotized, did some of the uncomplicated movements while kneeling in the center of the room. In the middle room, the men at the table were still alternately placing blocks on the table when directed to do so by the record. "Are you ready? . . . In trouble? . . . for the moment? . . . there! . . . Your move, one." When all twenty of the blocks had been arranged into one large, rectangular volume in the center of the table, the men remained motionless while the record continued to make comments and give instructions, finally ending in the middle of a word and revolving until the end of the part with only the repetitious sound of the needle sliding in the final grooves. The high-pitched sounds from the loudspeakers stopped. The voice—if not the actual words—of the girl in the room where the slides had been projected could be heard throughout the gallery: "Hackie, drive up here and let me listen to your meter sing. It alone has the voice of New York City . . ." When she finished the brief recitation, she, like the others, remained motionless until the bell, then joined the slow procession back to the control room. Before leaving the room, one of the men turned off the record player.

During the two-minute interval, the table in the second room was moved so that it was directly under the blue light globe that hung in the center of the space. The blue and white lights were on again in the third room.

With the bell beginning the fourth part, electronic sounds were again heard from the four loudspeakers. Two men and two girls, each carrying a musical instrument, entered the first room one at a time and stood side by side in a line facing the audience seated there. One had a toy ukulele, another a flute, the third a kazoo, and the fourth a violin. (None of the performers was a musician, and the particular instrument a performer used might change from performance to performance.)

The remaining girl carried a stool with a cup of water on it into the third room, set it behind the projection screen, walked to the other side and raised the shade. The audience in the third room could now look through the plastic partition and see the stool. When the girl returned to the central room, the third man entered, walking slowly and without expression as usual, carrying a pressurized spray can and a metal toy. He placed the can on the stool, entered the second room, put the mechanical toy on the table and set it in motion. About one foot high, it was the brightly colored figure of a Negro dancing on a drum; the legs jiggled and swung frantically and erratically when the toy was started.

The four people in the next room were beginning to play. Standing with erect dignity, the ukulele player strummed a few quick chords and stopped suddenly. The violin bow was scraped across the strings. The kazoo grunted and warbled. The flute blared shrilly and then went silent. The musicians were not playing a piece, but each was functioning independently with relatively long pauses separating the abrupt passages of sound.

Having set the dancing toy in motion, the remaining man was standing behind the plastic partition slowly striking wooden matches and carefully putting them out by dipping them in the glass of water on the stool. The spectators in the third room watched him through the plastic; some of those in the second room could get a partial view of what he was doing. Everyone could hear the sounds of the "concert," although many of the spectators could not see it. After solemnly striking nineteen matches, the man picked up the can that he had left on the stool and directed a white spray onto the plastic. The view of the spectators in front of the screen was increasingly obscured, and finally the man was completely hidden. (The spray was a kitchen cleanser that would evaporate, leaving the plastic clear again.) He stood motionless for fifteen seconds, turned, entered the second room, and switched off the mechanical toy. As he stood waiting for the bell, the "orchestra" could still be heard. They continued to repeat their unsynchronized sounds until the signal.

As the spectators were again changing rooms during the second fifteen-minute intermission, some of them perhaps inquired of their friends what had been going on in the other rooms and described what they had seen. Those in the first room noticed a table being set in place and twelve orange halves, twelve glasses, and a pressure juice-squeezer arranged upon it. At the same time, the mechanical toy and the table were removed from the second room, a can of paint and a brush were placed on either side of a canvas panel set in the wall between the first and second rooms, and an eight-foot-high wooden construction on wheels was left standing in one corner of the third room.

At the bell, another slow procession began along the corridor at the side of the three rooms. From the four loudspeakers came a fast and noisy jumble of sounds mixed with words: "Lionel trains," "I don't know, but," "pretty baby" and other phrases might have been discerned by some listeners in the babel and rush of sound from the unsynchronized speakers. The first girl to leave the control room walked slowly to the first room, paused in the doorway, crossed to the table, and began to squeeze one of the orange halves. The weather was unseasonably warm (it was October); the bright lights, the plastic obstructing ventilation, and the large

(rehearsal photograph) Part Four; Room 1: The orchestra (Shirley Prendergast, Rosalyn Montague, Allan Kaprow, Lucas Samaras). Note seated spectator seen through plastic-covered wall.

number of spectators combined to make it very warm and close in the gallery. The odor of the enamel in the opened paint cans was already permeating the space, and now the smell of oranges—perhaps more pungent in the heat—was added.

A man entered the second room and stopped. He placed the fingers of one hand over his mouth, pointing upward; his other hand was on his head, the fingers pointing down over his nose and eyes. He stood that way for ten seconds, put his hands down at his sides and smiled a broad, unhumorous smile.

A girl walked slowly into the third room, went to the construction in the corner, and began to wheel it into the next room. The long, box-shaped body was open at the sides and had mirrors in the front and back, a gallon paint can represented a head, and there were wooden arms on either side. In one "hand" were cards with numbers and letters (3, X) on them. (Kaprow called it the "sandwich man," and it seemed to be about to hand out its cards.) The whole thing rolled on old bicycle wheels that had no tires. The girl pushed the construction through the middle room (where the man was touching his tie, turning around, and touching the tie again) and into the room where the first girl was squeezing orange juice into a glass. A cord from the wheeled construction was plugged into a receptacle hanging from the ceiling, and a record player inside the box-body was started, blaring out an old, loud, brassy polka tune.

At the same time, two men and a girl were carrying placards mounted on sticks into the third room: the first stood at the far right of the audience, facing in; the second at the far left of the audience, facing in; the third stood next to the projection screen,

The "sandwich man" wheeled construction showing record player.

facing the audience. They began to read at random intervals from the placards: "Kiss me! Kiss me! Are you sure you . . . ?" "Four days . . . then defeat," "Hup!" (Each performer had a list of seven words or phrases taped to the placard. He was allowed to read them in whatever order and at whatever intervals he wished. Only three repetitions were allowed.)

When the wheeled construction passed through the second room, a man got up from his seat in the audience and walked to the canvas panel set in the wall. Another man left the audience in the third room and walked to his side of the panel. Picking up the brushes that had been provided, they began to paint on the canvas. Each had a single color (red and blue were used at one perform-ance, perhaps red and green at the next), and the paint would immediately stain through the unprimed canvas so that it was visible to the painter—and the audience—on the opposite side. One painter made only straight lines; the other, only circles. Each responded to the work of the other and attempted to integrate it into the abstract composition. (The number of lines and circles was set by Kaprow. He was angry when Al Leslie wrote four-letter words rather than doing what he had been asked to do. Not all the painters listed in the program participated. One evening Robert Rauschenberg and Jasper Johns substituted for Red Grooms and Lester Johnson. Johns used the lid of the paint can rather than the brush to make circles.) When the work was fin-ished, the painters returned to their seats.

In the first room, the polka record played; the girl squeezing orange juice drank each glass as it was filled and began to fill the next. The man in the second room knelt and rolled one leg of his trousers up to the knee, stood, knelt again and rolled up the other leg. In the third room, the three people were reading their plac-ards: "Would you kindly innocently raise your eyes a tiny, tweeky, single . . . ?" "My toilet is shared by the man next door who is Italian." The confusion of words and sounds from the loudspeakers continued for a while and then stopped.

When the three people who had been reading all stood quietly, the lights around the third room were again switched off, one of the performers pulled down the shade, and another quick sequence of slides was shown. These were essentially the decorative, freely lettered words and phrases that made up a "visual poem" (Kaprow called it "Mary Had Fleas"). The man in the second room, his trousers rolled up to his knees, was seriously brushing his teeth. As the girl in the first room squeezed each of the twelve orange halves into the glass on which it had been placed, she drank the juice. When the part ended, most of the performers were standing motionless, waiting for the bell before walking out.

(rehearsal photograph) Part Five; Room 1: The girl squeezing oranges (Rosalyn Montague).

After the two-minute interval, the sixth and last part of the Happening began. This time the first performers to walk down the corridor—two girls—turned into the second room rather than going all the way to room one. They stood side by side facing one of the audience groups. There was no sound. Two of the men entered the third room and took positions at either side of the screen. They began to perform movements that were somewhat synchronized: both turned, walked to opposite walls, then turned again and walked back to face each other; they both stepped simultaneously away from the audience and then toward it. After several movements, they stood facing the spectators, pointing across their bodies at each other and smiling.

Since there were no sounds and nothing was going on in their room (still filled with the smell of the oranges whose pulpy skins remained on the table), and the girls in the second room were motionless, the spectators in the first room could only try to catch a glimpse of the activity at the far end of the loft.

When the two men completed their movements, they walked slowly into the second room and stood facing the two girls. Behind them, the lights around the room were turned off for the last time, and a single slide was projected on the screen. It showed the expressionless mouth and chin of a bearded man (Kaprow). One of the men reached up and pulled a thread, toppling four long scrolls off a horizontal wooden bar suspended nine feet above the floor. The scrolls—two purple and two red—fell like a paper wall between the men and the girls, and all four began to read lists of monosyllabic words and expressions. (Pauses and duration were designated for two of the performers, while the other pair were free to vary these elements.) The voices mixed and overlapped in a babel: "eh?" "mmmmm . . . ," "uh," "But," "well," "oooh . . ." When the bell rang twice, indicating the end of the performance, the four performers, silent by this time, walked slowly in single file from the room. The last of the eighteen happenings was over.

COCA COLA,
SHIRLEY CANNONBALL? / *the script*

NOTE: Coca Cola, Shirley Cannonball? *was developed from ink drawings and working diagrams of the various pieces, movable and stationary. What is apparently an early sketch shows a tall box figure with a round smiling face on the front, a head wearing a top hat on the top, and arms protruding from the sides. The left hand is holding three balloons. In addition, there is a page diagraming and explaining the pitch, volume, duration, etc., of the various words spoken during the Happening. The following script is a combination of two separate sheets: one describing the sequence of action and the other detailing the exact steps that the "foot" should take. The steps for the "construction" have been lost.*

1. House lights out
   Voice and noise (tape) & drum boom twice

2. Center spotlight
   From two sides come the Hello Sam Spade and whistle
   then (light out)

3. Spot on left flat
   Leg moves. Light out (leg stilled)

4. Spot on left flat
   smile (head out) bottom hole right
   construction moves on left (light out)

5. Spot on left flat
   face turned (rachet sound) (stilled as light goes out)
   light out

6. Spot on right flat
   frown in second hole on right
   construction moves   light out

7. Spot on left flat
   hand and eye moved
   light out   hand and eye stilled

8. Spot on right flat
   smile in up hole right
   construction moves   light out

9. Spot on left, everything moved
   foot emerges (backs out of position)
   turns toward aisle and proceeds in a swaying motion (back and forth leaning with the body) to "walk" to the center. light out and

10. Spot on center—stands still. All movement in flat should be stopped by the time foot reaches center. After a moment foot, staying in one spot, begins to sway back and forth as before while from both sides in unison with his movements come the words "Tick" "Tock" repeated five times along with their respective pot and pan accompaniments. At the third "Tick-Tock," construction emerges from behind other flat and in a rhythmic hopping, twice as fast as the tick tock rhythm, goes up aisle to center, cans making noise at each hop. Construction stops at foot. Words from opposite flat. "Fat Baby" twice. Spots left and right on each figure. Dance between foot and construction,

    foot (swaying except where indicated)
    1. 2 steps right
    2. 1 hop left
    3. 3 sways
    4. 5 jumps up & down
    5. 1 step forward (not swaying)
    6. 6 jumps in a circle around construction (counterclockwise)
       foot should face own flat at 6th jump

    (At kicked ball, drum sounds.) and then return to flats.

(Spots should follow this, one remaining fixed in center and then all three out as foot and construction disappear.)

11. 3 lights on right flat & "ah" from other flat then one by one in measured rhythm, the written words of "Hello Sam Spade" are dropped into place in the holes on the flat and at the last word, from left flat face sound is heard quickly (rachet face spun). Lights out and house lights on.

Finis.

COCA COLA,

SHIRLEY CANNONBALL? / *the production*

ONLY TWO OR THREE feet separated the boundary lines of the basketball court from the high brick walls, and there was no space for the usual wooden grandstands, so the audience sat on what chairs and benches were available and stood, solidly lining both sides of the gymnasium. They might have been waiting for two teams to trot out to begin a game, but although this looked like the usual gymnasium in the usual small YMCA, the gathering was expecting something unusual. They were in one part of Judson Memorial Church, located just below Washington Square in the Greenwich Village section of New York, and they had already watched several of the various events, Happenings, readings, etc. (including initial theatrical works by Claes Oldenburg and Jim Dine), that were being sponsored by the church on that winter evening in 1960. (*The Ray Gun Spex*, which was the title of the program, were held on February 29 and March 1 and 2, 1960.)

The preceding works had been presented in other rooms, and then the spectators had been asked to enter the gymnasium. It was partially below street level with several large windows high up in one of the end walls. In a side wall, about eight feet above floor level, were two adjacent rooms where, during the more routine uses of the gym, spectators standing behind heavy wire screening could watch the activities below. But it was easily apparent that no basketball game could be played this evening: directly in front of each basket, braced to the backboards, were walls of wood and painted canvas.

The walls had been made by Allan Kaprow from some old canvas-covered stage "flats" that belonged to the church. Each was about eight feet high and ten feet wide. He had cut holes in them and added color here and there. The wall near the windows

87

was basically dull green and tan, several small holes pierced it on the left, and through larger holes in the lower left center, upper center, and lower right, a large cardboard hand, the white silhouette of a foot, and the round, cartoonlike features of a painted face could be seen. The wall at the opposite end was white with a wide vertical red stripe just to the left of center. Two square and four round holes were arranged in two very irregular rows across the canvas. Each hole was framed with more freely brushed red paint.

The spectators, somewhat self-conscious in their doubt about what was going to take place, studied the rectangular walls and looked at each other across the empty floor of the basketball court. Most of them noticed a cardboard cube that hung from a nylon cord about a foot above the floor. Each edge of the cube measured about two feet, and each side face had been painted with the circular outline of a ball. It hung near the boundary line in front of the screened balcony and at the top of the foul circle in front of the darker wall.

The houselights went out, and the exit lights above the doors glowed in the dark. Twice there was the deep metallic boom of a drum. A spotlight in the raised observation room went on and began to sweep its bright beam back and forth from one temporary wall to the other. Voices were heard from behind each wall: "Hell . . . ," called a man from behind the darker wall, holding the sound as if yelling over a great distance; "Ohhh . . ." responded an unseen man from behind the opposite wall; "Sam" (the first man again, holding each sound); "Spaaa . . ." (the second man): "d" (a loud final plosive from behind the first wall). There was hesitant laughter from the audience. The fictional Sam Spade had a large television following at that time. A low whistle came from the first wall, increasing in pitch. When it cut off, another whistle from the wall at the other end of the gymnasium picked up the same high note and carried it down into a lower register.

The spotlight lit the darker flat briefly: there was noise, and the cardboard leg moved suddenly behind its opening. The lighter wall was illuminated, and a face appeared in one of the holes close to the floor: those nearby could see that the man was smiling broadly. When the light hit the first wall, the cartoon face spun in its opening with a sudden raucous clattering sound; when it swung to the other wall, a real face, scowling, appeared in one of the upper holes and then was gone. In the first, the hand swung from side to side and aluminum foil rattled behind another opening. In the second, the smiling face again appeared briefly. Each incident, accompanied by noises from behind the walls, was over almost before the spectators had time to focus on what was taking place.

Then, as the light stayed on the darker wall, the various anatomical elements all moved sporadically, sounds were heard, and a large shape began to push out from behind the left side of the structure. As it got clear, turned around, and moved out onto the court, the audience could see that it was a giant boot or foot. Surprise and the awkwardness of the nine-foot figure caused scattered laughter again among the spectators. The sides of the boot, a wooden frame covered with cardboard, were black except for a curved top section of natural cardboard. The front and back edges—it was about two feet wide—and a bulbous, protruding big toe were white. Rocking forward and backward, the boot "walked" slowly toward the center circle.

The foot.

(Jim Dine was inside the figure. He and the others had rehearsed briefly the preceding evening, and he had memorized the
exact sequence of "steps" he would be called on to perform. During this short rehearsal, a tape recording that mixed electronic
music and poetry by Kaprow was tried out. It had been planned
to open the performance with it but it was discarded as being
"too corny," as being too much like the traditional overture.)

Standing in the center of the court, the boot tilted forward:
"Tick," called the man (Allan Kaprow) behind the wall from
which the boot had come, and there was the sharp clank of a tin
pan being struck. The boot rocked backward: "Tock," and a similar metallic noise was heard from the other wall. Four more times
the boot swayed back and forth, and the antiphonal "Tick-Tock"
was repeated. After the third slow repetition, the spotlight swung
to the opposite flat. There were intermittent clanking and banging
noises. Then another construction hopped out from the right side
of the wall: covered with white cloth with black and white streamers down its sides, it was the shape and approximate size of a
telephone booth (Claes Oldenburg was inside). There was a black
rectangle in the front, a black circle on the back. As it hopped
toward the boot, pausing briefly after a short series of jumps and
then going forward again, tin cans dangling from it on cords clattered and crashed.

The foot and the white construction were motionless, facing
each other in the center. "Fat Baby! Fat Baby!" the man called
from behind the wall in back of the construction, his voice abrupt
and the pitch rising and falling. (Kaprow specifically had him use
the inflection of "salt peanuts" repeated suddenly on a jazz record
by Charlie Parker.) Again there was scattered laughter from the
audience. The boot began an awkward dance: swaying from side
to side, hopping, and jumping up and down. Moving in a counter-
clockwise direction, it made a circle around the can-decorated
construction. As the construction started to return to the wall
from which it had started, the boot moved closer to its own wall
and approached the hanging "ball." Once the nylon cord running
over a pipe near the ceiling and down to the cube became caught
on the boot, but, with a little impromptu bobbing and swaying, it
was freed, and the boot began to rock back and forth in front of
the cube. Each movement was a little larger than the last, until

The foot circles the construction.

the boot tilted sharply back, "kicking" the "ball": the hanging
cube was yanked into the air, the drum boomed (Kaprow struck
a large metal barrel), and a shrill whistle sounded, its pitch increasing sharply. Once again there were laughter and scattered
applause from the audience. The boot made its slow way back
behind the wall from which it had started.

As the light swung to the opposite flat, cards were dropped in
sequence behind the six open holes. Those spectators who were
nearby could see that they spelled out: "Hel" "lo" "Sam" "Sp"
"ade" "!." There were sounds from the darker flat, and the painted
face spun noisily. Then all was quiet. The spotlight went off.
When the houselights came on, the spectators wandered out onto
the basketball court, talking among themselves, and, standing in
small groups, waited to be told what would be next on the
program.

A SPRING HAPPENING / *the script*

NOTE: *Several preliminary outlines for the Happenings that was eventually called* A Spring Happening *exist. Some are nothing more than lists headed "noise" and "actions." Most of the sounds and activities that were used in the performance are noted on these early lists, but others were discarded (such as "tape machine of laughs," "any visitor may shout once," "mirrors brought up to eyeholes," "cooking food"). Of the more complete outlines, the one printed here is neither the earliest nor the latest version.*

1. cotton clouds hanging shaken
   thunder blocks (boom! bang! bong!)

---

   all lights out   brights in tomb 2″ out on

---

2. flashing lights (sub theme) green or red if red or green room
   man back to eyes motionless slightly bent over . . . , turns
   around suddenly   chews on celery madly.

---

3. nude live figure | hanging black figure | baptism
       red paint   green paint

---

   all lights out   brights in tomb on 4″, out, on

---

4. figure falls   leaves drop covering it

---

all lights out   brights on in tomb 7″, out, on

---

5. fallen trees rise   are knocked down   rise again
   sound of zulu record

---

all lights out   brights on in tomb 10″, out, on

---

6. all darkness   door chimes sounded
   1–3–4–2–3–4–5–8–8–2–2–2–9–1

---

all lights out   brights in tomb 15″, out, on

---

7. dark, flash bulbs explode in faces of audience

---

all lights out   weak lights on in tomb 18″, out, on

---

8. person speaking babbling.
   nervous kazoo sits on chair   other person shakes mirror in
   face.

---

all lights out in tomb   20 sec. lights out, on

---

9. car horn starts constant sound, lawn mower starts, pushed by
   tar paper figure, moves through all eight rooms cutting swath
   through leaves blowing them all over

   lights out in cubicles

   bright lights on in tomb

finis

A SPRING HAPPENING / *the production*

WHEN THE BLACK CURTAIN was pulled to one side, and they were asked to enter, many of the people who had made reservations for A *Spring Happening* did not want to go into the narrow, gloomy tunnel; some refused. Perhaps two and a half feet wide and seven feet high, the dark passageway might have suggested a mine shaft with its regular ribs of wooden supports. As most of the spectators entered in single file, a few made a point of waiting until they could be the last ones—and therefore close to the exit curtain—in the event that the enclosed space became intolerable. When the curtain was dropped again, about twenty people stood one behind the other in the tunnel, crowded together like rush-hour riders in the New York subway. At about eye level in each of the black plywood walls to the right and left of them were two rows of small rectangular slits through which faint reflected light entered to alleviate slightly the absolute darkness of the long closet.

The Happening was being performed in the Reuben Gallery on East 3rd Street in New York just off Second Avenue. It was late March, 1961. When *18 Happenings in 6 Parts* had been presented two years before, the Reuben had been in a loft on Fourth Avenue, but now it had street-level space. In the preceding months, *The Car Crash* by Jim Dine and *The American Moon* by Robert Whitman had been performed in the new gallery. When arriving spectators entered the store with its glass display windows at either side of the door, they found the smaller front section partitioned into a lobby by a seven-foot wall of muslin sheets. One narrow section in the left side of the cloth wall was black. Above the black curtain a man could be seen, apparently walking on some sort of high platform, making arrangements for the performance. It was apparent that the space behind the curtains was wider and

94

much deeper than the lobby section. The lobby itself, in which the spectators stood talking in small groups, was bare except for two small tables filled with recording and sound equipment. When the limited number who had been allowed to make reservations were present, the black curtain was opened, and they were asked to step inside the passageway that was revealed.

Now the spectators were standing in the dark inside the long narrow tunnel. Crowded and in doubt about what would take place, they giggled and joked to break the uncomfortable silence. A light inside the enclosure went on, briefly illuminating the black walls, ceiling, floor, the black curtains at either end, and the row of figures within. Then it went out. On; the spectators looked at each other in the dim light. Off; they were left in darkness. Thirteen times—if anyone was counting—the light went on and off in short regular beats.

After a moment of darkness, a hanging light went on outside the closet. By turning to the right—most of the audience was still facing away from the lobby in the same direction they had entered—and looking through the rectangular slits, the spectators could see the large empty space of the room beyond the wall that confined them. At either side, hanging white curtains enclosed the space. The opposite wall, which was parallel to the side of the wooden "cattlecar" and about seven feet from it, had been painted red. Close to the floor on the left, higher up near the center, and bunched on the lower right, chicken wire, newspapers and cardboard connected by cords were attached to the red wall. In three seconds, the bare bulb that hung above the center of the space went out.

A light on the opposite side went on, and the spectators turned to their left. Looking through the slits in that wall, they saw another space of approximately the same size and shape as the one on the right. Before the light finally went out—it pulsed slowly on and off five times—most of them noticed that the facing wall on this side had been painted green.

There was a moment of darkness and silence: the audience standing with a certain decorum, waiting. Outside the tunnel, there was a loud jolting crash and rumble—a pause—and then more booming noises on either side. A man on top of the long closet was violently throwing large metal barrels down onto the tile floor. As each barrel hit, one of the three performers who were

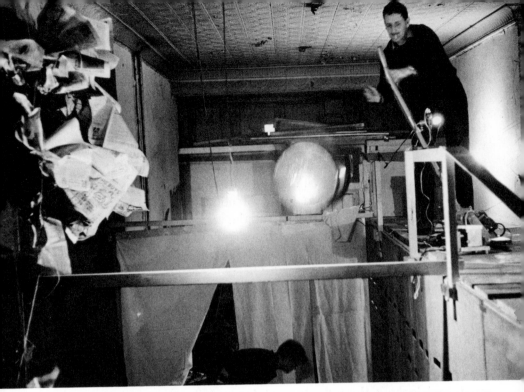

(rehearsal photograph) Barrel is thrown down from top of the tunnel. View is toward lobby.

participating in the Happening would dart quickly in from the lobby—their eyes had grown accustomed to the dark—and, with as much noise as possible, roll and push the heavy can out through the curtains. The spectators could make out little, if anything, of what was going on. The only light was that which filtered in from the street outside. Perhaps ten or fifteen barrels banged down in an irregular sequence, bounced loudly, and were rattled away to be lined up in the lobby.

As the reverberating, metallic rumble died away, the sound of an amplified tape recording grew gradually louder. Kaprow had used various electronic devices to achieve low, growling, machine-like sounds. The light went on again inside the tunnel; on either side, the spaces were illuminated faintly from somewhere above (a small work light, unseen by the audience). The loudspeaker was attached to the wooden roof just above the entrance, and, since even the floor on which the spectators stood was part of the enclosure, the whole structure vibrated as the volume increased. When the electronic sounds stopped, the dim light outside the slits went out, and the people were left with nothing to look at but the confining wooden surfaces and the other occupants of the black-hued closet. (A few times during the four or five performances, a spectator, unable to stand the oppressive restriction any longer, would force his way out again into the lobby and disappear into the night.)

In the darkness outside the walls of the structure, the sharp, clear, but suddenly stifled note of a bell was heard, first at the left rear, then, a moment later, at a different spot. One of the performers, moving back and forth silently and unseen in the dark, was striking a small handbell and then damping the reverberations so that the sound would not carry. Gradually, in an erratic pattern, the sound moved completely around the audience in a clockwise direction until it came from the right rear.

The light inside the enclosure went off, and new sounds were heard on both sides: there were hissing noises, and matches flared up here and there only to be suddenly blown out. Perhaps a flame would flash up directly in front of the slit through which a spectator was looking; the face of one of the performers might be seen briefly as he ignited a match and then immediately blew it out. At various heights and various distances from the plywood walls, the three performers—two men and a girl—struck matches and put them out as quickly as they could, making hissing, sucking and blowing noises as they moved about in the dark.

When the hanging bulb on the right of the tunnel began to flash rapidly on and off, there were no longer any performers to be seen. The masses of chicken wire, cardboard and newspaper mounted in front of the red wall began to shake and jump violently in the flickering light, making soft rustling and rattling noises. (The cords connecting the constructions ran through pulleys and out to the lobby where they could be manipulated by the man or men who, from the two small tables set in one corner, were controlling the sound and the lights.) After perhaps a minute of the irregular flashing of the light and the erratic twitching and waving of the hanging pieces, there was the loud, sharp screech of a power saw (operated by the man on the roof) as it bit into heavy wood and jammed. In the sudden silence, the light went out. Again, there was total darkness.

The light in the tunnel went on briefly, and the spectators— again somewhat self-conscious in the confined space—gradually became aware of low crackling noises. Another tape recording was being played over the loudspeaker on the roof of the enclosure. It sounded somewhat like wood breaking, popcorn popping, tinfoil crinkling, or perhaps a fire burning somewhere out of sight. Much softer than the earlier, noisy tape, it was still clearly audible. The inside light went out, and the outer areas on both sides were illuminated—the right by the bright hanging bulb, the left more dimly by the small light on top of the wooden structure.

Turning to their left, the spectators could see performers clearly for the first time. Two men wearing ordinary working clothes and sneakers stepped from the curtains at either end of the space. Both carried thick, slightly bent, and gnarled eight-foot-long clubs cut from tree branches. Very slowly they began walking toward each other.

On the right, a rubbing, bumping sound could be heard, and spectators turning to look out the slits in that side could see that a large cardboard box—it was perhaps five feet high and two and a half feet wide; large lettering on the side indicated that it had once held furniture—was slowly moving across the tile floor from the curtains outside the "front" of the tunnel.

On the left, the two men, moving in extremely slow motion, were jousting with each other—striking and parrying blows with the heavy wooden staffs. Perhaps one would gradually raise his club over his head and swing it down in a retarded arc at his opponent; the other, moving equally slowly, would shift his feet and raise his branch in both hands to catch the blow. When the timbers met, there would be no sound. Silently, the struggle continued. Perhaps one of the weapons fell and was retrieved. Perhaps the men struck their branches silently, but with apparent force, against the floor.

On the opposite side, the moving cardboard box bumped against the plywood wall of the tunnel, causing some of the spectators to turn. Then it backed away again, swaying and bouncing slightly.

Suddenly the two men surged into full motion: loudly they crashed their staffs against the green wall of plaster-covered brick, then slammed them down onto the tiles. After a moment of noisy action, they returned as suddenly to slow motion, silently repeating the activities they had just gone through.

(rehearsal photograph) The men with tree branches.

(rehearsal photograph) The shadow effect. At left, plastic covers the spectators' viewing slits.

The box, having bumped into the wall of the audience room several times, crept gradually out through the curtains into the lobby, and all of the lights went out.

In the darkness, a roaring noise started on top of the tunnel, and the whole structure began to tremble and shake. The man who had thrown down the metal barrels earlier was pushing a floor polisher over the wooden slats of the narrow roof. Inside, since the ceiling was perhaps a foot or so above their heads, the spectators could hear and feel the passage of the whirring and thumping polisher as it moved up to the front of the tunnel and then back again to the rear. When the machine was switched off, the quietly crackling tape sounds still could be heard for a few moments in the dark until they, too, stopped.

On the left side of the tunnel, a new light came on. It was seen to be behind a wall of cloth—muslin measuring about six feet high and perhaps twelve feet wide, attached to battens at the top and bottom—that had been lowered during the blackout. A moving shadow, vaguely human, was cast on the cloth, but as the spectators turned to watch it, transparent plastic was dropped over the slits through which they were looking. Two of the performers were behind the curtain: the girl wriggling, crouching, and twisting, always keeping her arms folded in against her body so that the images would not be too specific, and one of the men, holding a light in one hand and moving it freely to produce the constantly changing shadow. At the same time the other man darted in with a pot of soapy water and a sponge and began to wipe the frothy liquid over the plastic that now covered the viewing slits. The audience watched the huge, changing shapes of the shadow dance through the sliding blur of water and suds.

In the darkness that followed the sequence, the curtain—hanging from a pulley arrangement—was silently pulled up, the light inside the tunnel pulsed on and off five or six times, and sound again came briefly from the loudspeaker: high, thin wailing and heavy resonances alternated loudly. (The recording may have suggested breaking wood and clashing metal, but it was not actually composed from these sounds.)

The short tape ended, and again the audience was in darkness. The light on the left side flashed once. The light on the right side flashed once. Everything was quiet. The round white circle of a small spotlight began to wander over the walls. (The man on top of the tunnel was operating a small hand-held slide projector.) Slowly the beam moved around the spaces on both sides of the audience enclosure. Perhaps it seemed to be hunting for something. Suddenly it illuminated the naked, crouching figure of a girl, ragged green broccoli or collard greens hanging from her mouth. There were gasps and titters from the audience. But the circle of light did not stop, and the form was seen only briefly. Perhaps the spectators could hear the girl now as she ran a short way and stopped, looking around. Several times on each side of the audience (the view to the left was still obscured somewhat by the plastic), the light touched her, freezing her into immobility if she were not already motionless, but it never paused in its slow, steady movement. (The length of this sequence depended upon the performer, and, as she became more experienced and began to enjoy it more, the "scene" grew longer.) Finally the light shone full on the girl as she stood facing the spectators in the center of the space on the right. She was nude except for almost-invisible, waist-high tights of flesh-colored nylon. Broccoli or collard greens dangled from her mouth as she looked blankly up into the light without moving. In the silence, the spectators could be heard shifting, turning toward the illuminated figure. The slow boom of

(rehearsal photograph) The motionless girl is illuminated by the spotlight (Lette Eisenhauer).

a metal drum filled the room. (One of the barrels in the lobby was being struck.) Two men quietly stepped out of the darkness and stood motionless on either side of the girl. One of them held a blanket, and, after a moment, slowly raised it over the girl and let it fall, covering her completely. The men turned and disappeared into the darkness as the girl sank to the floor. The volume and tempo of the drumbeats were increasing, and the circle of light was still on the blanket. It trembled and heaved slightly at intervals. Then it was still. The drum continued to beat loudly. The spotlight went out.

A powerful roaring noise started at the front of the tunnel, and the black curtain was suddenly yanked open. In the beam of the flashlight that he carried, the spectators at that end could see one of the performers with a power lawn mower, its motor growling and its blades whirring. A powerful automobile horn in the lobby added its steady, supercharged, raucous shriek to the

(rehearsal photograph) The power lawn mower pushes through the tunnel (Steve Vesey, center).

sounds of the mower and the drum. Expressionless, the handle braced against his chest, the performer with the lawn mower began to push it into the tunnel—directly at the spectators. Those being threatened backed up, compressing the whole audience toward the lobby end of the enclosure. The curtain at that end opened, and a huge floor-model fan that had been placed directly in front of the exit blasted a powerful current of air into the space. After the hot, cramped, stuffy quarters of the tunnel, the cool air might have been very welcome, but the spectators apparently had no place to go: the large fan whirred at them from one side, and the roaring mower was pushing in from the other side. Just at that moment, the plywood walls suddenly fell outward. (Three large panels on each side, they were hinged at the bottom and tied shut with cords stretched across the roof. At the proper moment, the cords were cut rapidly and almost simultaneously by the man on the roof.) The spectators sensed that this was their way out and quickly stepped onto the fallen walls. The implacable mowing machine pushed along the passageway, forcing the last few people out of the enclosure. When the mower reached the lobby, the horn gradually died down, the drumbeat slowed and ceased, and the motor and fan were turned off. All the lights went on, and the audience wandered about among the skeletal supports and hanging curtains, seeing the space as a whole for the first time.

THE COURTYARD / *the script*

ACTION	LIGHTS
AS PEOPLE ENTER courtyard, a barely audible but insistent humming sound comes from various windows. Sound increases in intensity as small bits of tinfoil flutter down (wither from eighth floor or attic). Sound and foil increase for ½ minute, then peter out.	4 floods pointing upward
MAN WITH TRUNDLE CART comes in through glass doors and pushes through crowd, then goes out.	
TWO WORKMEN enter with brooms and large cartons . . . begin to sweep . . . hand out brooms to audience to clean up. Cartons are filled and dumped into crater by at least two trips up ladder by workmen. During this action, MAN WITH BICYCLE enters and rides through crowd, ringing handlebar bell in a quiet way.	floods go out
As cleanup ends, WILD NOISES are heard inside mountain (workmen collect brooms and leave)	spots on mountain
After a few moments, MOUNTAIN ERUPTS . . . tar-paper balls thrown out.	

VOICES AND ACTIONS from windows
. . . apartment noise heard . . . people lean
out of windows . . . flash lights, rattle dishes
and silverware, dust mops, etc. During this,
DISHES are thrown out of mountain,
breaking on courtyard floor. (Bicycle man
is still going around, ringing bell.)

> spots on mountain
> off
> 4 floods go on

All apartment activity stops. From windows
THREE MATTRESSES are lowered to
floor, followed by 5 or 6 cartons.

> 4 floods go off
> mountain spot
> goes on

TWO WORKMEN enter . . . go to mattresses and direct the action . . . carry mattresses and then boxes to top of mountain,
forming altar-bed . . . then they descend
and leave.

TIRE swings back and forth, is pulled back
just as . . .

> spot still on
> mountain

. . . GIRL IN NIGHTGOWN enters, carrying transistor radio . . . walks through crowd
listening to radio. She climbs up mountain
. . . reclines (changing positions) on mattress . . . radio is heard. (At this point, the
BICYCLIST stops his action and becomes
a part of the crowd until end of performance.)

TWO PHOTOGRAPHERS enter . . . look
for girl . . . shout "Where is she?" etc. . . .
find her . . . rush up ladder . . . ask her to
pose . . . flash bulbs go off . . . they thank
her . . . they descend and leave.

GIRL lights candle and holds it up . . .

ELECTRIC SAW sound starts high up . . .

TIRE is released and puts candle out . . .
GIRL releases white streamers down side
of mountain . . . SAW stops.

Sitting, GIRL catches and unties tire, clasps
it to herself.

SMOKE starts high up . . . SHIP DIS-TRESS SIGNAL begins . . .	floods on, pointing upward spots on mountain
From above smoke, TORN TAR PAPER floats down . . .	off
INVERSE MOUNTAIN descends . . .	halfway down, spots on mountain
Girl guides it over her body with the rope.	go on again

THE END

THE COURTYARD / *the production*

ON THE SOUTH SIDE of Bleecker Street, near the MacDougal Street intersection that marks the classic heart of New York's Greenwich Village, stands the Greenwich Hotel. It fills the whole block between Sullivan and Thompson Streets with its massive bulk of somehow-sinister whitish brick. Ten stories below the overhanging roof, small cigar and candy stores and a flamenco coffeehouse cannot quite dispel the subtle gloom of the huge presence, for the Greenwich Hotel is a slightly misplaced adjunct of the Bowery's Skid Row. For many years it has been the home of transients, bums, the down-and-outer, the old man with no place else to go. And although the hotel seems little used, and half of it stands empty, the presence and history of these people permeates all its spaces: the sterile marble lobby with its low stairs, the incredibly small rooms with space for only a bed, the dimly lit lavatories with their rows and rows of sinks and toilets where a silent man seems surprised and shuffles off into the shadow. But from a distance, where only the roof can be seen, the hotel might perhaps be mistaken for another part of neighboring New York University. Two giant skylights give it a certain grandeur. These skylights cover tall courtyards that rise the whole height of the building and allow some sunlight, however indirect, to filter through the hundreds of windows that open their slits onto the courts. It was one of these courtyards that became *The Courtyard* for Allan Kaprow's Happening.

In the fall of 1962, Kaprow attended a meeting of a committee hoping to convert the hotel into a theatre-residence hall for students and artists. The project eventually failed, but the character of the building's spaces had excited Kaprow and impressed him as potential locations for a Happening. He thought of perhaps using the miles of narrow hallways with their closely spaced doors.

108

He saw mattresses in some of the vacant rooms. And of course he saw the courtyards. He received permission from the committee to use one of the courts.

The courtyard was about seventy-five feet square, and the four stone walls, pierced by rows of narrow windows, rose straight up to the skylight ten floors above. Steps ascended to the court from one side and were covered by a low balcony which was reached by a few more steps from the yard itself. Double glass doors were centered in one of the adjacent walls, and the other two walls were blank until, at the second-floor level, the windows began. The floor of the courtyard was made of large squares of translucent glass.

Before seeing the space, Kaprow had had no specific ideas. As is his usual practice, he spent hours in the place he had chosen for the Happening meditating upon its possibilities. He sat upon the marble slab covering the circular radiator in the exact center of the court and thought of the unused mattresses in the rooms and of Beautyrest advertisements. He has mentioned remembering Gustave Doré's print—a better-known version of which was done by Van Gogh—showing a procession of prisoners around their oppressive exercise yard. Gradually the basic structure and pattern of the Happening were worked out.

The 23rd, 24th and 25th of November, 1962—the Friday, Saturday and Sunday following Thanksgiving—were selected for the presentation of *The Courtyard*. Publicity was begun. And on the Monday preceding the performances, carpenters hired by the Smolin Gallery, sponsors of the Happening, began building the two mountains that were required. The work progressed slowly. By Thanksgiving the structures were still incomplete.

On Thanksgiving, the evening before the first performance, the friends that Kaprow had called, and the friends of those friends, assembled in the courtyard of the hotel. Copies of the script were passed out, and Kaprow read through it, pausing as he went to discuss the material, to describe what would be needed, and to answer questions. This reading and discussion of the script was like the first rehearsal for a Broadway play, but Actors' Equity people would have had a month of work before they faced the New York audience. The Happening was scheduled for the next evening. The tickets had already been sold.

Although it was physically impossible to have a complete rehearsal this first night, certain elements of the script were tried out. Kaprow's original thought had been to open the Happening with the sound of moaning, but when this was attempted he found it to be "too corny" as well as relatively inaudible. Humming was then substituted with each person selecting his own pitch, and this effect was retained for the performances.

The "voices and actions" sequence was also rehearsed as completely as possible that first night. The performers, who were also responsible for the humming, were stationed at windows on the fourth, sixth and eighth floors, and it was found that actual words were not clear, so the idea of complete shouted conversations, as over the backyard fence or from a window to the street, was eliminated. These "voices and actions" participants were asked to bring mops, plates, clothes—anything they thought of to complete the tenement image—with them the following night.

(Another change had taken place even before this first meeting. Kaprow had wanted to use a motorcycle as a main element in the Happening but was not allowed to do so, and a bicycle had been substituted. The bicycle, he felt, was "too quiet," "ritualistic" and "symmetrical," while the motorcycle would have added a menacing quality and helped to strengthen and structure the noise pattern of the Happening.)

At 6:00 P.M. on Friday—two and a half hours before the audience would be admitted—the performers assembled for a final rehearsal. Some of them were there for the first time. Most of the time was spent making sure everything was in its place and that all the technical details of sound and lights had been worked out. The girl playing the main role climbed the completed mountain and called to Kaprow to watch. Her ascent up the shaking ladder should be more seductive, he thought, and he showed her what he wanted. He also demonstrated the type of posing he would like her to do on the top of the mountain. The mattresses were hoisted into a fourth-floor room, working lights and the various noise devices were arranged inside the mountain, the paraphernalia for the "voices and actions" sequence was taken to the upper floors and made ready in the narrow rooms. A trundle cart, called for in the script, had not been located, and a metal double-platform truck on which the performers had piled their coats was substituted. When Kaprow saw it, he thought the random heaps of clothes were perfect. But the bicycle had not yet arrived. It still had not arrived at the scheduled "curtain" time, and the first audience was kept waiting for fifteen or twenty minutes.

The courtyard was quiet when the audience entered. A few dim wall lights illuminated the space. Some of the translucent glass panels in the floor were lit from underneath and glowed dully. The spectators, limited in number to a hundred each night, moved slowly up the stairs and through the crumpled newspaper that covered the floor to stand along the four walls of the court. They looked with some awe, amusement, and expectation at the mountain that stood in their center. Twelve feet square at the base, it rose thirty feet in the air. The tar-paper covering gave it an awkward and sinister appearance. Most of the spectators, their eyes roving upward toward the huge skylight, noticed the smaller mountain, hanging ten floors above them. Also covered with tar paper, it was suspended from its base by a single heavy rope running through a pulley attached to the skylight. This hanging mountain was fifteen feet high, and a four-foot by five-foot opening in its lower, smaller end looked back at the audience.

After a few moments, humming, its exact source indistinct, grew gradually louder until its gentle presence was undeniable, and the vast verticality of the enclosure was accentuated by the soft floating fall of many small pieces of aluminum foil that tinkled

The courtyard seen from above. The mountain is center, hanging mountain, top center. Note spectators.

softly when they touched the stone walls and flashed dully with reflected light.

Then the humming subsided, the fall of foil gradually stopped, and the platform truck, draped with two levels of coats, sweaters, and hats, appeared from the doors at one side of the court, was pushed through the audience and made a clumsy circuit of the mountain.

Two men in their shirt-sleeves entered with brooms and bushel baskets and began sweeping up the crumpled newspaper and fallen bits of foil. Working at opposite sides of the mountain, they offered brooms to people in the audience, asking them to help. Reactions were varied. Most declined or began to sweep in an embarrassed, halfhearted way. Some helped eagerly; some volunteered. There was some laughter and a general shifting as the sweepers worked among the audience as well as in the large spaces that remained unoccupied near the mountain.

At this point a man on a bicycle entered through the glass doors and began to ride around the mountain in the opposite direction from that taken by the clothes-laden cart. After the first performance, Kaprow used him to make the standing audience shift position. He was "just a guy trying to get through the crowd," Kaprow said, and the slowly moving bicycle wandered among the people, moving them out of the way and punctuating its passage with the gentle tinkle of the handlebar bell.

As the bushel baskets were filled by the sweepers, the two workmen carried them up the shaking extension ladders tied to opposite sides of the mountain and emptied them into an opening in the top. These repeated trips up and down the mountain were not coordinated or patterned, and they occurred whenever necessary.

As the sweepers left, their confusion, comments and conversation passing away, spotlights rigged high in the courtyard windows illuminated the mountain, and an ominous rumble was heard from inside. In a few moments the mountain erupted. The spectators dodged as groups of black crepe paper balls, twenty-five or thirty in all, were hurled high above the mountain and fell among the audience. (Inside the mountain, one man stationed on a high platform was throwing out the balls, while another man swung a hammer around the inside of a large metal drum and crashed together a hanging series of ash-can lids.) Finally the eruption stopped, the metallic roar subsided, the spotlights were switched

off, and four floodlights—one mounted in each corner of the courtyard well above the heads of the spectators and pointing upward—
illuminated the rows and rows of small windows in the upper
walls.

Now the "'voices and actions" of a tenement neighborhood commenced. Dishes were being washed and a hammer was heard.
Figures appeared at various windows shaking mops, hanging out
wash, and placing and replacing artificial flowers in a window box.
Children were called, headlines were shouted, cats miaowed, and
the neighbor was asked if he had seen anything good on television.
("It didn't matter what you yelled," said one of the participants
later, "as long as you kept yelling.") As the spectators looked upward toward the noise, eight or nine heavy saucers were thrown
out of the mountain at random intervals and smashed on the tile
floor. Through the confusion from above, the exploding plates,
and the gradually shifting audience, the bicycle continued its
slow uninterrupted circling.

(When the bicycle rider stopped and got off during the first
performance, Kaprow explained that this broke the rhythm he
wanted and asked him to keep moving and to ring the bell less
frequently. At first Kaprow had told the hidden hurler of the
plates to extend his arm through openings in the tar paper, but
after the first performance he asked him to remain as unseen and
unanticipated as possible.)

As the voices and sounds diminished and stopped, the floodlights went off, spotlights again illuminated the mountain, and
the same shirt-sleeved workmen who had conducted the earlier
sweeping reentered and called up to one of the fourth-floor windows. The spectators backed away as one mattress and then
another were lowered by ropes to the floor of the court. A shouted
conversation was held between the men at the window and the
workers as the mattresses were untied, carried one at a time up
opposite sides of the mountain, and placed on top of each other
on the flat summit. (On the first night Kaprow had to come down
from the balcony where he was watching and verbally direct the
men on their early dumping of the sweepings as well as their
placement of the mattresses. He became part of the Happening.)

Then cardboard cartons were thrown from the window, crashing into the yard. These, too, were carried up the ladders where
they were stacked like a child's house of blocks on top of the

mattresses. The workmen were leaving, their job completed, when an automobile tire, attached by a rope to the hanging inverted mountain and until now secured at one of the windows, swung in a great arc and knocked the piled boxes off the mountain. The crowd cheered a little as the boxes tumbled down, and a cord attached to the tire pulled it back to its former place at the window.

Rock-and-roll music was heard. A dark-haired girl in a plain pink nightgown was walking through the audience with a small transistor radio held near her ear. ("You're having a love affair with the radio," Kaprow had told her.) She strolled languorously and with no apparent goal around the mountain and began to climb one of the ladders. Some of the spectators, getting into the habit of moving, changed position so that they could watch her. Once on top, the girl still seemed oblivious of the audience. She lay on the mattresses and struck poses—swinging a leg over the edge, stretching a bare foot in the air—as if for her own entertainment.

(Because the transistor radio lacked power, a larger radio inside the mountain was tuned to the same station. The timing was such that at two performances news was broadcast on that station rather than rock and roll. The girl changed the station, and the man operating the larger radio supported the volume as soon as he could find the new channel. One night a Spanish-language rhythm program was used.)

By this time the two workmen had donned jackets and ties. With "Press" cards in the bands of their felt hats and carrying cameras, they entered again as photographers, animatedly searching for the girl. Seeing her lolling on the top of the mountain, they clambered up, and, one photographer standing on each ladder, asked her to pose. Now the poses, all done in sitting, reclining, or lying positions, were those of a movie starlet posing for cheesecake. She turned and twisted. She smiled and tossed her hair back. When the photographers thanked her and descended, the final sequence began.

The girl in the nightgown, only partly visible from below as she lay on the mattresses, held a small electric light straight above herself and switched it on. From within the mountain a power saw began to whine and clatter. Again the tire swung down toward the mountaintop, and there were gasps from the audience as it

The tire knocks the piled boxes off the top of the mountain. Bicycle rider is at right.

The photographers and the girl on top of the mountain (William Mahin, Lette Eisenhauer, Charles Simon).

passed six or eight inches above the girl's body. As it passed, the light was switched off—the tire had extinguished it. On its back-swing, the long pendulum of tire and rope came to rest directly over the prone figure, and, turning, the girl unfastened four long streamers of white fabric, throwing one of them down each side of the black mountain. The noise of the saw stopped.

The girl sat up and hugged the hanging tire to her. Slowly the massive inverted mountain began to descend. A hand-held compressed-gas foghorn blasted its voice out from one of the upper rooms, and the harsh sounds of a dozen paper New Year's horns were added. Small bits of black crepe paper floated gently down in a dark snowfall.

At the first performance this climax was marred by the hanging mountain's refusal to be lowered. After much snapping of its heavy rope, which had become twisted, it was down far enough for a man to climb one of the ladders, reach up to the dangling structure, and pull it down over the girl.

But the mountain did descend. The girl disappeared into the rectangular opening in its lower end. One mountain rested on top of the other, their peaks touching. The girl was gone. The lights went out. The Happening was over.

The courtyard seen from above. The girl guides the hanging mountain down. Note white streamers down sides of mountain.

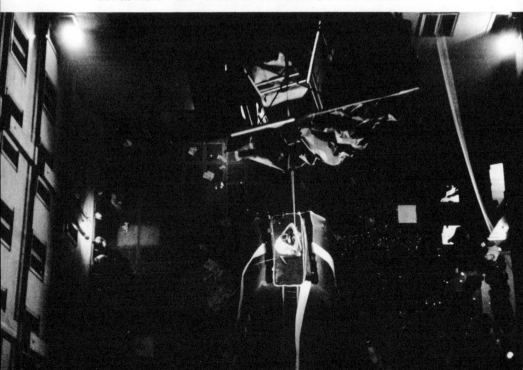

After a performance.

RED GROOMS

a statement

WHEN I WAS A KID, the big influence on me was Ringling Brothers, Barnum & Bailey, and the Cavalcade of Amusement which would roll in every year for the Tennessee State Fair. After that, I put on my own shoes in the back yard. *The Burning Building* on Delancey Street was an extension of my backyard theatre. I wanted to have some of the dusty danger of a big traveling show. And the chicken-coop creakiness of a backyard extravaganza. And the mysteries of the operations behind the proscenium.

The first big proscenium I ever saw was at the big old Rieman Auditorium in Nashville, where my interest in fire might have been ignited by the threat of the whole wooden place burning down. At any rate, firemen and their apparatus offered a good vehicle for my medieval melodrama.

The structure of my performances came from the idea of building a set like an acrobat's apparatus. The performer's actions would be improvised on the rigging around him. Since the action, or play, was directed by the environment, the sounds come from within, as on the street. The time of the act could take as long as

118

a man's dive from a tower into a flaming tank. And, hopefully, the meaning would be as direct.

From making sets I found the thrill of "3-D-ing" an environment, so that it enveloped the audience, would be something to attempt in my painting. Oh, the joys of a woodpile, cardboard, canvas, and glue, and paint!

All of the aforementioned is specifically describing *The Burning Building*. Since then I have been distracted and drifted far afield from my early one-track passion. Falling heavily under the influence of such a stage magician as Georges Méliès, to whose debt I owe a movie, made with Rudy Burckhardt, called *Shoot the Moon*.

Now to the delicate word "Happenings." In prehistoric times when I put on my play, *The Burning Building*, I was groping in the dark without that valuable word. Therefore, I must humbly bow to M. Allan Kaprow for the total invention of the word; and look with awe at the repercussions that it has caused.

LIST OF DRAMATIC WORKS:

Play Called Fire—August, 1958—Sun Gallery, Provincetown, Mass.
The Walking Man—September, 1959—Sun Gallery, Provincetown, Mass.
The Burning Building—December, 1959—Delancey Street Museum, New York City
The Magic Train Ride—January, 1960—Reuben Gallery, New York City
The Unwelcome Guests—an 8-mm. film—July, 1961—Florence, Italy
Shoot the Moon—a 16-mm. film—1962—New York City

THE BURNING BUILDING / *the script*

NOTE: *The original script for* The Burning Building *with the actual poem and word sequences has been lost. The following script, written in Florence, Italy, in 1961, to preserve some record of the performances, was spaced around two black line brush drawings. One drawing shows a fireman with an axe and a tall curved fire helmet; the other is of Grooms himself as "The Pasty Man" carrying a candle. The original paragraphing and punctuation have been preserved in the version presented below, but the layout has been altered.*

AUDIENCE SEATED * DOORMAN SHUTS DOOR, TURNS OUT LIGHT *
BLACKNESS

TWO FIREMEN COME OUT BEHIND THE RIGHT SIDE OF THE CURTAIN
AND DO A MAD FIREMAN DANCE IN SEMIDARKNESS * RETURN BEHIND
CURTAIN * GIRL IN WHITE BOX COMES OUT FROM BEHIND THE RIGHT
SIDE OF THE CURTAIN * DANCES ACROSS AND BACK * SHADOW OF HAND
COMES FROM THE LEFT SIDE BEHIND CURTAIN SLOWLY * REACHES THE
RIGHT SIDE OF THE CURTAIN, PULLS CURTAIN BACK * APPEARS THE
PASTY MAN WHO STEALTHILY CREEPS BEFORE THE WHITE CURTAIN
HOLDING A CANDLE * FOLLOWED BY THE BLACK FIREMAN HOLDING A
CLUB * PASTY MAN REACHES THE LEFT SIDE OF THE CURTAIN WHERE-
UPON THE CHIEF'S DOOR APPEARS * PASTY MAN KNOCKS THREE TIMES,
SOUND COMING FROM THE BLACK FIREMAN'S BOOT * HAND REACHES
THRU CURTAIN AND DOOR TAKES CANDLE * DARKNESS *

FIREMAN SOCKS PASTY MAN IN THE HEAD * PASTY MAN COLLAPSES
INTO THE FIREMAN'S ARMS AND IS CARRIED BACK ACROSS THE CLOSED
CURTAIN TO THE RIGHT * EXIT *

121

CURTAIN REMAINS CLOSED AND LIGHT BEHIND THROWS DANCING SHADOWS OF PASTY MAN, FIREMAN, GIRL IN THE WHITE BOX * SOUND OF TIN CANS AND RADIO STATIC * SHADOW OF PASTY MAN LEFT ALONE TURNING * HIS SHADOW DISAPPEARS *

CURTAIN IS THROWN OPEN BY PASTY MAN * THE SET IS SEEN FOR THE FIRST TIME: ON THE LEFT THE SOUND MAN SITS IN A RAISED ARMCHAIR VEILED IN PLASTIC * HE CONTROLS CANS ABOVE THE FIREMAN'S DEN WITH STRINGS, PASTY MAN CROUCHES WITH CANDLE ON RIGHT SIDE OF STAGE * SOUND MAN BEGINS TO READ A LETTER—

(Set: FROM R. TO L.—LEANING DOOR WITH AXE COMING THROUGH THE CENTER MAKING A HOLE FROM WHICH SMOKE BILLOWS UP; AN EIGHT-FOOT CARDBOARD FIREMAN CARRYING A HOSE; A RAISED PLAT-FORM SEVEN FEET IN LENGTH FORMING THE FIREMEN'S DEN WITH CANVAS WALLS; THERE IS A CLOCK ON THE WALL AND A DOOR; FROM THE CEILING HANG BLACK CANS, SPRINGS, AND BOOTS, AND A HOSE; BESIDE THE FIREMEN'S DEN IS THE BURNING BUILDING FROM THE ROOF OF WHICH STICKS OUT A YELLOW CARDBOARD HEAD; BLACK TEETH STICKING UP FROM THE FRONT EDGE OF THE STAGE AND JUTTING DOWN FROM THE CEILING. RED AND WHITE LIGHTS ALTERNATE ON AND OFF.)

(at same time WHITE BOX's face appears through clock—"Tick-Tock, Tick-Tock, Tick" PASTY MAN SEARCHES THE FIREMAN'S DEN WHILE THE SOUND MAN READS THE LETTER—"MY LOVE MY LOVE I AM WRITING MY LOVE I AM WRITING YOU TODAY I AM WRITING YOU TODAY AS IT IS RAINING OH MY LOVE MY LOVE I MUST BE LEAVING I MUST BE LEAVING YOU TODAY" * AS THE LETTER ENDS THE SOUND OF THE FIREMEN RETURNING IS HEARD FROM BACKSTAGE * PASTY MAN JUMPS OFF STAGE BEHIND THE CARDBOARD FIREMAN * ENTER FIRE-MEN * FIREMEN DO A DANCE, VERY ROUGH, LAUGHING * FIREMEN TALK "WOWWAWAWF HAWF HAWF" AND SOCK EACH OTHER * SIT DOWN IN DEN AND BEGIN EATING A PAPER TURKEY * GIRL IN WHITE BOX STICKS CANDLE FROM BEHIND DOOR UNDER SEAT OF RED FIRE-MAN. WHILE FIREMEN EAT BACKSTAGE NOISES BY PASTY MAN AND SOUND MAN, SIGNAL NOISES: "UNCLE SAM" "DICK TRACY" "MUD IN YOUR EYE" etc. UNTIL THEY GET TO THE WORDS "WATCH OUT, OPEN THE WINDOW THROW IT"—AT THIS POINT PASTY MAN STICKS HIS HEAD OUT DOOR WITH AXE HOLE AND YELLS "<u>FIRE</u>" AT THE AUDIENCE AS LOUD AS HE CAN!! * FIREMEN JUMP UP RUN AROUND BUMP INTO EACH

OTHER, FINALLY DISCOVER PASTY MAN BACKSTAGE AND DISAPPEAR °
WILD NOISES, CANS, YELLING ° PASTY MAN LEAPS FROM BACKSTAGE
INTO AUDIENCE ° RUN AROUND IN AUDIENCE MAXIMUM NOISE FROM
SOUNDMAN ° PASTY MAN DISAPPEARS BEHIND BURNING BUILDING °
NOISES STOP ° FIREMEN AND GIRL IN WHITE BOX STAND STILL BEFORE
THE BURNING BUILDING ° TWENTY SECONDS OF STILLNESS ° PASTY
MAN BURSTS THROUGH WINDOW IN BUILDING ° FLIPS AND LANDS ON
BACK ° STILLNESS ° BLACK FIREMAN PULLS CURTAIN CLOSED ° end

THE BURNING
BUILDING / *the production*

THE SIX-LANE EXPANSE of Delancey Street on the Lower East
Side of Manhattan glows at night with the neon of a Spanish-
language movie house, kosher delicatessens, a French-Roumanian
restaurant and the headlights of cars bound to and from the Wil-
liamsburg Bridge. At the point where the middle four lanes of
the wide street begin to rise to cross the East River, they are
spanned by a huge illuminated sign that reads: "Expressway to
Queens." Directly to the left of the sign is a small old unobtrusive
three-story building, 148 Delancey Street, with a bar on the ground
floor. It was on the top floor of this building—christened the
Delancey Street Museum—that Red Grooms presented *The Burning Building* from December 4 through December 11, 1959.

By the day of the first performance a set had been built and
seats arranged for spectators. Costumes had been made and props
constructed. Linoleum-print posters had been put up in certain art
galleries and in such artists' haunts as the old Cedar Bar in Greenwich Village—publicity during the "run" was to be primarily by
word of mouth—and an audience was expected, but there had been
no rehearsal. When early arrivals were knocking at the door,
Grooms was still explaining to the cast what he wanted them to
do, and walking them through their roles.

At the top of two straight narrow flights of stairs walled with
patterned tin, the spectators turned left and entered a small low-
ceilinged room. A doorman wearing an old overcoat and an under-
shirt with a necktie painted on it stood by the door. Long pewlike
seats (left by the boxing gymnasium that had previously occupied
the floor) had been arranged in rows, facing a curtain that extended from wall to wall and cut off the far end of the narrow
room. The legs of the seats had been sawed off or extended so
that spectators in the front row sat almost on the floor; those in

124

the last row were semistanding. The curtain was made of plain white muslin sheets hung behind a permanent cardboard frame cut like the teeth of a saw and painted black along the floor and ceiling and red along the sides.

At the first performance the doorman asked if anyone had any matches. (They were actually needed in the presentation and none of the performers could find any.) Because of the dingy cramped surroundings, the recent use of an unfamiliar word, "Happening," and the general lack of knowledge about what to expect, his question brought nervous laughter from the audience. Just as the other performers retained material that "worked," the doorman repeated his request at each following performance. Then, when he felt it was time to begin, he closed the door and switched off the light.

The blackout was not absolute. Enough of the abundant harsh light of Delancey Street filtered up through the poster-covered windows at the right of the audience for figures to be faintly discerned. In the semidarkness two men dressed as firemen pushed out from behind the curtain at the extreme left of the audience. They wore old overcoats, baggy trousers, heavy leather boots with painted cardboard puttees and large fireman's hats also made of painted cardboard. The low ceiling of the room, the dim light and the fact that the men towered above the first row of spectators, who sat almost on the floor, made them seem huge, while the darkness emphasized their absolutely white hands, white faces with red lips, and the cardboard axes they carried. In the four feet of space between the audience and the cardboard teeth that framed the curtain, the firemen began to dance. Usually they linked arms and spun in an awkward Irish jig, pounding their heavy boots against the floor and laughing in a deep, harsh, mocking manner. Then they might do short solo dances; perhaps they would hug each other and spin around. Frequently they would break out of the jig and, grunting loudly, pummel each other with the flour-filled socks they also carried. The fighting and pushing was so rough that sometimes one of the men crashed to the floor or into a wall. The hats fell, and puffs of white flour rose when a blow was struck. During some performances the audience enjoyed the fight so much that the men performed longer than usual—it was up to them to decide when to leave. (As one of them described it later: "You get that feeling 'now's the time to go.'") They went back through the curtain at the same place they had entered.

There was a moment of silence. A girl wearing a large cardboard box came through the curtain where the firemen had just disappeared. Holes had been cut in the grayish-colored box for her legs, arms and head. Her face, like that of the other performers, was stark white with red lips. She wore glasses, and her hair was brown and very long. Moaning softly, her long hair swaying as she turned, she began a simple tripping dance in the semidarkness, moving easily and without any set pattern around the open space in front of the curtain. After less time than the firemen had performed, she returned through the curtain, and the hushed groans died away.

Behind the curtain a match was struck, a candle flared up, and the huge flickering shadow of a hand, its outstretched fingers ex-

The girl in the box (Joan Herbst).

tending toward the audience's left, was thrown upon the white muslin. There was no sound. Very slowly the shadow moved toward the left edge of the curtain. When it got there, the curtain was pulled back, and the thin crouched form of a man holding a candle stepped carefully out. He wore white trousers, socks and a sleeveless white T-shirt. His face was covered with Clown White greasepaint; his lips were red, and two red marks angled back from the outer corner of each eye. His bushy hair was red. Very slowly and gradually the crouching white figure began to move toward the opposite side of the curtain, the wavering flame of the candle he held out in front of himself the only source of light in the room. As he stepped tensely away, the dark erect figure of one of the firemen moved out from behind the curtain and began to follow. Without a sound, the pair crossed slowly toward the right of the audience. When the man in white approached the far side, someone behind the curtain pulled it back far enough to reveal a door with the single word "CHIEF" visible on it in the light of the candle. The crouching figure raised his free hand and gestured three times as if knocking on the door without touching it. Synchronized with the movements, the fireman stamped loudly three times with his boot. On the third knock a feminine hand pushed through small curtains in the door and reached down to take the candle. The flame was blown out. At the same instant, the fireman struck the motionless white figure in front of him on the head with a flour-filled sock. As the candle disappeared through the hole in the door, the figure fell back into the arms of the fireman and was dragged quickly back the way they had come, both of them vanishing behind the curtain.

In a few seconds the candle was lighted again, and shadows again appeared on the curtain. Now they were the moving silhouettes of the figure in white, a fireman, and the girl in the box. Loud noises were heard: tin cans and chains clashed and rattled, a radio was tuned quickly from station to station, producing no clearly audible words, the feet of the dancers pounded the floor. Sometimes the shadows were gigantically enlarged—only long moving legs or turning and bobbing heads. At other moments entire figures could be seen. As both the single light and the performers moved back and forth, the shadows changed and swung. After a minute or so only the single figure of the man in white could still be seen. With his arms out to the side, he spun rapidly, tilting his body, his feet tapping a fast regular rhythm on the floor. Suddenly the candle was extinguished. The whirling shadow disappeared. Lights went on behind the curtain, and the man with red hair walked the sheeting open from left to right, revealing the setting for the first time.

At the extreme left of the audience was a real wooden door set at an angle through which the seven-foot cardboard figure of a fireman appeared to be entering. The upper central panel of the door had been broken away—apparently by the painted cardboard axe that thrust through it and jutted out from it—and a "flame" of red-painted canvas rippled up from the opening to turn into the billowing "smoke" of many black paper bags stuffed with paper that extended from the rear wall to the black teeth of the proscenium frame. To the right of center more painted bags "rose" from the painted red flames that flanked a cardboard burning building. Two rows of windows were indicated, and from the peaked roof, at about the same height as the hat of the large cardboard fireman, the flat cardboard head of a man protruded. Two platforms stood above the level of the floor. To the left of center, against the rear wall, a platform about a foot high, completely framed by its own inner border of jagged black cardboard teeth, contained a small boxlike table. In the wall behind the platform was an arched doorway backed by unpainted canvas and, to the left of the door, the painted face of a clock. To the audience's right, partially behind the door marked "CHIEF," was a three-foot platform on which a girl sat in a chair. She wore a large man's overcoat, white makeup, glasses, a false mustache, and her long hair fell from under a top hat. Transparent plastic curtains almost enclosed her, hanging loosely from a circular frame above her head. In front of her was a red cabinet with a radio on it, and cords from the platform extended to a series of boots, cans and chains that hung near the low ceiling. The dominant colors in the set were red, black and tan. Two hanging red bulbs and one white bulb flickered erratically, creating light that was alternately white or various degrees of red. (Inexpensive capsules inserted in the sockets produced the random effect.) When the curtain was fully open, there were no performers to be seen except the motionless seated girl on the raised platform.

The familiar crouched figure of the man in white entered from the right corner where the curtain was now bunched and, extend-

The Sound Man. Door marked "Chief" is at right (Sylvia Small).

ing a candle, crept stealthily about the set. Now he was seen more
clearly in the irregularly pulsing light. The seated girl began to
read slowly from a piece of paper: "My love . . . My love I am
writing . . . My love I am writing you today . . ." The painted clock
face in the rear wall was removed, and the face of the girl in the
box appeared repeating, "Tick-Tock, Tick-Tock, Tick-Tock . . ."
As the man in white moved carefully about, the reading girl's
voice continued evenly—"Oh, my love . . . My love I must be leaving . . ."—and the "Tick-Tock" of the human clock added counter-
point. The crouching figure stepped up onto the low platform and
appeared to search for something by the light of the candle. "I
must be leaving you today . . ." read the girl. "Tick-Tock," repeated the face in the clock. Loud stamping noises and the
raucous guttural voices of the firemen were heard from behind
the rear wall of the set, the reading ended, the clock was silent,
and the figure in white leaped off the platform, disappearing behind the large cardboard fireman.

 The two firemen entered through the archway behind the plat-

The firemen crouch at the table "eating" the paper turkey. At right is the burning building with the cardboard head of a man protruding (Bob Thompson, Jay Milder).

form. They stamped down from the raised level and tramped noisily around the playing area pushing each other, laughing roughly, and grunting. Then they jumped back up on the platform to crouch at either side of the table, pull apart a stuffed-paper turkey with their hands and pretend to eat. As they ate, they emitted a continuous stream of growls and satisfied rumbles.

A man's voice from behind the set to the left and the girl seated in the chair on the raised platform began to alternate short staccato words and phrases: "Abraham Lincoln," one might say; "Dick Tracy," the other would answer. Names of states and of comic-strip characters were the most common material, randomly mixed. The series had the rhythm and incisiveness of a football quarterback calling signals. (The words were read from sheets of paper rather than invented each evening.)

At the same time a small striped piece of cloth on the wall near the floor behind one of the firemen was moved aside, and a girl thrust a candle out. She held it under the fireman's posterior as he ate the turkey. At the moment he felt the heat and jumped up, the man in white pushed aside the red canvas "flame" that masked the broken panel in the left door and yelled, "Fire!" (It had been his voice alternating with that of the seated girl in the word sequence, and this was the final word in the series.)

The girl on the platform began to yank various cords, causing the hanging cans and chains to crash and clatter. Then she added the blaring random noises of the radio to the general din. The firemen stamped around, gesticulating wildly, and disappeared out the archway. From behind the set, yelling voices merged with loud banging and clanking of tin cans and buckets. After a moment the four figures of the man in white, the two firemen and the white girl in the box burst from behind the set and leaped over the black row of cardboard teeth into the audience.

A noisy awkward chase developed in the front portion of the space where the spectators sat as the four darted clumsily after each other, running this way and that. The bulky costumes (ex-

The chase. Girl in the box, The Pasty Man, a Fireman. In the background an axe juts from door; "smoke" rises (Joan Herbst, Red Grooms, Bob Thompson).

cept for that of the man in white) were a hindrance, and there was not much space for the performers to move. Perhaps some of the spectators noticed when the white figure moved quickly back into the set and disappeared behind the burning building. The audience still watched the halting, rushing movements of the other three performers, who, after a moment, stopped, apparently realizing that the subject of the chase was gone, and turned toward the set. Suddenly, through a cloth panel in the front of the cardboard burning building, the flying figure of the man in white dove, somersaulted, landed flat on his back and lay motionless. The two firemen and the girl in the box froze in rigid positions. Everything was perfectly quiet. After a moment, one of the firemen walked to the curtain and pulled it closed, signifying the end of the performance.

The Burning Building played in about ten minutes. It was never timed and the duration changed according to the performers' attitude and the audience reaction. Performances were given on eight consecutive evenings. Usually only one performance was

The Pasty Man dives out of the burning building (Red Grooms).

given in an evening, but the number varied with the number of spectators. There were four performances on "opening night." Once there was an audience of one: on a particularly cold midweek evening only Jim Dine arrived, but the performance went ahead as scheduled. It was halted halfway when members of the card-playing club that met twice weekly in the loft below came up to complain about the noise and the fact that their ceiling was falling down.

ROBERT WHITMAN

a statement

(Rewritten from a recorded interview.)

THE THING ABOUT THEATRE that most interests me is that it takes time. Time for me is something material. I like to use it that way. It can be used in the same way as paint or plaster or any other material. It can describe other natural events.

I intend my works to be stories of physical experience and realistic, naturalistic descriptions of the physical world. Description is done in terms of experience. If somebody says something is red, then everybody knows what that means because they have seen it. They have had that experience. A story is a record of experience or the creation of experience in order to describe something. The story of something is its description, the way it got that way, its nature. The intention of these works has to do with either re-creating certain experiences that tell a story, or presenting experiences that tell a story, or showing them. You can re-create it or present it or show it. You can expose things. All these things have to do with making them available: you make them available to the observer, so called.

The stories do not come from the objects, necessarily. There

134

might not be a story if there were not people. It is in the nature of what we do to listen to people and watch them and see what they are doing, respond to them. If I am making an object, and I want to find the story of that object, one way to do it is to see what people do when they are involved with it, have people involved with it, and be involved with it myself.

At a certain point, fantasy is an object in the physical world. It is like a street or rain. It is a product of physical events. It is a part of nature that can be described. The fantasy exists as an object, as a central physical entity, and as part of the story that you tell about other objects.

Since time is the material I use to describe these things and is essential to their nature, the chronological order of a piece develops naturally. I can let the order of events develop in a practical way. If you build anything you have got to start somewhere. You cannot start building a house on the second floor. Once you have the basic house built from the ground up, you can finish off this room or that room in any order. There is a certain rigid order in the nature of the piece and there are other things that can be practical matters or matters of choice.

Time is the medium that I use to demonstrate what I know about, what I think people need to know about.

THE AMERICAN MOON / *the script*

WHITMAN DOES NOT PREPARE a "script" either for himself or for his performers. He sometimes makes notes—pencil sketches, watercolors, captions, verbal notation. Those for *The American Moon* are typical.

At that time, Whitman's method of work was to leave exact details "undetermined until the actual moment of building," and these pages were primarily suggestions to himself about images that he felt were significant, but they contain at least germinal forms of every important image in the Happening except the final ones. Effects were noted, forms and shapes illustrated in color, and a suggestion of the structure was indicated by the page that combined notations on the use of motion pictures, balloons, and human action (divided into "floor piece," "hanging piece," etc.).

A number of the ideas in these notes were never realized in production. Some were discarded for esthetic reasons. A quick line sketch in pencil shows a circle filling one of the archways through which the audience watched the action, and huge letters spell out, "Big balloons in cave—Bang." Balloons were thrust into the openings of the "caves" but were withdrawn rather than exploded.

Other images were excluded because they could not be realized physically. For example, another pencil sketch shows two human figures in profile, their heads apparently touching the top of the familiar arch and their legs blurring into multiple positions. The large caption reads, "Running thru the space." In a description of *The American Moon* that he prepared later, Whitman wrote:

People are seen running through the space. They are only seen from

137

the waist down. They are suspended and pulled across the space. They are running faster than they are going. From this the space is filled with bodies shooting around in all directions. They are hung from the top by huge elastics so that they can spring around in all directions.

In order to carry out the first "gravity-defying event," actors would have to wear some sort of harness and be suspended from a horizontal rope or cable while they "walked on air" with perhaps only their legs visible to the spectators. In an attempt to achieve this, large bolts were sunk into the gallery wall to anchor a line. The difficult job took several hours. Finally the rope was rigged, tested by concerted pulling, and judged to be secure. But when one of the workers flipped the rope, the wave rippling up its length somehow hit the terminal with enough force to fire one of the bolts across the room like a bullet. The project was abandoned.

Another image that never took physical shape was the "Big Wheel" on which a standing person was centered. The wheel could theoretically be tilted from the horizontal to the vertical so that the rigid figure was parallel to the floor. One of the sketches shows two figures standing out from opposite sides of the wheel like some sort of human axle. Again the technical problems were too great.

THE AMERICAN MOON / *the production*

STARTING IN LATE November, 1960, and continuing into December, about ten performances of *The American Moon* by Robert Whitman were presented at the Reuben Gallery. Large pieces of paper in various bright colors bulged from the walls of the lobby, their curving surfaces and rough arrangements perhaps suggesting the strange artificial rocks of an amusement park tunnel of love. The visitors stood around a monolithic paper-covered structure in the center of the room, waiting.

When it was time for the performance to begin, eight or ten spectators were allowed to enter through a flap door in the wall that divided the lobby from the rest of the store-gallery. They found themselves in a tunnel about four feet wide and six feet high. The only light now was the flashlight carried by the girl who was leading them, and, after they had made their way through twenty or twenty-five feet of enclosed passageway with red walls and roof, the beam directed them through another flap door to one side and into chairs in a similar, but shorter, tunnel. In the darkness they could hear other segments of the waiting audience being led in. The later groups did not have as long a journey to find their places, and soon everyone was seated. Arranged in four rows of two or three people each, each group sat in the dark, knowing they were separated from the rest of the audience, hearing noises around them, and waiting for something to happen.

Three weeks before the first performance, Whitman had started work in the gallery. He had already completed the film that was to be a part of *The American Moon*, but now he began to build the complex structure that was, in itself, to be the most important experiential factor in the Happening. Using primarily scrap lumber and spending almost all his time in the gallery, he erected six tunnels, three radiating outward from each side of an oval central

139

area. Each tunnel was to contain its own small audience of from eight to ten spectators who would watch activities taking place in the central space. No one in the tunnels could see the complete space, and those in each tunnel would have a different view of the action. The sides, movable roof and rear of each tunnel were walled with kraft paper painted red. Curtains were hung over the front openings. Directly over the curtained ends of the tunnels and almost encircling the oval central area were catwalks, accessible by ladders, for the use of the performer-stagehands.

It could be said that rehearsals began two weeks before the first performance. The people who were going to participate—friends and others who had expressed interest—began to stop by the gallery after the first week of building. Whitman would tell them what he expected them to do during the performance, or, busy with his work, just let them become familiar with the space he was creating. Occasionally the whole cast would gather, and at the first two such meetings Whitman described the Happening, but no actual physical rehearsal took place. Later, run-throughs of the complete Happening were held. If something needed correction or improvement, Whitman would pause while it was repeated, and then the run-through would continue. Sections were never rehearsed separately. The overall "flow" was more important to him than specific details.

For the performances an additional but temporary tunnel was erected across the central space, joining the middle tunnels on each side. In this way members of the audience could be seated in the tunnels farthest from the lobby without seeing the performance area or the radial arrangement of the tunnels. When the audience was seated, the temporary tunnel was removed, and the performance was ready to begin.

The expectant audience heard a loud, harsh metallic buzzing from the darkness. Tape-recorded, it lasted for forty-five seconds. Then a light went on in the central space. The people in each tunnel found they were facing two curtains through which could be seen only vague shapes and light. The outer curtain, made of burlap, was slowly raised. (These burlap curtains, thrown over the railings of the catwalks, would prevent the audience from seeing anyone on the walks.) Now the audience was looking through curtains of transparent plastic on which were glued standard-sized sheets of typewriter paper. The sheets were not continuous, and between them the spectators could begin to discern the opposite tunnels and to make out shapes on the floor of the central space. The rows of rectangular paper and the grid formed by the narrow spaces between them resembled multiple-paned windows, but in this case the strips were transparent and the panes opaque. Then the plastic curtain, too, was slowly raised.

Across the open space, which had no visible ceiling or walls, the spectators could see one or more tunnels like their own where seated spectators looked back at them. The floor of the revealed space was covered with large irregular heaps of colored cloth. In the dim light a streamer of cloth began to twist and swing as it rose upward; the ascending column broadened as a wide mush-room shape was pulled into view, followed by a pointed oval, like a mouth or the shield of some African warrior. The piles of cloth on the floor became animated and rose as three separate figures. Moving about the central space and into the openings of the tunnels, the three figures could be surmised to be costumed performers, but their shapes and movements were decidedly nonhuman. A mouth figure with painted teeth spun and darted and scuttled close to the floor like some strange crab. A tall limb-

The cloth-covered figure in the opening sequence. View is from inside one of the tunnels. Two other tunnels may be seen opposite.

less tube swayed, twisted, and suddenly jumped. A huge heap of used upholstery cloth wove and bobbed and lunged, dropping and scattering bits of cloth. Then the forms moved outside the limited field of vision—several feet at each end of the central oval, near the walls, were used by the participants as "offstage" space for preparations and waiting—and the lights went out.

In the darkness the plastic curtains were again lowered over the front of each tunnel. Unseen 8-mm. projectors, directed through holes in the rear wall behind each audience group, beamed a color film onto the mosaic of white paper rectangles glued to the curtains. Each of the six projectors showed the same film and were started at the same moment by two master switches, but exact simultaneity was not attempted. The space between the many small paper screens produced a grid effect on the image.

The motion picture itself opened with a cloth-covered figure rising slowly in the center of an autumn-tinted wooded area. The figure, looking perhaps like a multicolored cloth haystack, moved slowly, with one sharp sudden leap, toward the camera and past it. The camera panned the fall foliage, predominantly green and yellow. In a dark and slightly underexposed shot, the figure rose slowly from behind bushes and sunk from sight again. Then a similar cloth figure was seen hanging in the air, apparently supported by wires like a marionette, and being jerked along. Two white helmet shapes filled the foreground. Several such marionettes appeared in succession. The last one began to shed its piled coverings one at a time, and the scene again shifted to the woods where the white helmet shapes, also of cloth, swung and floated among the trees, carried on the ends of long wooden poles. Two red semicircles on a common base and a yellow mouth or pointed oval form accompanied them. Finally one of the white shapes was raised and lowered in an open space. It flew toward the camera like a cloth-tipped javelin, landing somewhat to the left.

During the screening of the film, lights were occasionally flashed on in the tunnels, briefly destroying the image. Occasionally someone would walk by the rear of the multiple screen and push it so that it rippled. At times, too, the center lights were momentarily switched off so that the spectator could look past and through the image at the front of his cave to see, from the rear, the pictures on the opposite curtains. If a projector malfunctioned, perhaps "losing a loop" so that the image jumped and blurred chaotically, the curtain was raised so that the opposite image could be seen.

When each film finished—their endings were not simultaneous —the plastic curtain of that tunnel was raised so that the white light of the projector was beamed into the central area, illuminating another huge cloth-covered ball similar to those seen in the film. Soft noises came from the ball. (The sounds were based on a script which the concealed performer was reading with the aid of a flashlight.) When all six projectors lit it, the cloth heap rose slightly and moved off, still making the noises. The projectors went dark, and the central lights came on.

Suspended like the ball of a pendulum from two ropes attached somewhere above, a large pile of red cloth was swung back and forth across the central space. Secondary ropes slanting down from each side alternately pulled it in its arcing passage. The red covering began to drop away. Slowly at first, and then with a rush, the layers of cloth dropped and were thrown aside, and there sat a bearded man swinging across the empty space. The lights went out, and noises were heard in the darkness.

(Whitman considered all sounds that occurred, whether intentional or "accidental," part of a noise pattern that was an integral element of the Happening. Sound of various sorts was a natural concomitant of the visible occurrences in the central space between the tunnels, but equally as prevalent were the sounds made by the performer-stagehands as they made unseen adjustments and preparations. Their "backstage" pattern of operation was carefully worked out and, at least at particular moments, very exact. One of the performers recalls pausing every evening at a certain place in the performance to hold a flashlight directly above her head. The light was taken by someone above her on the catwalk— a transfer that had been found necessary during rehearsal—but she never knew to whom she was handing it. Since the wooden catwalks were only a couple of feet above the heads of the seated audience, and no particular effort was made to prevent or conceal noise, the audience units were often engulfed by sound. Their vision was limited by the tunnel, but sound was heard from all directions.)

At this particular moment sound was caused by the raising of the tunnels' roofs. The lights were turned on in the tunnels, and the cloth of which the roofs were made was slowly pulled up and back, opening the center. Past the red of the roof, now slanting upward, each audience looked up into a yellow cone several feet above. The flat-roofed tunnels had been transformed. About ten seconds later, all the lights were turned out.

Illuminated by the abrupt, sweeping, erratic light of flashlights swung randomly and turned rapidly on and off, two figures were seen in the central area carrying balls of plastic about five feet in diameter, stuffed with crumpled paper. Moving purposefully and quickly in the lightning-like flashes that glinted from the plastic, they threw the balls into the tunnel entrances, obscuring the view of those inside. After a moment someone removed each ball and threw it into a different tunnel. (Although it might not have been sensed by the spectators, each of the two performers would place balls at random in the tunnels on one side of the central space and remove those that had been placed on the opposite side, alternately placing and removing.) After a few minutes of this activity, the center lights were again turned on, showing the space to be empty.

The woman rolling over the man.

From each end of the oval central area the stiff body of a person, arms at sides, rolled quickly out. The figures, one male and the other female, collided in the center and rolled back out of sight. Again they rolled out, collided, and rolled back. On their third appearance, the girl rolled abruptly over the man, and each continued across the space. Repeating this once more, the woman rolling over the man, they returned to the sides from which they had started. Now when they appeared they began a kind of prone hopping, face down and bodies held rigid, perhaps suggestive of the tremors of a *grand mal* seizure. They hopped toward the center, circled each other, and the lights went out.

In the darkness a whirring and buzzing noise was heard. Some may have recognized the sound of a vacuum cleaner. When the lights came on, plastic stretched across the central floor was beginning to rise, swelled and blown by wind within it. (Four unseen vacuum cleaners, two at either end of the oval, were inflating a huge plastic balloon made from polyethylene sheets taped together.) In the dim light, the transparent skin, rippling and glowing as it rose, might have reminded one of a Portuguese man-of-war: just as the jellylike fish is almost invisible in the water, the immense balloon approached invisibility. From above, a snow of crumpled sheets of newspaper began to fall, some pieces pausing briefly on the top of the balloon before they slid off to collect on the floor at both sides. Finally the balloon was inflated. It was about six feet high and the ends could not be seen by the spectators within the tunnels. The space was almost completely filled, yet without substance. Then, for the first time in this sequence, human figures appeared. A man and a girl squeezed between the balloon and the tunnel entrances, and crawled under the plastic. The transparent material glistened as it hung in folds over their reclining forms. Another man (Whitman) came out wearing a short leather coat and stood in the middle, staring into the balloon, his hands resting on the shiny surface. After several moments in which no one moved, the lights went out.

The huge bag of air was quickly deflated in the darkness and rolled up. When the lights came on, Whitman asked the audience to come out of the tunnels into the central area. All may not have heard the invitation, but as they saw what others were doing, they followed, and soon everyone stood in the space the balloon had just filled. The lights went out and then on again. A few feet

Man and woman under the large balloon. View is from above (Lucas Samaras, Simone Whitman).

Man looking into the balloon.

Audience standing in the central space, watching rigid man on swing. Projection screen curtains can be seen above the three tunnels at right, draped over the railing of the catwalk (Lucas Samaras).

above the heads of the spectators, the rigid horizontal body of a man hung on a trapeze, his hands gripping the verticals of the ropes. Near each end of the tall oval space, a large ball made of many layers of variously colored cloth bounced and swung at the end of a rope and did an eccentric dance in the air. Then the lights went out. From the darkness, expressionless faces appeared, rising above the railings of the catwalks, lit by the explosion of flashbulbs and the sudden momentary beams of flashlights. The order and rate of movement of the performers as they rose into potential visibility from behind the railings and sunk back again into obscurity, as well as the timing of the illuminating flashes, were random.

With the disappearance of the last face and the last flash of light *The American Moon* ended. After a moment of darkness, the lights came on again and the standing audience was left to find its way out through the tunnels and back to the lobby. It would be much simpler than the passage in. Now they were familiar with the spaces that Whitman had created.

MOUTH / *the production*

ONE EVENING IN EARLY April, 1961, two Police Department
detectives, walking along East Third Street on New York's Lower
East Side, noticed, in one of the stores, what looked like a huge
mouth with pink flesh, red lips and rows of white teeth filling the
space from wall to wall and from floor to ceiling. Beyond the
mouth, through the opening between the teeth, they saw movement. The door to the store was open; the detectives went in,
walked carefully through a gap in the lower row of teeth, and
looked around. Immediately behind the mouth wall through
which they had passed and along both side walls to their left and
right—in the relative position of teeth within a mouth, although
they probably did not make the association—were about fifty
folding chairs facing toward the center of a space about twenty-
five feet long and ten feet wide. Except for a column of aluminum
foil that stood at the edge of the entrance, the space was empty.
The rear wall, opposite them, was made of cloth fastened to the
ceiling, slanted backward at an angle until about seven feet from
the floor, and then dropped vertically. At the point where the
cloth wall slanted back, a pulley arrangement fastened to the
patterned tin ceiling supported a hanging, white, cloth-covered
structure about six feet high that bulged at the top and tapered
toward the bottom in the approximation of a heart shape. At the
right and left sides of the rear wall were cloth and paper partitions jutting into the room, and overhead, hanging from horizontal
ropes, were a six-foot arrow and an equally large white shape
that could have been a cloud. But there were no people to be
seen.

From behind the scrim wall that created a "backstage" area,
one of the performers noticed two unfamiliar pairs of black shoes.

148

The rehearsal for Robert Whitman's *Mouth* was about to begin. Everyone was in place, silent, waiting. But these shoes were not a part of the Happening. Whitman went out to speak to their occupants. The tall men in snap-brimmed fedoras had just identified themselves when they realized that people were apparently hiding throughout the strangely remodeled store. Someone was standing behind a curtain at the left side of the rear wall. Someone else was inside the contraption that dangled from the ceiling. And there were probably other people behind the cloth wall. What was going on? Why should these people want to hide from the police? Whitman, reticent about mentioning theatrical performances, explained that it was "moving sculpture" and that the various people were needed to operate the movements. Apparently satisfied, if a little confused, the detectives were leaving when one pointed at the chicken-wire-and-aluminum-foil column that reached almost to the ceiling. "What is it?" he asked. "A tree," answered Whitman. "What's the matter," said the second detective to his partner who stood looking up at the leafless metallic trunk, "don't you have any imagination?"

Mouth was performed seven times at the Reuben Gallery on the evenings of the 18th through the 23rd of April, 1961—there were two performances on Friday evening. Four or five full rehearsals had been held and most of the time during them was spent working out the movement patterns and placement in the limited space. It was important that everything have an assigned place so as not to interfere with the succeeding business. Some of the more difficult sequences, such as the opening "dance," were rehearsed separately, and much rehearsal time was spent working out the "backstage" technical operation of the performance. The day before the first performance, the floor and the folding chairs were painted—the floor was flesh color near the walls with a redder central "tongue" area, the chairs were white—and *Mouth* was ready to be performed.

The spectators passed through the opening in the mouth wall— a wooden framework covered with chicken wire and papier-mâché—and found seats inside. General white light illuminated the space. Lights concealed behind aluminum foil shields on either side of the rear scrim wall colored it red. At the center of the rear wall, the large white hanging structure (a rectangular

framework given a general heart shape by chicken wire and covered with white muslin) swung slowly from side to side, pulled
alternately by ropes attached to the main rope from which it
depended. Until the entire audience was seated, there was no
other movement.

Then the large white cardboard silhouette of a bulbous cloud
hanging at the left end of a horizontal rope running parallel to
the rear wall and a foot or so from the ceiling began to be pulled
very slowly to the right. The arrow, hooked onto a similar rope
track that stretched from the right side of the mouth wall, behind
the audience, to the left corner of the curtain wall (where the
cloud was beginning its travels), also began to move. The arrow,
about six feet above the tile floor, was somewhat lower than the
cloud. After some time had passed and the slow-moving cloud
was about halfway in its journey to the opposite wall, the silence
was broken as a girl entered through the rear curtains beneath the
cloud. Hindered by a tight skirt, she was running in an eccentric,
precipitous fashion, changing directions sharply, her high heels
making a steady staccato rhythm on the tiles—a rhythm which
was interrupted only at the moments when the struggle for equi-
librium was lost, and she fell. Crisscrossing the space at a constant
rate, she circled behind the pendulum, timing its swing. At moments she seemed about to fall into the audience seated in double
rows on three sides of the area. While she "danced," the cloud
and arrow were still moving, and she timed her exit for the
moment the arrow was about to touch the curtain wall toward
which it was traveling. The point of the arrow reached the small
curtain, the section of cloth shot up in the air, and three girls
tumbled to the floor. All the lights suddenly went out.

After a blackout of perhaps ten seconds to allow the girls to
exit, the lights were again turned on, and a rectangular yellow
cardboard car containing two girls, both dressed in street clothes,
pushed its way from behind the scrim curtains. The crude car,
almost six feet long and three and a half feet high with motionless
painted wheels and four oval faces of different colors painted on
its windshield, was propelled by its occupants. The girls bounced
up and down as they pushed and carried the framework on a
slightly wandering drive along one edge of the playing space and
parked near the aluminum tree at the farthest possible distance

The three girls fall as curtain is raised. Hanging arrow is seen at left, pendulum in center.

The car drives out (Chippie McClellan, Trisha Schlicter).

from the scrim wall and the pendulum. Getting out through a flap door in the left side of the car, the girls carried a picnic lunch to the center of the acting area, where they spread a cloth and sat down to eat. (The meal—sandwiches and perhaps a Thermos of coffee—varied each evening, depending upon which of the pair had prepared it. It was actually the performers' dinner, and they did not just pretend to eat.)

While the girls picnicked, perhaps saying a word or two to each other if it was necessary but nothing extended or animated and nothing that could be clearly heard by the audience, the roundish painted papier-mâché heads of two animals poked through openings in the scrim wall and watched them. Then the animals came out slowly and partially circled the girls. The large animal, a five-foot-tall orange mountain of chicken wire and papier-mâché looking like an elephant without a trunk, came first, animated by an unseen performer inside. The small animal—stiff wooden legs three feet long and a flat back covered with strips of brown and green cloth—was carried out by an expressionless girl and left in place. Both animals were now between part of the audience and the picnic, and their white heads with black eyes, ears, and noses and red-rimmed mouths with rows of sawlike teeth were turned toward the girls. Spectators leaned and shifted to see around the animals and the car. The girls paid no attention to the animals and continued to eat. There was no sound.

Two more girls joined the one who had placed the small animal. One girl wore a basic muslin dress to which leaves had been glued. The dress of the second was covered with aluminum foil, and that of the third had ragged white fur attached to the front. At first the girls alternated sudden quick motion with moments of motionless standing. ("Like a squirrel in the woods," as Whitman describes it, that scurries quickly and then freezes into semi-invisibility.) The timing and direction of these movements were completely spontaneous and any overall pattern depended upon chance. Each girl would try not to move at the same moment as any other, and the audience could not anticipate who would move next or when they would move.

When the picnickers were finished, one of the girls picked up the cloth, wrappers, and Thermos, got back into the car, and "drove" off, exiting through the scrim wall. The remaining girl did

The picnic. The large animal and the pendulum are in background.

not notice the watching animals or the moving figures. She lay down beside the pendulum, which was still swinging, and went to sleep. The bottom of the pendulum was only about a foot from the floor, and it partially obscured her. Red pieces of cloth about the size of an envelope began to fall from the bottom of the swinging pendulum and scatter over the floor and over the recumbent girl.

The three silent, sporadically moving girls were joined by a fourth who wore a long full dress of white muslin that had been soaked in water. Water dripped from the dress, leaving a trail behind her as she began to move in the same fashion as the others. (It was the same girl who had just taken part in the picnic. She kept a hot plate backstage to heat the water so it would not chill her.)

Soon the shifting "stop-and-go" pattern began to change. One

The picnic. Small animal is at left. Three costumed girls are beginning their "stop-and-go" movements.

of the girls had reached a predetermined spot near the aluminum tree and started to rock back and forth. Using this as a cue, the others worked their way toward the same spot, still alternating quick movement and frozen waiting. When they got there, they commenced swaying or rocking movements at various tempos. The "water" girl spun in circles, and drops sprinkled the nearby spectators. Then one of the girls, her hands at her sides and her body straight, began to step quickly so that she bumped into the girls near her. This, too, was a cue, and all the girls moved in the same way. Grouped together in one spot, the four girls spun and turned and bumped each other and rebounded. As the energy of their movements increased, the lights went out. Above the sleeping girl, the pendulum still swung. The motionless animals still watched.

After a moment of total darkness, during which the animals were taken off and the performers left the playing area, the pendulum was illuminated from inside. On its swing to the left it glowed red; during the right half of its arc, it glowed blue. The alternation of colors continued for quite a while. ("As long," says Whitman, "as I felt like doing it." He was controlling lights and directing activities behind the scrim wall.) Then all the lights went off, and the scrim wall was lit from the rear by flashes and flickers of moving red light. (Whitman and the others behind the scrim were using hand-held lights and sheets of red gelatin to create the effect.)

The general white lights were turned on again. From behind

Three of the four costumed girls in movement sequence (Chippie McClellan, Simone Whitman, Judy Tersch).

The pendulum glows. Arrow is silhouetted by light. Large animal looks out from "backstage." In right center is aluminum foil tree.

the scrim came a procession of three dark tube shapes, seven or eight feet tall. (The unseen performers within them raised their hands above their heads to support the tubes and shuffled slowly ahead in single file, their movements restricted by the cloth.) Swaying slightly and rhythmically, the three tubes made a clockwise circuit of the playing area and disappeared again behind the curtains.

There was another total blackout. After a moment, the beam of a flashlight illuminated the pendulum, now motionless and seen as a rectangular space containing a chair. (While the lights were out, the two horizontal ropes used to swing the pendulum had been released and the whole structure turned so that what had been its back now faced the audience.) A girl came out and sat in the chair, facing front. The flashlight flicked off, and again nothing could be seen. Creaking sounds came from the darkness. Now seen to be near the ceiling, the pendulum glowed with blue light. (The same lights that had previously alternated the colors as the pendulum swung were used. They were hidden between the wooden framework and its covering.) While the lights were

The reversed pendulum is lighted. Head of small animal is at left (Simone Whitman).

out, the pendulum had been raised and now was lowered slowly, the seated girl still facing toward the front. When it reached the floor, the lights again went out. After another moment of darkness and noise, the pendulum structure again illuminated itself when high above the floor; this time it glowed red. The girl sat in profile. The pendulum was slowly lowered, and again there was a blackout when it reached the floor. Now when the light again went on after the moment of darkness—both red and blue combining to make purple—the raised box was empty. The empty box descended. When it was down, the general white lights were switched on.

All of the girls who had been performing pushed through the scrim curtain and, for a brief moment, hopped toward the opposite wall and toward the audience. Again there was total darkness.

When the lights came on, the pendulum was motionless, the playing area was empty, the Happening was over. If the audience lingered, not sure whether to expect anything more, someone would call out, telling them that the performance had ended.

FLOWER / *the production*

Flower BY ROBERT WHITMAN probably was given more performances than any other Happening to date. On weekends
during March, 1963, it was presented twenty times. When the
spectators entered the large store or ground-floor loft on Great
Jones Street, a few blocks east of Washington Square Park in New
York City, they passed some of the machinery of the production
on the way to their seats. The front section of the store was partitioned off with white curtains, now partially drawn back to
allow entrance, and in the center of this lobby-backstage space
was a wooden stand that held a motion-picture projector and a
slide projector. To the right was a table which was obviously the
control center for various lights and sound equipment. And to the
left, close to the curtains, was a large rectangular structure about
six feet tall, its purpose or use not easily discerned.

Walking through the opening in the curtains into the main
portion of the high-ceilinged room, the spectators found two long
rows of chairs, perhaps thirty-five or forty in all, facing each other
across a central space about eight or nine feet wide. The rows of
chairs were about four feet from the longer walls and parallel to
them. These side walls had been painted with brightly colored
vertical stripes. (With each performance more stripes would be
added; their density continually increased during the "run" of the
Happening.) In the center of one of the side walls, a motion-
picture projector had been placed on a wooden stand. Near one
corner at the front end of the room was a huge, red flower construction, its cloth-covered petals folded toward the audience in
a partially closed position. On the floor in the opposite corner was
a large, bulging burlap bag. The rear end of the room, opposite
the entrance, was obscured by a white sheet, and, on all four sides,

large, white muslin curtains had been hung, their lower portions pulled up toward the center of the room, revealing the walls and allowing entrance.

When the audience was seated, the sliding curtains at the front were closed, and all of the lights, located primarily in a square wooden framework suspended over the center of the space, went off. A flashbulb exploded at the front of the room, and the spectators turned in that direction. Another flash went off some distance away, momentarily revealing the figure of the man who had triggered it. In the extremely faint light coming from the control area, the man could be seen as he crossed the twenty feet of open space at the end of the room and stopped at what was apparently a spectator seated at the end of one of the rows of chairs. Leading the onlooker to the center, he posed him, illuminated him briefly in the white flash from a camera, and walked with him back to his seat. Then he moved to the front again, directing his flash at the large burlap sack that lay in the corner. A light above the sack went on, and the performer disappeared behind the curtain.

The sack moved, and a column of narrow pieces of green cloth, perhaps resembling the tail of a kite, slowly rose from it like a snake being charmed by a fakir. Now some of the spectators had to turn in their seats or stand in order to watch the movement. Obviously pulled up by a hanging wire (the thin plastic cord was almost invisible), more and more cloth ascended and began to hang in loops near the ceiling. Sometimes the cloth pulled free leaving the brown bag behind, but at about half of the performances the bag, too, rose in the air to hang amid the drooping coils of fabric. The light that had focused attention on the activities of the sack and its content went out.

The spectators, already turned toward the front of the room, saw a colored picture of woods projected onto one of the curtains there. It was the first in a series of slides of landscape and nature. When the subject changed to details of facial anatomy—an open mouth, an ear, a nose—a motion picture made from the slides but having a bluish cast was thrown on the adjacent curtain from the rear, and the motion picture and the slides continued side by side, presenting identical material. During this sequence, the projector that was visible to the audience was switched on, throwing motion pictures of a person in bed onto the sheet at the opposite end of the room. For a while, all three projectors were functioning at the same time. Then the slides and the motion picture of anatomy were switched off.

A dim light went on overhead. The movie of the person in bed continued to run. Suddenly two people burst out from between the curtains where the simultaneous movie and slides had been shown. Holding on to each other, they spun into the space between the spectators. They were a man and a girl—the man in ordinary street dress with a coat or jacket, the girl in slacks and a bulky sweater—who were pulling furiously at each other. The man was able to yank off the girl's sweater, revealing another one (or a shirt) underneath, and it became apparent that each was simultaneously trying to pull off the other's clothing. Jerked this way and that, perhaps falling, the pair battled, spinning around the space. The floor became littered with sweaters and shirts that had been forcibly removed. Although the man was usually more successful, the girl did not give up her own strenuous attempts to remove his jacket and sweaters; then, without any apparent winner, the pair, who had worked their way back to the front of the room, disappeared through the curtains.

The curtains did not reach to the floor, and, after a moment, a man rolled a large, round white shape under them. The head and bare legs of a girl protruded from opposite ends of the stuffed, cloth ball. Leaving the figure motionless in the aisle between the spectators, the man rolled out another girl whose covering was blue. The two girls were passive and only cooperated slightly in movements that the man initiated. When he helped them to their feet, the stuffing within the bulging costumes sank to the bottom, leaving only the head and feet of each girl visible outside the roughly pear-shaped mass. Stepping to a folding chair at the opposite end of the rows of spectators, the man picked up a pile of folded clothes and began draping pieces of cloth around the "shoulders" of the two motionless, expressionless girls. Perhaps a yellow cloth was placed on the blue figure, hanging down one side. Perhaps a blue piece was wrapped around the upper portion of the girl in white. A rectangular piece of white material with a round hole in the center for the girl's head was perhaps placed around her; the red outline of painted hands could be seen as it hung down. Several layers of cloth were attached to each girl. Then the man walked off, and the two girls were left alone.

One of the girls hopped suddenly and again was motionless.

The other girl hopped. With pauses of about three seconds between their small jumps, both girls, their faces expressionless, began to move in small, abrupt bounces away from the curtains through which the man had disappeared. The rate of hopping became slightly faster, and they began to spin quickly as they jumped. Alternating motionless pauses with the hop-spins, the girls moved out of the space between the spectators.

The man entered and guided them back to the center. Stopping them some distance apart, he began slowly and gently to remove the cloths that he had placed around them. Pulling cloth from one and then from the other and dropping it on the floor, he moved back and forth, his motions becoming more energetic. Then he roughly seized the front of one of the pear-shaped costumes and ripped it open. He reached inside, pulled out crumpled newspapers, and scattered them on the floor. The girl remained motionless, her face blank. The man crossed to the other girl and tore open the front of her bulging cloth covering. Again he pulled out crumpled newspaper. Faster and faster, he moved back and forth between the two impassive figures, grabbing out armfuls of newspaper, flinging the paper out violently onto the floor, burrowing into the lower recesses of the container and scattering the stuffing in all directions. The space between the spectators became completely filled with torn and crumpled paper. Suddenly several men and girls (all available performers were used—there were usually about four or five—and the number varied from performance to performance) rushed out from the curtained area at the front of the room. Grabbing large armfuls of the littered newspaper, some of them carried it around the audience rows or threw it directly over the heads of the seated spectators into the spaces between the side walls and the chairs. At one side, a man with a staple gun (Robert Whitman) was attaching bunches of paper to the wall. At the other side, one or two of the performers were dipping handfuls of the crumpled newspapers into a bucket of paste and pushing them against the wall: the glue did not hold, and the paper fell to the floor, but still the attempt to cover the wall was made. (Even when they knew it would not hold, the bucket of paste was retained because Whitman felt that the activity of forcing the material against the wall was more important than the actual sticking, although, preferably, he would have

The man pulls newspaper out of the costume of one of the "ball girls." Spectators are seated at left and right (facing camera: Walter DeMaria, Suzanne DeMaria).

Newspaper is pushed against the wall behind one row of spectators. Note movable cloth wall and painted stripes.

liked to achieve that, too.) Now the areas between and behind the rows of spectators were filled with performers, all of whom—except for the two passive girls—were involved in furious activity: paper was carried, thrown and pushed against the wall; the man with the staple gun had succeeded in attaching large clumps of paper to the wall on which he was working, and he was attacking the motion-picture projector, which was still running, and its wooden base, stapling paper there, too. The man who had been removing the stuffing from the cloth containers that the girls wore was almost finished with his job. Perhaps he placed one of the girls on the floor where she lay among the scattered papers. Perhaps he shook one of the costumes violently to make sure it was completely emptied of paper. When all the stuffing had been removed, he carried the inert girls out of sight. For some time, the almost-frantic activity with the paper continued. (Whitman was able to control the duration of the sequence itself. When he ceased stapling and exited, the others soon followed.) When the last performer disappeared, a jumble of crumpled newspaper hung from the wall and lay scattered around, over, and behind the two rows of chairs.

At the end of the first part, all performers move the newspaper out of the central space.

At the end of the room, the motion picture was still being projected; the spectators turned to watch it. After several minutes, the film ended. Everything was quiet. Suddenly the folding chair from which the man had previously taken the cloths to use in "dressing" the two costumed girls was yanked up into the air, and a rectangular wooden box or stand came crashing down. (A rope connected the chair and the box, and when the suspended box was released, it fell and abruptly pulled the chair up to dangle in the air near the ceiling.) The lights went out. In the darkness, someone was heard saying that the first part of the piece was over and that the second part would begin after a short intermission.

While the spectators stepped outside or stood near the projectors and sound equipment in the control area where they could watch the preparations, the performers began to sweep up the scattered newspaper and remove it from the walls where it had been stapled. The projector was moved to the back end of the room, and the hanging sheet which had served as a projection screen was removed. Now a brown cloth about eight feet square could be seen: in its center was the shiny white, heraldic silhouette of a three-petaled flower. Two large, bulging burlap bags were suspended, with some effort, from light ropes with hooks at the end that had been hanging over the central area between the chairs throughout the performance. When everything was ready, an announcement was made to the spectators, the information was passed along, and the audience was again seated. The lights went off.

A light went on at the front end of the room, and the spectators could see that a curtain had been removed, revealing the rectangular structure that some of them had noticed on the way in. Perhaps four feet wide and six feet high, the element was a solid white. From its base, a beige or coffee-colored cloth began to rise around it. (Again the plastic wires that were used were almost invisible.) Slowly and evenly, the cloth was pulled up until the whole rectangle was covered. Suddenly, three large cardboard flowers—one red, one yellow, and one white—sprang up from the top of the structure. (They were pushed up on poles by unseen performers.) The light went out, and again the audience was in darkness.

The dim light over the central space went on. A girl entered at the front of the room. She was wearing a one-piece dress of shiny white material that left her arms bare, and, as she began to walk slowly and impassively about the room, another girl, and then another, similarly dressed, entered. Four girls, all wearing the same type of simple white dress, were soon wandering randomly around and between the audience rows. Their faces were expressionless, and occasionally their hands moved carefully, making adjustments in their costumes. Now the dresses were no longer white but showed passages of bright red at the shoulder. As the girls walked, their clothing changed color: they progressed from white to red to blue and then to gold. (Although each girl went through the four stages which lasted about a minute each, they did not make the changes simultaneously, and as time passed there was less and less chance that all four would be the same color at the same moment. The costumes were designed so that the upper, blouse portion could be slipped off the shoulder and dropped down to become a skirt. The lining of the blouse, now exposed as a skirt, would match the color of a second blouse that had been under the first and was revealed. Of course the opposite procedure could be followed and the skirt raised to become the blouse.) At any of the intermediary, transition stages, two or more colors could be seen, and, since changes were only made gradually as the girls walked aimlessly about, this was most frequently the case. Although the light was dim, the eyes of the spectators were growing accustomed to it. They watched as the combinations of colors became more and more complicated. (When each of the girls had moved through her sequence of color changes, she began to twist, pull and turn the layers of her costume in order to find new arrangements. Even after many performances, new possibilities were being discovered.) Then a metallic rattle was added to the sound of high heels clicking against the floor. One of the girls had picked up a pressurized can of spray paint and was shaking it. Soon all four of the performers, without breaking the tempo of their random pacing, had walked to the spot near one wall where the paint had been placed and had picked up a can. (The decision to begin the next sequence was made by the girls. It was based on feeling, established in rehearsal, rather than on a particular physical cue.)

Now the girls began to add vertical stripes of colors to those that were already on the walls behind each of the two rows of spectators. From five basic colors—red, blue, green, yellow and white—four had been chosen. Each girl would spray on a long, soft-edged vertical line of bright color and then walk to another spot, perhaps at the opposite wall, to repeat the process. The rattle of the metal agitators in the cans provided random auditory accompaniment, and the spectators were aware of the acrid smell of the paint.

A strange figure appeared at the front of the room. Shaped somewhat like a huge yellow ice-cream cone about seven feet tall, it had a wide rounded top and shiny cloth sides slanting in and and down to the floor. (The original plan was to have a man walk out with an umbrella and raise it. Yellow cloth attached to weights would fall, covering him completely. But the mechanical problems of the device were never completely solved, and, after the first performance, the performer entered already enclosed.) The yellow shape moved past the two burlap bags hanging in the center of the space, stopped in front of the large white flower emblem at the back of the room, and collapsed. Perhaps the spectators got a glimpse of the performer as he folded the umbrella,

The yellow figure moves past the hanging bags between the rows of spectators.

crouched under the folds of cloth, and moved to one side, disappearing behind a small panel.

With the entrance of the yellow figure, the four girls had ceased their painting, and, without hurrying or breaking the random pattern of their movements, had returned the cans to their original place. Now changes again were appearing in the costumes as the girls moved about.

The cloth curtains that hung over the upper walls at the sides and curved out like the limp sails of a large ship now began to descend. Slowly the pieces of wood that held the lower edges of the white muslin were lowered toward the floor. When the bright stripes that the girls had just painted had been completely obscured, similar curtains at the front and back of the space began to come down. The red flower construction at the front and the white flower silhouette at the rear were both hidden behind the hanging cloth. The four performers and the audience were completely enclosed within blank white walls. Long streamers of green cloth attached to the ceiling had been held up by the side curtains, and as the cloth walls descended, the streamers, knotted and twisted together, swung out and down. The girls walked around and untangled them, filling the space with hanging strips of ragged green cloth that reached to within a few feet of the floor.

The four girls continued slowly to change the colors of their costumes as they wandered about the room. The dim white light went off, and red lights mounted in the central hanging frame went on, illuminating the white walls, the audience, and the walking girls. After perhaps a minute, the red lights were switched off; yellow lights went on. The girls continued their slow movements. Blue lights replaced the yellow, and then various combinations of light—blue and red, red and yellow, yellow and blue—were switched on. Each color remained on for half a minute to a minute, while the girls crossed between and around the rows of spectators. Then the lights went out.

For a minute, the audience sat in the dark inside the four blank cloth walls of the inner room Suddenly there was a loud crash, and the building vibrated. (In the control area, Whitman had raised a heavy wooden skid—the kind used to facilitate the loading of trucks—as high as he could and dropped it onto the floor.) Loudspeakers at either end of the room blared out a steady stream

The man empties cloth from one of the hanging bags. The four female performers are wearing the costumes that "changed" colors. Large flower emblem is in rear. Green cloth "vines" hang from ceiling. Cloth wall at side has been lowered.

of complicated noise, the lights went on, the cloth walls at the ends of the space lifted back into their original position, a man dragged in a burlap sack and, moving quickly to the two hanging sacks, began to open them. The noise (actually a recording of hissing steam from a radiator, although it could not be recognized as such) stopped and another sound replaced it: comments of shoppers, clothes hangers squeaking and squealing as they slid on display racks, the voices and sounds of a department store. The man spilled multicolored pieces of cloth out of one of the hanging sacks; perhaps unhooking the second bag and lowering it to the floor, he dumped out more rags. The four girls gathered around the piles of cloth, picking through them as if looking for something. The man moved to the third bag, opened it, pulled out still more cloth, and then helped a girl out of the burlap container. She stood motionless as the man and the four girls in the brightly colored costumes began to wrap and cover her with the pieces of cloth. In a while, she was completely encased: all of the variously colored cloth from the three bags was hung and tied around her, and she became a huge, ragged pillar of fabric. The motionless figure was left alone as the other performers disappeared into the control area. The department-store sounds stopped. The lights went off.

The red flower construction that had been visible at the front of the room throughout most of the performances was illuminated. Slowly and erratically, the huge petals opened, folding back. The eight extended red ovals stopped moving, and for a moment nothing happened. Then the burlap circle that formed the center of the flower bulged. Something began to push through. A mass of rags poured out and lay in a multicolored pile on the floor. More cloth spilled out. Then the heap of fabric moved, and parts of it rose slowly into the air. At two separate places, cloth was pulled from the pile and lifted up. (As in earlier effects, the plastic cord was almost completely invisible.) At some performances, additional pieces of cloth would cling to the brown and yellow fragments to which the cords were attached, making ragged bunches of various sizes, but most frequently the two pulled free from the pile and rose independently. For perhaps a minute, usually at different heights, the crumpled brown and yellow pieces of fabric hung in the air. There was no sound. Then the light went out.

At the opposite end of the room, lights illuminated the large, white three-petaled flower emblem. A curtain of heavy yellow-brown kraft paper, weighted by a wooden batten across the lower edge, was lowered in front of it. Slowly, the flower was obscured by the stiff crinkled paper. Then another, lighter curtain began to descend in front of the paper. This was a print cloth, solidly covered with a repeated design of red roses and their green leaves. When the colored print covered the heavy rumpled paper, all of the lights, including the colored ones, were switched on. For the first time, the space was brightly illuminated.

All of the girls who had previously performed—except, of course, the girl who still stood motionless within the pillar of cloth—appeared suddenly, smiling, laughing and throwing yel-

The petals of the red flower open.

low daffodils. In a moment, they were gone again, running off to disappear behind the curtain at the front.

Flower was over. If the audience was not aware of it, perhaps someone in the control room said something. When the spectators began to stir and stand up, the girl wrapped in cloth shook off her covering and left the performance area. As they moved out into the street and dispersed into the night, many of the spectators were carrying yellow daffodils.

The girl completely covered with cloth (Simone Whitman, Joseph Schlicter, Suzanne DeMaria).

WATER / *the production*

When Robert Whitman visited Los Angeles in the summer of 1963, he decided to do a Happening there. He was fortunate to find a multicar garage on an alley off North La Cienega Boulevard not far from the growing concentration of art galleries that made Cienega well-known. He painted the garage walls silver and covered them with plastic sheeting; he bought twenty used inner tubes—the huge ones used in truck tires—and built a construction out of them. A small cast was assembled and rehearsed; announcements were sent out, and a full "dress rehearsal" was held with an audience made up of those who would not be able to attend the regular performances. But the landlord also read the announcement. Not having had a very clear idea of the purpose for which the garage was being used, he was disturbed to see that "performances" were to be given, and, citing the zoning regulations, refused to let the show go on. It was the day of the first scheduled performance. Perhaps more than a hundred phone calls had to be made announcing the cancellation to those who had made reservations. Each evening Whitman went to the garage to try to explain to those who had not been informed. Nothing could be done except to postpone the production for a couple of weeks and look for another place.

But another place was not easy to find. Whitman searched Los Angeles and many of the neighboring suburbs such as Venice, where Claes Oldenburg was living at the time. Finally he accepted the offer of space at a private home in Westwood: a substantial house with an attached double garage behind it, there was a sizable paved area in front of the garage large enough for cars to turn around or to park. This would become the "stage" and the "auditorium." The garage would serve as "backstage."

First, a seven-foot wooden framework was built around three

sides of the almost-square paved area, and plastic sheeting was hung from the framework to make a solid transparent wall with an entrance facing the driveway. From the top of the wall, another wooden framework about three feet wide slanted down toward the center; when covered with plastic, it formed a roof under which the audience would stand. Lengths of white muslin were fastened across the open doors of the garage. The final large building job was the construction made from truck inner tubes. The tubes were stacked in two six-foot columns at the center of the muslin (garage) wall and held in position by vertical wooden beams cross-braced at the top and bottom. More white muslin was wrapped around these two columns, and a final tube, sprayed silver, was folded into the space between them. About three feet above the pavement, the right and left sides of the silver tube touched each other. With the addition of many sets of Christmas-tree lights—not easy to obtain in Los Angeles in the summer—and three buckets hung over the playing area, the "setting" for *Water* was complete.

Some replacements in the cast had been necessary because of the change in "theatres." The primary members were still available, however, and only a couple of rehearsals had to be held at the new location. Certain changes in the production had been made. Now there were no silver walls behind the plastic, and the area was more regular than the previous indoor space had been, but most of the performance elements were exactly the same.

Water was presented on the 20th and 21st of September, 1963. Two performances were given each night. In the darkness of the California evening, the unusual plastic-enclosed space was lit by the ordinary light from the rear door and windows of the nearby house. Sporadically the members of the audience found their way up the driveway and into the structure, where they stood along the three frame walls inside the plastic. The central space was empty except for a garden hose that had been apparently dropped at random on the concrete in front of the cloth-covered columns of inner tubes, one end disappearing under the muslin wall fronting the garage. When the spectators were assembled, the garage light directly above the columns went on. After a moment, water began to flow from the curving hose. The Happening was beginning.

For what may have seemed like a long time, there was no movement except for the quietly flowing water. Then there was a stirring of the inner-tube columns, and something began to push through the folded silver tube anchored between them: it was a man. Slowly he worked his way out, pausing to hang head downward when his body could be seen. Yellow watery liquid splashed out over the figure and splattered on the concrete. (Whitman had used finger paint for color because he was sure it was nontoxic; unseen within the garage, he was throwing a bucketful of the mixture.) After a moment, the man moved again and wriggled out until he was lying full-length on the wet surface.

Carefully and purposefully, without any particular facial expression, the man stood, picked up the hose, and held it up in front of himself. His tall figure was dressed in sneakers, plain trousers, and a slightly rumpled white shirt. He didn't move. There was only the sound of the water as it arched up from the hose and splashed down on the driveway. Then he became animated again, carried the hose to another spot, and inverted the nozzle on top of his head, standing motionless as the water coursed through his hair, moved in sheets over his face, and soaked his clothing. Two or three more times he moved to different spots and took different motionless poses with the hose. He might turn it

(rehearsal photograph) The man pushes through the silver tube between the cloth-covered columns of inner tubes (John Weber).

against his chest or hold it straight out in front. (There was an understanding that variety should be obtained, but no necessary poses or places had been set during rehearsal. At each performance the details within the measured and orderly pattern of movement and pose were somewhat different.)

After a certain number of poses, a blond girl came between the pillars of cloth-covered inner tubes. The silver tube through which the man had squirmed now hung free, dangling from a rope, and she merely pushed it aside as she walked in. She wore an ordinary white shirt, a skirt, and tennis shoes. At about the same time as the girl's entry—or perhaps somewhat sooner, depending on the audience's attitude—Whitman, who remained unseen throughout the performance, turned on a soaker hose that had been placed along the top of the enclosure. Very gradually water from the many small holes in the hose began to trickle onto the slanting plastic roof under which the audience stood and drip down off the edges: it was raining.

The movement became continuous as both the man and the girl performed a series of washing actions. Using lather from a push-button can of shaving cream or a bar of soap that had been hidden with other accessories under the columns, he washed himself, rinsing with the hose. She washed her hair with shampoo squeezed from a tube and perhaps stood under the dripping artificial roof to rinse off the foaming lather. At one point he took off his white shirt, revealing a similar shirt underneath, and, walking to another spot, continued to wash. Although they carried out their own separate movements without conversation and with only the incidental facial expressions that would naturally result from such energetic activity, they sometimes came together: she might scrub the back of his shirt, or he would wash the back of hers. With another push-button can he put a thick white lather of whipped cream on her face and then licked it off. Or she went through the same procedure, decorating the front of his shirt with whipped cream and then licking it. (This section, like the preceding solo section, was indeterminate in sequence and location and was determined only in the type of action.)

At this point each began a new series of activities that were more or less independent. She was to inflate three balloons with water, and he was to shower himself with the contents of the three hanging buckets. (At times these independent series coin-

The girl and the man washing. Furled projection screen hangs in background (Laurie Weber, John Weber).

cided so that while she filled each balloon, he was tipping a pail, but this was not required, and it usually did not occur that way.) She thrust the hose into a balloon and began filling it. He walked under a bucket that hung seven and a half feet above the ground halfway between the corner where the audience had entered and the garage wall, pulled the hanging cord, and spilled purple liquid over his head. The color ran over him, soaking his white shirt. When the balloon was full, he took it from her, carried it through an opening in the muslin wall to the right of the columns, and disappeared, returning in a moment empty-handed. His help was not needed with the second balloon because she kept its opening pressed tightly around the hose until the water pressure burst the rubber, but he carried the last balloon out, holding it stiffly in front of himself and applying slight pressure so that the water spurted up into the air in a fairly continuous fountain. Meanwhile he had two more buckets to empty over himself: a bucket of milk that hung six and a half feet above the concrete in the corner close to where the audience had entered, and a bucket of green liquid in the opposite corner, whose height, five and a half feet, forced him to recline under it. If he had not doused himself with green by the time he removed the final balloon, he would return to go through the procedure, but his second exit was a cue for the entrance of four girls who were waiting in the garage behind the muslin.

The girls were completely enclosed in burlap except for an arm or a leg: two showed arms and two showed legs that protruded through the covering. Before the girls put them on, the burlap costumes were shaped like balls and now hung in folds around them, covered by large sheets of transparent plastic that slid and glittered like liquid. (The earlier production in the garage had included three girls: one with a bare arm showing, one with a leg, and a third whose bare lower back could be seen through a round opening. But with a change in performers there had not been time to rehearse a replacement in the difficulties of moving in the third outfit—she would have had to enter backward while holding the burlap tightly across her back—and the costume was regretfully eliminated.)

The girls, entering one at a time, in an order they had worked out during rehearsal, attempted to burst into the playing area and rush across the space, but they were extremely handicapped by

The man empties a bucket of purple water over himself (John Weber).

the layers of cloth and plastic, and the bracing on the floor between the two pillars of tire tubes became a formidable obstacle.
The trailing burlap soaked up water, becoming heavy and ob-
stinate. It was difficult to see out of the costumes. The girls had
been directed to "pick out five places [as targets] that involve
crossing the space five times," and, as fast as they were able, they
struggled about to complete the instruction. There were collisions.
Occasionally one fell, got up, and swayed ahead. At the same
time, the blond girl, rather than leaving the playing area when the
balloons had been filled, was wistfully wandering from one spectator to another, smiling at them and perhaps touching them
gently. Following the additional directive that each girl include
among the five crosses—at a time of her own choosing—a brief trip
offstage, the bulging, glistening figures would now and then disappear through the muslin wall and reappear a moment later to
continue crossing the space. Two of the girls, for a very functional
reason, had been asked to make two such exits: after the second
exit, they returned, pulling long lengths of cloth.

The cloth was part of the same muslin sheets that covered
the inner-tube columns; as it was pulled, it came away from the
tubes, hiding them behind a cloth wall. The girls, aided by the

One of the costumed girls covered with burlap and plastic.

man, who was almost unseen inside the yards of muslin, hung the cloth from cords stretched like clotheslines across the playing area. Now the audience was faced with a roofless, cloth-walled box that almost filled the space. One side of the box merged with the garage wall; the other sides were parallel to the sides of the enclosure within which the audience stood. The burlap-and-plastic-covered girls were gone. The light went out.

Shadows appeared on the hanging cloth. A face, a hand, what looked like a girl sitting in a bathtub—the shadows constantly shifted, disappearing from one wall of the enclosure and moving to another. There were silhouettes of the man with the hose, a girl eating an apple, a leg or an arm being washed. (Within the muslin screens, Whitman was making the shadows with a flashlight. Around him were the three people whose shadows he was projecting. By moving closer or farther away, he could change the size of the image, and they moved slightly, too, so that shadows could be thrown onto all three walls. When Whitman felt he had done enough with the shadows, he switched off his flashlight and went back into the garage to turn on the main light.)

Three of the four burlap-covered girls who had been seen a short while before moved slowly to positions outside the perimeter of the cloth enclosure. Despite the hanging cloth, most of the audience could see two of them as they began very slowly to remove their costumes. As it did to all the performers during the Happening, light illuminated most clearly and brightly the sides of their figures that were toward the garage. The girls shed the plastic sheets (if they had not already fallen off during their previous exertions) and began to climb out of the burlap. The girl whose arm showed pushed her head through the same opening and slowly worked the cloth bag down over her torso, finally stepping out of it. The two girls who each exhibited a bare leg stepped through the opening with the other foot and gradually worked the baggy material off over their heads. Underneath the burlap the girls, who were in their early twenties, wore plain street clothes. (Whitman has said that he wanted "clean-cut American teen-agers.") As soon as one girl was free of her costume, she ran to unhook the hanging cloth that had been used for the shadow projection and put it out of sight behind the columns of tubes, which could now be seen without their previous covering. The cloth was in two sections, and, although one of the girls might dismantle both parts, the three were able to adjust their disrobing so that they all finished at approximately the same time, and usually at least two of them did the work of once more clearing the central area. Then they exited through the opening to the right of the columns.

A girl the audience had not seen before, shoeless and wearing a bright print dress, began to climb on and through the structure of black inner tubes. Even though wooden beams ran up within the columns, holding them in position, the inflated tubes were far from rigid. They sagged, twisted, and slid under the weight of the climbing girl. From somewhere above, soapy water flowed constantly down the tubes, making the rubber even more slippery than it would be ordinarily. (Unseen by the audience, a man was using buckets full of detergent and the hose to create the waterfall.) For a minute or so the girl climbed inside and out of the glistening tubes, then the light went out.

Christmas-tree lights, stretched in a zigzag pattern across the plastic roof under which the audience stood, were turned on. They were not the common flame-shaped bulbs that burn constantly but "twinkle lights" that blinked on and off at random

(rehearsal photograph) The girl climbs through the inner tubes as soapy water pours down over them (Simone Whitman).

intervals and in random order. These particular bulbs were shaped like flowers with five petals, and the center and the petals, which were of different colors, lit alternately. The artificial rain was still falling from the plastic roof. The girl who had been climbing through the inner-tube pillars walked to the center of the space and unfastened a sheet which had been tied, rolled up, to a cord across the playing area. It fell vertically, its upper edge fastened to the cord, its lower edge weighted. Whitman, who had gone from the garage into the house through a connecting door, let the lights blink quite awhile. Then he switched on a motion-picture projector that had been set up in a second-floor window. The color film was projected onto the hanging sheet, which was at right angles to the garage, and the image could be seen clearly from both the front and the back. Those in the audience who did not have a good angle of view could, if they wished, move to the side or step onto the playing area itself through an opening in the "rain." As soon as they realized what was going on, there was some shifting among the spectators opposite the garage.

The brightly colored images filled the seven-foot screen. First there were pictures of water: rain, rain falling into a bubbling hot spring, the feathery white spout of a geyser, a single solid stream from a hose falling into the flat green water of (perhaps) a swimming pool. In a brief sequence, the flow from the hose, seen from very close, was photographed from different angles. Then the same girl was seen in an orange dress, a red dress, a yellow dress, walking or simply standing against (usually) the solid green background of a hedge. When this series began, the girl who had lowered the screen stepped into the projector's beam carrying a folded umbrella. It was the same girl whose life-size image appeared on the screen, but, while in the film she wore dresses of solid colors, now she wore the print dress that had been completely soaked when she was climbing through the tubes. The spectators on one side saw her fairly clearly, while those on the opposite side only saw her shadow. When the image on the screen sat down, the real girl sat, too. Suddenly the screen was empty, and, in the harsh white light from the projector, the wet, bedraggled girl was seen clearly. When the pictures began again, the girl on the screen appeared in various single-hued suits and dresses. Sometimes she walked out of the frame and then, without any apparent movement of the camera, walked back wearing a different dress. Once the camera had been turned so that the image of the girl stood on the left edge of the frame. A moment later she appeared standing upside down. Several close-ups of a large glass of water packed with ice cubes were followed by more views of the girl, now occasionally wearing a bathing suit. When the girl on the screen stood in the rain holding an umbrella, the real girl raised the umbrella she carried. A foaming waterfall was shown, and the real girl closed her umbrella and walked to one side. There were pictures of water cascading over rocks, a curtain of mist, a great downward rush of water filling the whole screen. Then the motion picture was over, and the girl raised the sheet again.

In the darkness the small colored lights continued to twinkle, and, for quite a while, water fell from the edges of the roof. Then the blinking lights went out. The water was turned off, and the sound of steady dripping began to subside. The white main light on the garage above the columns went on, and, as he had at the beginning, the man began to squirm headfirst between the columns. The pillars were now bare rather than being covered with muslin, and he merely pretended that the central silver tube, previously held tightly in a folded position from behind and now hung from a single rope, was unchanged. Although he stopped halfway, as he had previously done, no yellow liquid splashed over him. He continued out until he was lying prone on the drying floor. Since the constant dripping had ceased, there was a pronounced silence. Carefully and purposefully, without any particular facial expression, the man stood, picked up the hose, and held it up in front of himself. No water came out. After a moment he carried the hose to another spot and inverted the nozzle on top of his head. To emphasize that the water had been turned off (although Whitman did not really approve of the action), he pointed the hose toward nearby spectators. In general he repeated the sequence of alternating formal poses and movement with which *Water* had begun. The blond girl entered as before, and they went through another series of washing actions. But now there was no lather from the soap and the push-button cans. The actions were pantomimed and they went through the motions of rinsing with the empty hose or under the quiet eaves. When the sequence had run its course, Whitman turned the light off. The performers left, and when the light came on again, it marked the end of the presentation.

a statement

(Rewritten from a recorded interview.)

I CANNOT TALK ABOUT theatre because I have no background except acting out everything in everyday life. That is a complete, comprehensive background, because it happened every day of my life. The Happenings then became an extension of that, rather than an extension of my painting. The visual side of the Happenings was the extension of my painting, but there were other things involved, since I think on two levels. I think on the visual level, which has nothing to do with the way one talks. But these things had to get across with talking, too—as literary ideas seen in a visual way—so that there were two levels. And my only preparation for that was acting out everything through my life. I felt that it was the most natural thing to do—to do the Happenings. When I did *The Car Crash*, it related to my paintings only because I was doing a Happening then, and that is what I was painting about, and I thought it would be nice to tie them in. There was no other relationship.

Kaprow once said, "You're the one who does the funny Happenings." He likes classification—that there was someone who did

"funny Happenings." But they were not funny. *The Car Crash* was not laughed at; the spectators tittered like they do at nudes in museums—kids get embarrassed and laugh.

The first "Happening" I did was called *The Smiling Workman*, at the Judson Church. I had a flat built. It was a three-panel flat with two sides and one flat. There was a table with three jars of paint and two brushes on it, and the canvas was painted white. I came around it with one light on me. I was all in red with a big, black mouth: all my face and head were red, and I had a red smock on, down to the floor. I painted "I love what I'm doing" in orange and blue. When I got to "what I'm doing," it was going very fast, and I picked up one of the jars and drank the paint, and then I poured the other two jars of paint over my head, quickly, and dove, physically, through the canvas. The light went off. It was like a thirty-second moment of intensity. It was like a drawing. I did not have to think about it. Claes said, "We're going to have these Happenings," and I said, "OK. I'd like to do one." And that is the one I was going to do. It was just a thought I had. It was a thought. For me, it was the most pure that I did.

I did not think it was funny. What I was doing was not a humorous situation. I think it was funny to see it, but I do not think obsession is funny or that not being able to stop one's intensity is funny. If I had performed it for an hour with that sort of intensity, I do not think it would have been funny. It took the form of a blackout or a vaudeville act. The nature of the medium did that, not the intent.

The next one I did was called *The Vaudeville Show*, which was a crowd-pleaser and one that was quite pleasing to me to do. I had a stage built. It was like an old-time stage with two flats of canvas on each side, and over the top it said, "Jim Dine's Vaudeville" in Dayglow color. There was a tape recording made for that. It was all kinds of crazy things: organ music, me talking—it was a collage on tape. I came out with a red suit on and cotton all over me, my face painted yellow. To the music that was going on, I pulled the cotton off and just let it fall to the floor until there was no cotton on me. Then I walked out. As soon as I walked out, inanimate objects became actors. Two people behind the flats operated a dance of strung cabbages and carrots and lettuce and celery. That stopped quickly, and red paint was poured down the flats on each side and onto the floor. That was another "act." The final act was: I came out with my red suit on and a straw hat on this time. On each arm I had a nude girl made out of cardboard so that each of my arms became their inner arms. These were made like puppets—Javanese puppets. I did a dance. I do not even understand how I did that dance. I could never do it now. But I did this dance that people cheered. And they tore my clothes off. Encores! And I ripped off my tie and threw it to the audience. It was an incredible scene. In the sense of audience participation, I have never felt it stronger—with someone else or with me. People remember it as a fantastic night. It was the same night Whitman put on *E.G.*, which I was in. Mine was the finale.

The next one was *The Car Crash*, and the final Happening I did was called *The Shining Bed*. The music was important in that. It was a 33 record of a Palestrina chorale played on 78, and it sounded like The Chipmunks singing it. It played through the whole performance, very softly. The Happening opened with one light and the audience seated around a bed. The head of the bed was covered with foil and was strung with Christmas-tree lights that were not yet turned on. There were long silver spikes made out of foil at the end of the bed. There was a big piece of paper over the bed. Then they lifted the paper off, and there I was as Santa Claus with a blue face and no beard, under the covers of the bed. I lay there for a few minutes as if I were waking up, while the music—The Chipmunks—was playing softly in the background. Then I quickly pulled a piece of polyethylene from the foot of the bed up over my face and made certain movements with a flashlight in my crotch very quickly. Throwing the plastic off, I sat up, went to the end of the bed on my knees, took batter out of a bowl, and put it all over the spikes. It was a repulsive situation. When that was over, I reached down with my head between my legs into a bowl of flour and pulled my face up quickly. It was white instead of blue. The lights went off, and the people were in darkness for a short time. From underneath my pillow, I pulled a gold baby doll and put it on the pillow. I disappeared. The Christmas-tree lights, which blinked, came on, and the Palestrina music on 78 got very loud. The baby was just sitting there. Then it was over. That was my best one—the one I liked the best. It was the most beautiful one.

I had to do it all myself, and I did it without rehearsals. We always had one rehearsal, in which my wife would see me go through it. I would not really do it. I wanted to save that performance, but she would see me go through it and say, "Well, this looks different. Maybe you could get closer toward the lights"—something like that. But that is all we ever did in rehearsal.

Now I feel that I would never want to appear in my own works again, but then it was important because I did not trust anyone else, and I did not feel that what I was doing was of a public-enough nature to even tell the people what to do. That is where I think the clue is to the fact that they were so personal and so much related to acting out one's life rather than art because I was not able to even transmit my ideas to anyone else to have them do it.

The name "Happening" was a great crowd-pleaser. People knew what they were going to see. If it said "Happening," they were going to see Whitman, Dine, Oldenburg, or Kaprow. People sometimes say about my painting, "That's a real Happening." It is ridiculous. It is Kaprow's word, and it does not refer to me. I do not really know what it meant. But if it meant what he did, it was not what I was doing, so it was not true of me.

What I did was not understood for the most part. I do not feel that there was enough of a perspective between art and life in them. I felt they were too closely allied with me. That would be all right in paintings because people would have time to look at them, but these were too temporary. Everybody I ever talked to was completely misinterpreting them.

I stopped doing Happenings because I felt anyone could do anything and be liked. It was becoming so chic. The audiences were laughing at everything. And I also felt that it was taking too much from my painting, which I really wanted to do.

THE CAR CRASH / *the script*

NOTE: *Two separate scripts for* The Car Crash, *one for the action and one for the words spoken by the seated woman in white (Pat Oldenburg), are combined below.*

TRAFFIC SOUNDS BEGIN. Car comes out and does swirling motion light dance. After an interval two white people enter and try to hit each other with right-angle beams. They somehow keep hitting the car by accident. Each time the car is hit, he winces and makes noises. Soon they start hitting each other more regularly always using one light on the sex organs, the other on the face. They keep getting closer to each other, eventually ending up in the center where they focus on each other and turn slowly, subtly with bodies and lights held rigid for the count of 60 (possibly 120). Car sounds off. Lights on.

Two white people go to respective banging places and begin banging piece. Car is moving slowly around room honking. On cue (not yet determined) Pat begins speech while banging continues as accompaniment and honking becomes varied. Towards the end of her speech, car stops honking, takes balloon out of pocket and blows it up slowly. When it breaks, speech stops. Lights out.

THE CAR IN MY LIFE IS A CAR WITH A POLE IN THE HARM OF MY SOUL WHICH IS A PRETTY CLANK . . . (loud) MY CAR IS MY HERTZ SPOT OF LOVE TO ZOOM THROUGH THE WHOLE TRANSMISSION OF MY LOVELY TIRE HOLD TIME OF GOODSHORT GASSSSSSS, HOW SWEET IS SHORT SMELL OF EARTH NOISE WHEN THE SPARK

189

PLUG LIE OF WHOLE SHORT MAKE MY GARNU FLACK OUT OF
SHORT WEAVING MOTORS COME IN GAS HOLE OF TIRE RACK, TOOL
SMELL, AND CUZMY JERK ON OF OIL SLICK IN THE MIDDLE OF A
GOOD TIME OF DAY, WHEN ALL THE CARS OF MY MY MY MY HORN
HONKS ON THE HELP NOISE OF ALL OUR TIME TRUNK LOCK
CADILLAC MANIA FOR THE FORD IS THE CRUNCH OF THENORD
OFALL THE SHOOT FAST TIME NOISE OF OUR CAR

repeat

Traffic sounds (crash) for approx 2 min. Spot on wringer. Car
cranks out help, Pat is saying help softly, one white person is
banging softly, other is passing out help signs. Pat gets louder,
keeps saying help in a drone until it is very strong. Spot goes out.
Traffic off. White people and car put flashlights on Pat who begins
second speech. When she starts stammering, fluorescent comes on,
. . . spot on blackboard where car is.

OH MY OH MY GUM SHOT DAMN DAMN DAMN OH SHOT OH
CROTCHO OOOOOOH MY CAR IS THE WARM PART OF A SOUL BEAR-
ING THE GOOD OH MY GAAAA . . . WHERE IS MY MOTOR, SOUL,
HELL, HARD PART, COME ON GOOD TIME NIGHT TIRE REAL OF THE
GRAND TIME IN GHREE ON FOUR OF OUROLD GRAAAAAGGH, OH OH
OH MY SHIP IS THE LONG TWELVE VOLT LOVE TOUCH OF YOUR
PIT AND TAKE IT DOWN THREE THOUS OUR LONG LIFE IN THE
SPRING OF SEATEARS MAKES MY CAR TALK WITH BIRD CREASE ALL
OVER MY WALLS PUT FORTH IN A SHARP TOOL GREASED AND
GREASED TO FIT A HEART WHO SAYS I'M ON OUR ROAD TOLL
MAKING MILES FOR THE VOLTS TO CHARGE THE GREASE SPOT OF
MY MY (stammer)

Car begins to stutter and draw cars and erase them. Two white
people stand and cough, gag, stammer and stutter. Develops into
chorale which builds up then gets quieter and more jerky. Car
walks off slowly, while Pat and white people are still talking softly.
Two people exit quietly . . . Pat still talking softly and irregularly.
Traffic sounds on. Pat stops talking and sits there. Traffic sounds
for 30 sec.

END

THE CAR CRASH / *the production*

IN EARLY NOVEMBER, 1960, the Reuben Gallery, which had just moved into a small store on East Third Street in New York, presented *The Car Crash* by Jim Dine. Entering the gallery, the visitor found himself in a small room, the walls of which were solidly lined with drawings and paintings by Dine. All of the works contained crosses—usually the blocky symbol of the Red Cross—and some had tirelike circles. The white, freshly painted display room was simple, neat and clean, but as the spectators passed the small table at which the proprietress of the gallery was accepting contributions for the production and stepped into the rear room, they were surrounded by an unusual and visually complex Environment.

Folding chairs filled most of the floor space. The wall to the left of the entrance was almost invisible behind shelves that overflowed with jumbled rolls of felt, linoleum, and cork, from which loose, curling strips escaped in streamers. On the temporary rear wall (made from heavy kraft paper and scrim) was a horizontal electrical conduit, a tire with a glove lying on top of it, and several limp, hanging bags from a vacuum cleaner. The right wall was also partially hidden by tall thin pieces of metal tubing and strips of wood which were propped against it. A satchel overflowing with stringy cotton waste was suspended at the end of a rope, and a few light bulbs with tangles of accompanying wires dangled down. Several large cardboard crosses hung from the ceiling throughout the room. The crosses were red, white, or silver. Everything else in the room was white. Paint had been splashed and splattered on the walls, and sections which were not solid white were covered by a fine white grid of vertical drips. Even the floor was white.

The main group of chairs faced the doorway through which

191

the spectators entered from the lobby. At least one row of chairs lined each of the other three walls, leaving a narrow U-shaped aisle with its base toward the front, connected with the main entrance. Thus the largest segment of the audience sat in a central group while others faced them from the front and sides. There were about forty or fifty chairs in all, and most of them were filled at each of the five performances.

As the first spectators took their seats, they noticed a motionless girl with a white face and long brown hair who appeared to be about eight feet tall. The ladder on which she was seated—just to the left of the doorway as the spectators faced it—was invisible under the white muslin sheeting that descended from her shoulders to the floor. In the corner at the opposite side of the entrance, a blackboard had been set up.

(Dine has explained how he was "a little anxious about sullying it [i.e., the entirely white Environment] with people." He had worked at the "setting" for several days, primarily utilizing materials that had been left in the store by the previous tenant. When the cast assembled for rehearsal, three days before the first performance, they found the white room virtually complete. Since they were told exactly what was expected of them at the first meeting, since the author himself had a central role, and since there were simple "cueing" and clear divisions between segments, only one hour of rehearsal was needed each of the three days. At the dress rehearsal the costumes fit well with the white room, but Dine briefly considered giving the spectators white caps and smocks to wear in an attempt to preserve the purity of the Environment.)

When everyone was seated, the lights went off abruptly. Honking horns and street noises were heard (a record was being played). Parallel rays of light flashed into the room through the front entrance, and a figure entered the dark room with two small lights on his head. As he moved slowly down the aisle, swinging the beams from side to side, the spectators could see that it was a solidly built man (Jim Dine) wearing a raincoat and a rubber shower cap that had been sprayed silver. His face was silver with dark lines circling his eyes and nostrils; his lips were bright red. Holes had been cut in the golf cap that he wore, and two flashlights jutted out just above the small brim.

In a moment, another pair of light beams entered the room from the rear. A figure dressed in white, holding a flashlight on each hip, walked through an archway ripped in the white paper that made up part of the rear wall. It was a girl wearing men's clothing (white trousers, white shirt, and white tie), her long, black hair tied back in a ponytail and her face hidden behind a papier-mâché mask with oval eyeholes and a half-open mouth. The circles of light swept across the audience, momentarily illuminating the watching faces and flickering on the white walls. As the girl turned the corner of the aisle, the beams struck the man in the silver raincoat, and he moaned loudly as if in pain. Then the two figures moved past each other at the front of the room.

Another man entered through the rear arch. He wore a girl's white formal dress with a flaring skirt. His arms, shoulders and back were bare, and the dark hair of his chest could be seen over the low-cut bodice. The mouth of the white mask that he wore was rounded, and the lips protruded slightly. A flashlight was pressed under each arm, which made his movements somewhat stiff as he walked toward the front of the room. The three pairs of lights slid and darted about as the figures wove slowly back and forth in the narrow aisles. Car horns could still be heard. When the masked man or woman occasionally caught the silver man in the beams of their flashlights, he would grunt, moan, or cry out. He attempted to elude them, but the moving lights touched him several times.

Then the silver man disappeared out of the front entrance, leaving the playing space to the masked pair who slowly approached each other from opposite sides of the room. Their slow, sinuous movements were partially controlled by the position of their lights as they swung from side to side and began to slide the beams over the other person. Completely revolving once or twice, the masked white figures approached each other until they were only a foot or so apart. For a moment they wove from side to side, playing the beams of their flashlights over each other. Then both performers switched off their lights, and the sound of horns stopped.

Almost immediately the hanging bulbs went on, brightly lighting the room. The masked white figures had disappeared. As a loud, metallic clatter began from behind the rear wall (the two performers in white, who could see through the scrim wall without being seen, were banging pots and pans), the man in the silver coat, no longer wearing the flashlight headdress, entered again

The man dressed as a woman enters from behind central audience group. Girl dressed as a man is at right (Marc Ratliff, Judy Tersch).

from the front and walked back and forth making honking noises. The "eight-foot-tall" girl in white, who had remained motionless through the flashlight sequence, began to speak, raising her voice to be heard over the noise.

> "The car in my life is a car with a pole in the harm of my soul which is a pretty clank . . . my car is my Hertz spot of love to zoom through the whole transmission of my lovely tire . . ."

Her tone was pleading, her face mobile and expressive at the top of the white column of cloth. When she finished the short speech—". . . trunk lock Cadillac mania for the Ford is the crunch of thenord ofall the shoot fast time noise of our car"—she began again from the beginning. The silver "car" crossed to the blackboard, stopped honking, took a white balloon from his pocket, and began to blow it up. Just as the girl finished the second recitation, the man burst the balloon with a pin. The crash and clatter "offstage" stopped abruptly, and again the room was plunged into darkness.

The sound of a car starting was heard (again on record), the brake was released, the clutch engaged, and the sound of the motor and tires changed as the driver shifted into second gear, then into third and picked up speed. The volume increased as the unseen car accelerated in the darkness. It suddenly was heard skidding out of control, the shriek of the tires amplified loudly. Abruptly there was silence. The lights came on again.

Mounted directly above the blackboard was the wringer from a washing machine, and the man in the silver raincoat and shower cap stepped up on a folding chair and, smiling slightly, began to turn the handle. Paper towels pushed out from between the rollers. As they hung down, it could be seen that the word "Help" was painted across them, repeated over and over in large, black, block letters. "Help," the seated girl began to say quietly. The girl dressed in men's clothing entered quickly from the rear archway and began to tear off the towels, handing them to members of the audience who were seated nearby. The voice of the seated girl became louder. When perhaps ten or fifteen towels had been ripped off and distributed, the lights went out again.

High above the floor, the face of the tall girl in white was illuminated. The two masked performers, standing at the rear wall—the man in the archway, the girl under the hanging white satchel at the end of the other aisle—were angling the beams of their flashlights at her over the seated spectators. "Oh my oh my gum

The audience during the first speech by the seated girl in white. The man-woman and woman-man can be seen in rear doorway. View is from entrance to lobby. The girl speaking is out of sight to the right.

The seated woman in white (Pat Oldenburg).

The man in silver at the "help" machine (Jim Dine).

The second speech of the seated girl in white, lit by flashlights (Pat Oldenburg).

shot damn damn damn . . ." Without any competitive noise, her
sweetly suggestive but intense voice could be heard clearly.
". . . who says I'm on our road toll making miles for the volts to
charge the grease spot of my my . . ." As she began to stammer,
the flashlights flicked off, and, after a brief moment of darkness,
the bright general lights came on.

The man in silver was standing by the blackboard, a large, thick
piece of chalk in his hand. With a few quick moves, he drew the
outlines of a large car in (perhaps) yellow, then added a window-
eye and a huge smiling mouth. As he worked, the soft chalk
crumbled and broke, falling on the floor. His heavily-made-up
face contorted as if with the effort of his drawing, and he uttered
a series of noises that sounded as if he were about to say something
but could not quite begin a word. He erased the car and drew
another in a different color. Again it had human connotations. The
masked man and woman were standing in their places at the rear
of the room, and they, too, began the strange stammering sounds.
The stationary white woman joined in. With increasing excite-
ment, the man at the blackboard drew, erased, and redrew cars
in various colors. The sketches were becoming smaller and less
specific; the volume of the grunts and semiverbal utterances by

The man in silver drawing on the blackboard (Jim Dine).

all four of the performers grew louder and louder. "Uh, bu, bu . . . woo, ech, heh . . . ayee, hee, doow, ugh . . ." From all corners of the room, the fugue of sounds became more intense. The man in silver rubbed out the cars and turned away from the board. The noises he was making gradually began to subside. In a moment they stopped completely, and he walked slowly and quietly out the front entrance. The others continued the vocal cacophony, but gradually their energy decreased. The masked performers stopped the sounds and disappeared. The girl at the front of the room was silent.

Although the spectators were not yet aware of it, *The Car Crash* was over. At every performance they sat quietly for several minutes. Finally some of them began to get up and move about, and the general exodus began. The presentation had lasted for fifteen or twenty minutes. Above the heads of the departing spectators, the woman in white remained in her place.

CLAES OLDENBURG

a statement

WHAT I DO AS A "happening" is part of my general concern, at this time, to use more or less altered "real" material. This has to do with *objects,* such as typewriters, ping-pong tables, articles of clothing, ice-cream cones, hamburgers, cakes, etc., etc.—whatever I happen to come into contact with. The "happening" is one or another method of using *objects in motion,* and this I take to include people, both in themselves and as agents of object motion.

To present this material, I have worked out some structures and techniques which parallel those of the presentation of the static object. The static object is shown by me as one of a number of related objects, in a particular "real" place—itself an object. For example, *The Store* (1961, New York), containing 120 items approximately, within a real store (107 E. Second St., New York). Or, *The Home,* which I am now developing, with items of furniture and appliances, etc. (*Bedroom Ensemble,* 1964, a room at the Sidney Janis Gallery, New York) though a real house or apartment has not yet been set up. I present in a "happening" anywhere from thirty to seventy-five events, or happenings (and many more

objects), over a period of time from one-half to one and a half hours, in simple spacial relationships—juxtaposed, superimposed—like those of *The Store*. The event is made simple and clear, and is set up either to repeat itself or to proceed very slowly, so that the tendency is always to a static object.

In some pieces, I tried setting up events into a pattern, a pseudo-plot, more associational than logical (*Ray Gun Theater*, those after *Store Days II* especially. March–May, 1962, New York). In the first "happening" I did, *Snapshots from the City* (March, 1960, New York), the events were fragments of action, immobilized by instantaneous illuminations. Otherwise, the "happenings" have been one pattern or another of discrete events: in *Blackouts* (December, 1960, New York), the events were illuminated at different stations across a long stage. In *Fotodeath* (February, 1961, New York), the events repeated themselves in superimposed lines of movement. In *Gayety* (February, 1963, Chicago), the events occurred at stations within and around the spectators In *Stars* (April, 1963, Washington, D.C.) events moved in and out

201

of sight along a right-angle stage. In *Autobodys* (December, 1963, Los Angeles), the audience (in cars) surrounded a rectangle on which widely spaced events occurred.

An individual event may be "realistic," and this may be quite direct, evolving on the spot with a player and certain materials and objects, or a reconstruction (of something I might have observed the day before or read about or dreamed, or of which someone else may have brought the account) or it may be, at an opposite extreme, an enigmatic, fantastic event, with altered objects and altered (costumed) persons. I mix realistic and fantastic events, as the imagination does, and I consider the imaginary event as real as the "real" one.

In the process of altering an object or event, I use various methods, some of which are purely whimsical, others having a rationalization, such as the alteration of real (tangible) furniture into its appearance (visual perspective).

The effect of my "happenings" will be missed if my specific intention and technique are not understood. Spectators will look for development where none is intended, or be bored by the repetition. Or the term "happening" by its vagueness will raise an expectation unlike the effect encountered; for example, spontaneous effect or an improvisation or a spectacle of some sort.

My aim is the perfection of the details of the events rather than any composition (except in the later *Ray Gun Theater* with its "poetic" arrangement of incidents), and the composition is merely a practical structure (usually "real" f.ex. "snapshots" "blackouts" "circus"—a structure which is an object in itself).

The audience is considered an object and its behavior as events, along with the rest. The audience is taken to differ from the players in that its possibilities are not explored as far as that of the players (whose possibilities are not explored as far as my own). The place of the audience in the structure is determined by seating and by certain simple provocations.

The place in which the piece occurs, this large object, is, as I have indicated, part of the effect, and usually the first and most important factor determining the events (materials at hand being the second and players the third). "Place" may have any extent, a room or a nation, and may have any character whatsoever: old, new, clean, dirty, water or land, whatever is decided.

There is no limit to what objects or what methods may be used to arrive at events. An account of the "rehearsals" or making of particular pieces will show the strategies employed to achieve results.

INJUN / *the script*

NOTE: *During the preparation of Injun, Oldenburg wrote the following description for himself.*

The spectators experience the house from the outside, perhaps they walk around it first. Then the house from the inside.

They meet in the lobby of the museum with some doubt as to where the thing will take place. It is generally known something will come and get them. Which then happens: the tornado and possibly another form, with a hundred feet of rope comes to the door. The lights dim and the rope is stretched the length of the lobby people hold on to it, it has knots and a procession starts out the front door down the drive up the bank and into the yards of the houses. As the people go, the lights are turned out in and around the museum so that the area is very dark. There will be streetlights and streetsounds of course and the flying of the planes above.

There occur stations of activity along the way like night patrol or Coney Island fun house. Inexplicable pastoral scenes: boxes tumble off the roof of the garage. A spotlight plays down in the garden on some people moving around in bags? Someone is talking on the porch of the children's house. Perhaps a hanged man. Something is being done inside the garage which cannot quite be seen, perhaps a murder or a foal delivered. Legs protrude from the ceiling of the barn. People lie in the grass.

On the back porch there is going on an argument of some sort,

204

a shadow play, one can barely make out. Things are being thrown. The Tornado leads the people around the house. They see up and inside through the windows the activity there. Things are thrown out the window. Inside music plays. Curiosity developed. fragments. Cry of a baby, flushing toilet. House sounds. coughing crying singing dancing. eating . . .
Feathers fall, shots, screams etc. sentimental sings A windup phono Loudspeaker talk. Record wiretap?

On the street side and behind in the yard shapes are moving back where the spectators walked something is still going on in the garage. There is all around them considerable suggested activity. Then the lights in the house go out. The spectators are led to the rear of the house and slowly into the house through a ramp at the backporch. Slowly as if all one investigating the strange house. The tornado which led them out has now disappeared and there is another leader and perhaps a prompter. They are led counter-clockwise through the kitchen the dining room the front room and back through the front bedroom, the hall past the second bedroom and the toilet and onto the porch looking as they go into and through the rooms. This first turn there is no activity in the house and it is quite dark.

The second time around. The light goes on in the far front room like a stage. There is moaning from parts of the house and a clear song from somewhere. The Injun is in the front hacking at something. Doors close in the hall rooms and there is knocking from behind them. In the front bedroom a man sits up in bed which is full of bricks. The spectators return out again.

The piece is divided into these trips through, let us say five to be made.

Thus five trips, six rooms, of cumulative intensity, until finally the whole house is alive with activity. It is then the front door is opened and the walkers diverted outside on the front porch and down, to dissolve and wonder if its over. Then a black Cadillac drives up. Shooting some bodies are dumped. a lot of running. This too quite inexplicable like things is. . . .

Then the general sense of it being over. The actors in the house drift out the back of the house and return to the museum. . . .

The path is this:

From the lobby through the gate to the yard of the CH [carriage house] then on and between the two houses (all very slowly). Little action in these areas at this point. In the driveway a car with dim lights filled with newspaper. Intimations. Calls from window etc. All quite slow. . . . Perhaps use CH windows too. Then up front porch and thru front door. Rooms in use will be front room, kitchen, bedrooms 1 and two and bathroom. The corridor and second front room for spectators who may mill about as they desire until instructed to leave when the back door will be opened not the front. All along there has been scurrying action in the porch glimpsed through the doors, but now the doors open and the action increases in the back yard, the garage and finally the garden. The spectators are pressed to walk in the direction of the museum. The apotheosis a body thrown into the garden and the confused motion of the Tornado from Yard MH [main house] thru to Garden . . . then subsidence and audience led back. The signal it is over is when the lights go on in the Museum again (someone sent ahead). . . .

The first bedroom is the man's bedroom. The second is the woman's The Front room is for eaters and livers. The kitchen is for argument and the bath for murder. The entrances can be made in and out of windows . . Need ladders . . .

INJUN / *the production*

THE DALLAS MUSEUM FOR CONTEMPORARY ARTS no longer exists, but in 1962 it was located on Cedar Springs Road not far from the center of Dallas. When the museum organized a "1961" exhibit which was to include many of the major artists who had shown work in New York during the year, they also invited Claes Oldenburg to present a Happening. He accepted. A large room on the second floor of the building occupied by the museum was set aside for the production. Publicity was begun.

When Oldenburg arrived in Dallas a week and a half before the scheduled dates for the presentation, he had only very general ideas of what he would do. Somehow the Happening would be related to the place itself, what "the West" meant to him. For several days he sat in the space he had been given, but he could not crystallize a concept that satisfied him. Time was running out, and the pressure was intensified by the fact that several items of plaster food which were to be exhibited on the first floor in a re-creation of his New York store had been damaged in shipment. Day after day he worked many hours repairing them.

One day Oldenburg wandered out of the museum and across the long driveway that connected it to the road. Walking up a shallow hill, he discovered three buildings that he had not known were on the museum grounds: two single-story frame houses and a garage-like shed. He investigated. One of the houses was used on Saturdays for young people's art classes. The other was empty and apparently unused. Walking through the empty house, he remembered a scene from a Wallace Beery movie that he had seen years before. Beery, playing the part of a Civil War veteran who had just returned to his farmhouse where an axe murderer had slaughtered his whole family, had gone from one room to another

207

picking up parts of the dismembered people. The concept for the Happening began to clarify itself.

Oldenburg asked the museum authorities if he could use the house. "Yes," they said, "but it's occupied by Mexican squatters."

"No, it's not. I went in."

"They must have gone. I suppose they left it in a terrible mess. They probably took all the light bulbs with them."

"No," he answered, "it's very clean. It's in perfect shape."

Most of the remaining time was spent in finding props and costumes and in transforming the house. There were no steps to the back porch of the house; the museum built some. The Frank Lloyd Wright Theatre offered Oldenburg lights, costumes, and performers, but he declined. As was his usual practice, found materials were used. The discovery of large rolls of heavy paper in the shipping room of the museum spurred the work. A member of the cast brought materials from her attic. Cheap "farm" dresses were found in an old store. Within a few days, the physical aspects of the Happening were created.

The performances themselves took shape at the last minute. The Happening was to be given on the 6th and 7th of April, 1962—Friday and Saturday evenings. Most of the details were worked out at a rehearsal on Thursday night. (On Saturday, after the first performance, a film was made to record the piece, and this served as further rehearsal, allowing certain points to be clarified.)

On the designated evenings, spectators gathered in the corridor of the museum. In one corner some of the visitors noticed a long rope tied at intervals with pieces of cloth. Single-page programs were distributed. "INJUN," the title read, and below it, in clarification, "Country piece for a house, a yard, a shed and a lean-to." The designation "Happening" was not used on the program. Twenty-three performers were listed: eleven women in one column, twelve men in the other. The spectators were asked to wait in the corridor of the museum until they were "picked up," and an outline of the presentation was given:

PART I

1. A Walk to the House (5 min.)
2. A Walk Through the House (30 min.)

PART II

Yard — Shed — Lean-to
Injun in Movement (20 min.)

A terse note at the bottom of the sheet read: "Please follow and obey masked leaders." Although it indicated that the "country piece" would not take place in the museum, the program did little to clarify the spectators' expectations. The audience waited.

Outside the brightly lit corridor, it was dark. Spectators near the glass doors or waiting on the steps outside watched three strangely dressed men engaged in some sort of silent game. Two of them wore ordinary work clothes, had cloth bags over their heads, and carried long sticks of wood. The other was entirely covered with brownish-green mosquito netting. Large, irregular, rock-shaped lumps (actually cotton wrapped with tape) were twisted into the netting on all sides of the figure. Thin white streamers of torn cloth hung down and fluttered when he moved. At a short distance, the man inside (Oldenburg) was practically invisible as he stooped under the folds of cloth, and in the darkness of the museum grounds only his general shape could be seen as he ran, suddenly stood still, crouched and hid. After several minutes, the three figures entered the corridor where the people waited.

The spectators were requested to grasp the rope wherever there was a knot of cloth and to follow the masked men: they were the "leaders" to whom the program referred. (Two hundred reservations had been made. The rope was two hundred feet long, and the muslin knots were spaced a foot apart. Originally it had been planned to put the name of each spectator on a knot, but this proved impractical.) All the lights on the grounds had been turned out. Following the hunched, brownish-green figure, the line of spectators moved slowly out of the museum into the darkness.

Very gradually the procession made its way across the driveway and up the slight rise toward the houses. There was little cooperation among the two hundred people: while some attempted to step ahead, others would be pausing, and the rope would not move. The masked men prodded the line with their sticks, urging it on. Spring rain had softened the ground, making more difficulty for the spectators. High heels sank into the wet dirt. The hunched figure covered with netting swayed and darted around the column, disappearing and reappearing suddenly.

The file of people passed through an opening in an old wire fence. To their right, a girl wearing a simple print dress had been tied to a post. She did not move. Ahead of them to the right was an unpainted frame shed with a peaked roof. A flat-roofed extension jutted from the side wall and on this extension, outlined against the night sky, sat the hunched, motionless figure of another girl, her hair teased out in a huge mass. To the left were two houses, and from the screened back porch of the nearer one came the deep, steady thump of a washtub bass.

The spectators moved past the bound girl and turned left between the houses. The house that was now on their right appeared to be occupied. In the lighted rectangles of the windows, the passing column could catch glimpses of various people as they moved about inside. A large jet plane suddenly roared low over the dark yards. (The museum was close to Love Field, one of the busiest airports in the country. At unexpected intervals throughout the evening, jets, either landing or taking off from the field, would add their sound to the performance.) The spectators were noisy: they made jokes, called loudly to each other, laughed nervously, and complained. Gradually, the awkward, struggling column moved around to the front of the house. There the people were directed up the front steps, where they let go of the rope (the original plan to have them retain their holds as they passed through the house was not practical) and stepped into the house. When all the people were inside, the doors were locked.

The front room extended to the right of the entering spectator. No windows were visible. The walls were solidly covered with sheets of newspaper, and the floor was hidden by a tangle of newspapers and refuse. Pieces of broken furniture protruded from the rubble. Partially covered by a patterned piece of cloth, a small man with a mustache lay in the center of the room, his head propped against a bale of hay. He was wearing pajamas, and he played a violin that had only two strings. Occasionally, he appeared to sleep. (Oldenburg had been thinking of the recluses' rooms that he had seen as a reporter in Chicago. One rich old lady who had been one of the first female lawyers in Chicago had filled a mansion with torn newspapers and law books. Her possessions and furnishings were hidden under five feet of torn paper. After she died in a small rented room around the corner from the mansion, Oldenburg had seen the bed in which she had slept cross-

The first room (Harold Pauley).

wise—she had been a small woman—the sides of the hollow that her body had made encrusted with food.)

In addition to the man with the violin, there was another figure in the room. The legs of a man wearing long underwear could be seen beneath a huge, ragged cardboard construction. Crumpled kraft paper formed a cowl around his head and body, hiding him almost completely as he moved slowly about the room in a stooped position picking up things. Sometimes he went to a corner and stood still.

The two hooded men carrying sticks directed the spectators into a corridor that connected the front room with the rest of the house. As they passed along the corridor, the people could look through a doorway to their right into another room. The walls of the room were covered with old, flower-patterned wallpaper. The board floor was bare except for two sets of white long underwear stuffed with newspaper, and two large white balls of cotton covered with tape. A dark-haired girl with stark white makeup lay on the dummies. (The performer was determined to wear the makeup—she claimed to have studied with Marcel Marceau—and

Oldenburg did nothing about it.) She wore long white underwear under a dark sleeveless dress, slacks, high-heeled shoes, heavy bracelets and a large neckpiece. From time to time she crawled and slid along the floor, pushing the lumpy white shapes and rolling the balls about. Or she would stand suddenly and throw the dummies against the walls. A girl in colorful striped pajamas and high-heeled shoes sat on the windowsill, looking wistfully out at the night, oblivious of the other girl. Occasionally she got up, gently kicked a little bell around the room, disappeared into the closet for a while, and then returned to the window.

On their left, the spectators passed a doorway that was covered with a semitransparent plastic sheet dotted with scattered black spots. A man's voice, a radio, and sounds of movement could be heard from the other room. Now and then the swaying shadow of a dancing girl appeared on the plastic.

Farther down the corridor, another doorway opened on the

(rehearsal photograph) The second room (Carolyn Higginbotham, Flora Reeder).

(rehearsal photograph) The dancer standing in the plastic-covered doorway (Joan Key, Howard Doolittle).

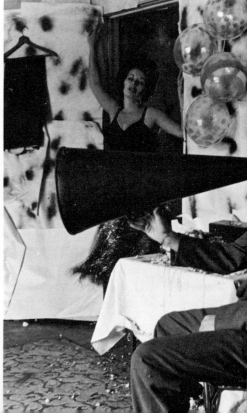

right. This was the bathroom. Looking into it, the spectators could see the bathtub filled with soft mud. A man wearing long underwear threw handfuls of mud against the wall and ceiling and decorated the small room with long streamers of toilet paper.

At the end of the corridor, the path laid out for the audience passed through the door to the back porch, along the outside walls of the screened enclosure, and back into the house itself through the same door. (This was a last-minute innovation, devised to relieve crowding in the house.) It was dark on the porch. Torn pieces of heavy kraft paper hung from the ceiling, making a shifting maze through which the people pushed their way. In the center of the porch, inside a fencelike structure, was the man in the brownish-green net who had come for the audience at the beginning of the performance. Almost invisible under the layers of cloth, he thrashed about and grabbed at the legs of passing spectators. He improvised a stream-of-consciousness monologue, pouring out disjointed, irrational statements. Sometimes he sat quietly. Sometimes he scrambled around his enclosure like a monkey.

(rehearsal photograph) The man covered in brownish-green netting moves into the left section of the shed (Claes Oldenburg).

Looking out through the porch screens, some of the spectators noticed that there was activity in the shed behind the house. The shed was divided like a two-car garage, and in the left section three girls in simple print dresses moved aimlessly or lay on the hay that was piled against the rear wall. In the right section, a man slowly rolled a solid six-foot wheel from side to side. The people on the porch moved around the costumed figure in the center and back into the house.

Rather than passing back down the corridor, they turned to their right and entered the kitchen. Paint-splattered kraft paper had been stapled loosely to the walls (and over a window and door) softening the regular outlines of the room. A sink poked through the paper on the right. Near the far wall, a table had been constructed from two sawhorses and a plywood panel and covered with a layer of cotton batting. A girl, almost hidden under a disordered pile of old clothes, lay on the table. Jutting up from behind the table were two long rusty metal bars, their ends encased in ragged masses of concrete. At one side stood a small cupboard with a circular mirror and a broken, paint-splashed rectangular mirror on it. A bucket filled with water was nearby. A wide board was propped against the wall, and from it hung a baseball catcher's mitt, a doll, and a woven Mexican hat. The floor was scattered with torn bits of white foam rubber which looked like popcorn.

The girl stirred, shook off the heap of cloth. She rose into a crouching position on the table, her knees drawn up to her chin, and began to move along very slowly, pushing the cotton batting onto the floor. When the panel was clean, she got down and walked to the mirrors. Her black and white blouse left her midriff bare, and she wore a bouffant petticoat over white tights. Picking up a wide roll of masking tape from the stand, she tore off strips and fastened them across her mouth until the whole lower part of her face was covered. After a moment, she slowly removed the tape. Then she lifted the decorated board and, standing behind it, danced slowly around the room with it. Using an oil can with a long spout, she squirted more black paint on the paper walls or washed her feet with a scrubbing brush in the bucket of water.

The walls of the next room were also covered with heavy paper, but here smaller sheets had been used, overlapping each other. The walls, the semitransparent plastic which covered two windows on the right, and the plastic stretched across a doorway on the left were all spotted with large black dots of paint. A bunch of spotted balloons hung on the wall. There was a dresser with a mirror and a table covered with a white cloth. On the table were a radio, an electric fan and a bowl filled with small pieces of white foam rubber. As they moved into the room, the spectators found that there was action on both sides. To their left, seated next to the table, a thin man in a baggy suit and a wide-brimmed hat was speaking into a megaphone. He improvised a long rambling account of his life. After a long while, he slumped forward over the megaphone and remained motionless. A brunette girl in a cellophane hula skirt danced nearby. When she moved into the plastic-covered doorway, her shadow was cast on the plastic. The fan blew her skirt when she passed. From time to time the girl would search through the pockets of a pair of men's trousers that hung near the doorway, twist the dials on the radio to change the station and volume erratically, or, moving to the dresser, use a pressurized can to spray her hair.

To the right of the spectators was another performer, only her head visible above a huge, crumpled, boxlike costume of brown kraft paper. As she moved about the space, the heavy paper brushed against the spectators and rustled as it rubbed along the paper-covered walls of the room. Behind her, light shone in through the plastic which covered the windows, and loud noises were heard. (Cars had been maneuvered so as to throw the beams of their headlights on the house, and several men with sticks were banging at the window frames. At the first performance, they became too enthusiastic and smashed a window. Neighbors called the police, reporting a riot at "the Mexican house.")

Then the spectators passed into the other front room of the house. It was very dark. The walls were entirely covered with black paper, and in the center of the room a huge chicken-wire-and-paper construction that hung from the ceiling and reached to within a few feet of the floor filled much of the space. Four big men in work clothes lounged against the dark walls. In the rear, frequently obscured by the hanging construction, a girl walked back and forth. A few large sheets of crumpled aluminum foil had been attached to the close-fitting white jersey and tights that she wore. Occasionally she would sit against the wall or, picking up a hammer, noisily smash glass that filled a tub in the corner. From time to time, the four men would plunge suddenly toward the center of the room and wrestle violently on the floor under the construction.

The cycle had been completed, and the spectator was now back in the room that he had first entered with its newspaper-covered walls and littered floor.

Plans had been for the people to pass through the house several times at a set rate. Each time they went around they would see another segment of the repeated pattern. During rehearsal the night before the first performance, stand-ins simulating an audience carried out the procedure smoothly, but when two hundred people entered the building, movement was far from fluid. If something were particularly interesting, the spectators would bunch up, watching it. Or a group would stop and wait for one of the activities to be repeated. The two masked attendants attempted to keep the crowd moving, pushing them with their sticks, but the spectators showed little cooperation. It was very noisy. Sounds of the performances—violin, radio, voices—could be heard throughout the house. People yelled at each other, joked and milled around. A photographer pushed through the crowd with his assistant, who was dressed in a black cloak and carried a mirror globe which, it was hoped, would allow them to shoot photographs in the limited space. When the shadow of the hula dancer appeared on the plastic in the doorway, men would grab at it. On the back porch, spectators analyzed what the caged figure covered with netting was saying, and he, in return, would mimic and twist their comments. The doors were locked. It grew very warm. The house throbbed with activity.

When half an hour had passed, the girl who had been alternately washing her feet, putting tape over her mouth, dancing with the decorated board, and squirting paint from an oil can onto the wall coverings in the rear room took off her petticoat—she was wearing tights—and lay down on the floor.

The door of the back porch was unlocked, and the audience was directed down the newly constructed steps into the open space behind the house. Several men wearing rough costumes made of burlap hung with streamers of torn white cloth and carrying long sticks to which newspaper had been attached wandered about the open space between the house and the shed. White shapes began to drift down over the heads of the spectators in the yard. Performers were throwing balloons covered with newspaper off the roof of the house. Visible in the darkness, they bounced softly and drifted about the space. When they broke, the costumed men would pick them up and put them on their sticks.

(At this point during the first performance, police with flashlights climbed over a fence to the left of the audience. Investigating the "riot" call, they began to question the performers in the burlap costumes. A police car pulled up at the side of the house behind the standing spectators, but the action did not stop. The police soon realized that they were part of a performance and gradually moved around to join the audience. The radio of the police car was heard throughout the remainder of the Happening.)

The man in the brownish-green net costume reached through a hole and pulled the girl who had been lying in the kitchen onto the porch. Spectators still inside the house watched her disappear suddenly. Carrying the motionless white figure in his arms, he climbed off the porch through an opening in the screening, put the girl down on a sheet of plastic to the left of the spectators, and pulled her to a spot near the shed. Then he left her and entered the left section of the shed through a hole in the wooden wall.

Illuminated by dim blinking lights, the three girls in simple print dresses were moving about the hay-strewn space when the stooped brownish-green form entered. He reached up and connected a bright, hanging bulb which also blinked on and off erratically. The spectators watched through the open side of the shed as the man and the girls started to fight, the net and cloth costume of the man swinging wildly as he flailed his arms, the girls darting about striking at him and throwing hay. Balloons wrapped in red-painted paper flew through the air. Buckets of red paint and plastic bags filled with red paint had been placed around the shed and were now used in the struggle. Red liquid splashed the crudely whitewashed walls and splattered the four frantic figures. Suddenly the girls fell into the hay and lay motionless. The hunched figure hung with irregular taped balls and long ragged streamers of white cloth moved slowly back to the girl he had left lying on the plastic sheet and dragged her across to the center of the shed.

Inside the right section, a man dressed in white, his back to the audience, began to roll the huge circle of plywood from side to side. Sheets of metal had been fastened to the walls at either side, and the thick plywood struck with a loud metallic crash. Back and forth it went, shaking the small building. After a few moments, the net-covered figure stalked into the shed again and thrashed wildly at the operator who collapsed. The large wheel fell slowly against the rear wall.

Again the costumed man pulled the motionless girl along on the plastic sheet, stopping near the low addition attached to the right wall of the shed. A spotlight illuminated the roof of the smaller shed. To the right, held vertical by a wire running to the addition, was a tall canvas construction. Randomly painted green and brown, it bulged at the top, resembling a tree or a giant ice-cream cone. (This was a "tornado" that, in the original plans, was to have come for the spectators at the beginning of the performance. When it was stuffed, it became too heavy to move.) To the right of the audience, a record playing the music of a Mexican mariachi band was heard from the screened porch where the washtub bass had played earlier.

Lifting the girl in his arms, the green figure carried her up a ladder onto the almost-flat roof and laid her down. Water began to flow from a hose that hung against the tall peaked wall of the large shed. It ran across the low roof and poured in a waterfall off the right side near the canvas construction. Four suits of white long underwear, stuffed and daubed with red paint, were dangling from the overhanging eaves of the taller shed. The man snatched them down and threw the damp, headless, handless and footless bodies at the spectators. Then he crouched at the rear corner of the roof, dropped to the ground, and disappeared.

The girl who had been motionless for so long stood up and took down a costume hanging from the eaves. Putting it on, she began to dance vigorously, hopping up and down. Long hanging sections of the costume (made from old window shades) flapped wildly as she moved. Then she picked up a pair of shears and, kneeling, cut the wire that attached the large construction to

The netting-covered man throws a stuffed suit of long underwear down onto the spectators from the roof of the small shed (Pat Oldenburg, Claes Oldenburg).

the shed. It fell, landing with a heavy thud, and the spotlight went out.

Thinking that the Happening was over, some of the spectators began to wander away, but others watched silent activities in an overgrown sunken garden just to the right of the shed. Several performers, including the man in brownish-green netting, were running with long streamers of kraft paper. For a few minutes they wove about in the darkness, then lay motionless on the wet ground.

The spectators began to find their way back to the museum. The house was again without a tenant. And it was much dirtier than it had been when the Mexican family left.

WORLD'S FAIR II / *the script*

First Part: The People Come In.

A long table in the center of a long space. As the people arrive they take places around the table, which is silver and which is heaped with old magazines which they may read while waiting for the performance to begin.

Second Part: The Table

Table is cleared by Letty. She stacks the magazines and carries them off to the back. She wipes the table. She may have a sort of uniform on.

INTERROGATION

Lucas and John enter carrying Dominic in a suit stuffed with paper and debris as if dead. They place him on the table, slide him. He is in the middle and they go through his pockets, laying what they find on the tabletop around him. Turn him over etc. When his pockets are empty they push him to the edge of the table and carry him out.

DISSECTION

Lucas and John reenter with a trunk. Same procedure: they slide this on the table and go through it laying the objects out on the tabletop. They then carry the trunk out.

PLANNING

Lucas and John reenter with a cloth in which are many blocks and things for the construction of a model such as an architectural model. They either set the objects out among the others or lay the cloth on the top and set the piece on the cloth. When this is finished they leave.

Letty comes in, puts on a record and cleans the tabletop, putting the things into a barrel or bag and carrying them off. Lucas, John, Dominic and Claes carry off the tabletops and the horses, leaving the floor in roughly the same area covered by the tabletops. Letty sweeps floor, lowers the lamps to the floor, presses people back with her broom.

Third Part: The Floor

WALKING

Lucas comes out, tippytippy, very small steps, walks around. John comes out with his feet attached to boards. Dominic comes out with his feet in huge burlap bags. They walk around. Each carries a shopping bag full of stuff. Letty comes out lies down and wearing old-fashioned cotton stockings moves her legs on the floor.

DROPPING

The bags open at the bottom and the stuff falls out, as all keep walking. Complex of debris and feet.

DANCING

Pat appears, does a slow floor dance, to be choreographed. If the floor is now too crowded all but Pat and perhaps one other person may leave the stage area. In her dancing, Pat grabs the ankles of people watching or pinches toes or tickles them in some way with a long feather . . . or something. Pat leaves.

RUNNING

Lucas enters violently and runs around.

Letty comes in and sweeps the floor, takes the debris away. Plays record.

Fourth Part: Walls

AUDIENCE AS WALLS

John and Dominic and Lucas bring in boxes or big sheets of cardboard and press them against the audience all around the playing area.

VEIL

Ladders are set up at either end of the playing area. Letty and Pat (or Max) climb them and cut the string holding the muslin over the heads of the audience, which gradually falls so they are covered over by it.

VEIL WITH LIGHTS

Dancing with boxes continues in the playing area. A solo or a duet, unseen by the audience also except they barely see it and sense the shadows.

VEIL WITH DARKNESS

The lights are extinguished except for two blue lights. The dance continues. Noises and music.

PRESSURE AND POKING

Big soft pillows and ends of broomhandles are gently poked at the audiences bodies through the muslin.

Letty and Max or John lean over the audience and cut down muslin, which falls on floor. Letty turns over lights so they shine up.

Fifth Part: Ceiling

Above stage area is a corresponding area of chicken wire. Onto this is now hung by everybody the forms representing the fair or the city. When this is completed everyone retires, and the performance is over. Someone may lie on the floor while the pieces are being hung up.

WORLD'S FAIR II / *the production*

DURING THE WINTER AND spring of 1962, Claes Oldenburg presented ten Happenings in a store he had rented on Second Street between Avenue A and First Avenue in New York. He called the store the Ray Gun Manufacturing Company. Each Happening was given single performances on Friday and Saturday evenings, and the following week was spent preparing another presentation. *Store Days I, Store Days II, Nekropolis I,* and *Nekropolis II* were performed in February and March. Late in March, Oldenburg went to Dallas where he created *Injun;* the Happenings in the store resumed in late April and May with *Injun I, Injun II, Voyages I, Voyages II,* and *World's Fair I.* (Despite the paired titles, the works were entirely different.) The final Happening of the series, *World's Fair II,* was given on the 25th and 26th of May, 1962.

As with the other Happenings in the store, the audience was limited to thirty-five. When the spectators arrived, the long narrow front room of the store was almost entirely filled by a large table made from two sheets of plywood resting on sawhorses and painted silver. There was a single chair at either end of the table, and the display area inside the front window created a raised level, but essentially there was no place for the audience to sit. Three evenly spaced lights hung at about head height from the ceiling and illuminated the table from above, their conical shades suggesting, perhaps, the archetypical pool hall at night. Higher on each cord was a small blue light. The table itself was littered with cheap secondhand magazines: girlie magazines, confession magazines, comic books, Spanish-language picture novelle, teenage romance magazines. Crowded around the table, the spectators read the magazines as they waited for the performance to begin.

223

The People Come In: Spectators looking at magazines before the performance.

When he felt that the audience had waited long enough, Oldenburg walked out from the rear room from which and to which all entrances and exits would be made. He stepped up on one of the chairs. "The piece will now begin," he said. "It is entitled *World's Fair II,* and there are four parts: Table, Floor, Walls and Ceiling. It will take about forty-five minutes. There will be no intermission." He climbed down and disappeared through the curtained doorway to the back room.

A whiny bagpipe tune, played at less than its intended speed, was heard, and a brunette girl stepped through the curtains. She was dressed in a sleeveless white middy blouse with red trim and a drooping red bow, Bermuda shorts with broad vertical black and white stripes, full-length natural beige stockings of heavy cotton, black high-heeled shoes, and a brimless cap with a band across the crown that looked somewhat like a bellboy's cap. (The costume was not ready for the first performance, so those who attended that evening saw only the usual street clothes.) She walked to the table and began stacking the magazines, taking them out of the hands of the spectators. Passage along the sides of the table was not easy since only two or three feet separated the table from the walls of the narrow room, and the room was crowded, but she silently moved around collecting the magazines and making several piles on the table. Occasionally a spectator would want to keep the magazine he was looking at or would take it back once she had taken it, but the uniformed girl was persistent. Jostled and pushed by the crowd, she made a second circuit of the table, picked up all the magazines in one tall stack, and carried them off. The bagpipe music was still playing, and in a moment the girl returned with a cloth and a feather duster and began to dust the table, rubbing diligently at any spots. Then she left the room again, and the music suddenly stopped.

Two men entered carrying the sagging inert body of a third man between them. The first man wore a blue summer suit that had been faded by age or the sun until it was a luminous pink or lavender. He wore pink sunglasses. The second man was dressed in a pale blue suit and a black and white striped shirt. Both wore wide, gaudy, colorful ties. The face of the dark-haired man they carried had been painted a stark white, which gave him a clownish aspect, and his baggy suit, spattered and daubed with several hues of paint, bulged awkwardly. The two men moved slowly through the standing audience, crossed the ten feet that separated the curtained doorway and the end of the table, slid the motionless body onto the silver surface, pushed it into a straight supine position, and shoved it to the center. For what may have seemed like a long while (it was actually about half a minute), the two silent expressionless men sat motionless in the chairs at either end of the table, gazing fixedly at the white-faced figure lying directly under the lights.

The man wearing sunglasses clambered up on the table. Reaching inside the jacket of the rigid body, he slowly withdrew large pieces of stiff crumpled cloth. Perhaps from a side pocket, he removed a baby rattle or a pair of sunglasses; from a rip in the clothing he extracted a thimble. After several objects had been discovered and set carefully aside, the other man, too, climbed up on the table, crouched at the feet of the supine figure, and also began to search the body. Deliberately the expressionless men removed a wide variety of small objects: a string of beads, a souvenir scarf, a brush, playing cards, a flashlight. The audience could easily watch the movements of both men. Some discoveries and actions brought an obvious reaction from the surrounding spectators: a rubber glove withdrawn from the shirt momentarily resembled viscera, the whitened lips of the inert man were pushed back and his teeth and mouth examined, a shoe was removed and the space between the toes investigated. (A certain competition for audience response and approval developed between the two men, and although there was no visual or verbal exchange and each concentrated on his own work, they vied with each other. Oldenburg had not specified what objects he wanted used or where he wanted them hidden; he and all three of the performers "loaded" the "body" with objects found around the store—detritus from the previous seven Happenings produced there.) The table near each of the men was littered with their small discoveries when, on a prearranged signal by one of them, they climbed down, slid the body to the end, swung it into its earlier sagging position between them, and made their way out of the room.

After a moment the two men returned, walking in the same way, again carrying something between them. It was an old battered suitcase with the lettering *DOM* on the top. They lifted the suitcase onto the table just as they had done with the body, slowly slid it to the center, and clambered up to sit at either end of it. The ropes that held it together were untied; the suitcase was opened. It was seen to be entirely filled with a jumble of refuse: a short length of rubber hose, an old funnel, a bottle, paper play money, an empty beer can, a piece of cloth with the number 6 on it. Carefully the men began to remove the various items, studying each before setting it aside. Again their activity continued for quite a while without any communication, each working independently. The pile of objects on the table grew. The suitcase was still half full when the men closed and tied it, stood on the table, slid the case to the edge just as they had done with the body, jumped down, and carried the suitcase out between them.

This time when the men returned, they carried a sagging white sheet between them, which they spread over the object-littered table. Using the items of refuse that were left uncovered and reaching under the sheet for others, they began to arrange the materials. Crouched on the table, intent upon their work, the men were building what some spectators would recognize as a strange toy city or a miniature world's fair. Where the cloth was swelled by an object underneath or where it was pushed and bunched up by one of the men, hills and valleys were formed. Roads were made with paper money and bits of paper; cans and bottles became buildings and towers; plastic flowers were turned into trees. (Again there was no obvious emotion, no communication or contact between the performers, but again competition developed. Each strove to outdo the other in imagination and creativeness. Sometimes one would take part of the other's construction to use in his own work.) Some of the spectators were restless after the previous extended episodes. The men worked quickly and then walked out, leaving their miniature landscape for the audience to study.

Once again the bagpipe music played at reduced speed was heard, and the girl in the middy blouse and striped Bermuda shorts entered, pulling a large barrel of brown cardboard, the handles of a mop and a broom protruding from it. With the barrel at the edge of the table, she began dumping objects into it,

The Table: The "body" is searched (Dominic Capobianco, John Weber).

The Table: The "body" is searched (Lucas Samaras, Dominic Capobianco).

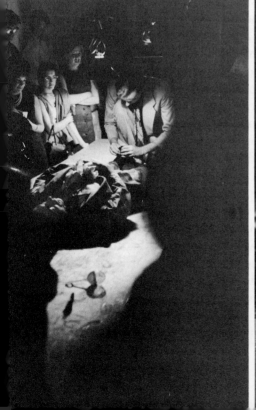

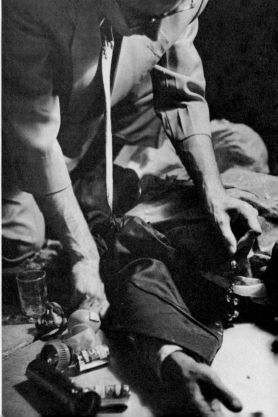

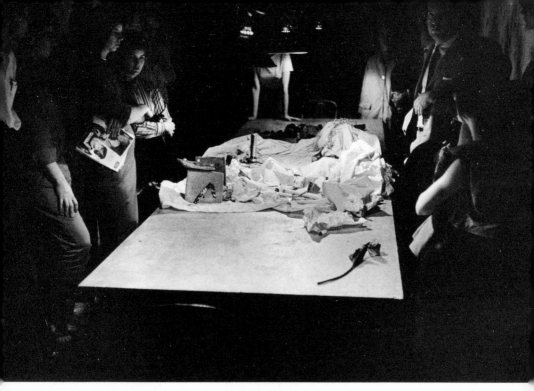

The completed "world's fair" landscape.

bunching the cloth and its construction to stuff it into the container. As she slid the barrel away, four men entered and began to disassemble the table. First the two pieces of plywood that made up the top were carried off and then the four sawhorses that served as legs. With a broom, the uniformed girl cleaned the vacated space, sweeping at the shoes of any of the standing spectators who even threatened to encroach upon it. The long cords of the three hanging lights had been looped up and held by clips, and the girl lowered them until they were only about two feet from the floor. A moment ago the room had been brightly illuminated. Now the conical shades made three round pools of light, leaving the walls and the audience in semidarkness, lit only by reflected light. The girl disappeared into the back room and the music stopped.

The figure of a man began to run rather quietly around the dimly lit room. Although it was not too dark for the spectators easily to see that he was dressed in a suit and carried a weighted shopping bag in his arms, only his feet and ankles were ever in direct light. He would take a series of short, quick, running steps forward or backward on tiptoe, stop for a moment, and then take more quick steps. The gentle intermittent bunched rhythm of his white tennis shoes could be heard as he moved in and out of the pools of light. Frequently when he would pause, several large nails would drop from the bag and clink on the floor. (There was a small hole in the bottom of the bag that the performer covered and uncovered with his hand.) Then another sound—a steady, dull, thumping noise—was heard. The form of another suited man appeared, his feet in cardboard boxes. One box reached to his knee, the other was not as high. Awkwardly he stamped about the space, raising his boxed feet with every step. A third man appeared, and a third sound was added. On his feet this man wore enormous burlap bags stuffed with paper. Each was perhaps a yard long and a foot and a half high. (As with the box shoes, cords attached to the strange footwear and held in the performer's hands aided maneuverability.) The bulbous cloth shoes with their paper stuffing added a soft, rubbing, shuffling sound to those of the other men who were moving around the space. (These were the same three men who had performed in the first "scene" on the table. The flashy ties and the dark glasses had been removed, and,

The Floor: Note position of lights (John Weber, Dominic Capobianco, Lette Eisenhauer).

although his face was still covered with white paint, the "body" no longer wore the baggy, paint-marked suit.) Then the staccato click of high heels was heard. The uniformed girl ran quickly to one of the hanging lamps, sat, and placed her legs into the pool of light. Sliding quickly in a crab walk to the next illuminated area, she swung her legs directly under that light, holding them slightly off the floor and bending or straightening them as if posing for a pinup photographer. For a few minutes the four performers crossed and recrossed the rectangular space where the table had been standing: the girl's legs brightly lit, the various shoes that the men wore moving in and out of the light, the sounds and rhythms mixing. The girl left first, running quickly through the curtained door, and the others followed. Except for scattered nails, the central space was empty. The three circles of bright light made a regular pattern in the semidarkness.

A girl with long hair wriggled into sight along the floor. She was wearing a ruffled blouse that left her arms bare, a dark skirt, silk stockings, and tennis shoes. Slowly she pulled herself across the nail-strewn floor on her stomach. Occasionally she would twist sinuously onto her back and wriggle forward, or, in a prone position, spin rapidly, her arms and legs slightly raised. When she reached some of the surrounding audience, she tickled someone's foot, placed nails in a spectator's shoe, or tied the laces of adjacent shoes together, then crawled slowly and tortuously to another point on the wall of watching people. Perhaps she ran her hands up a girl's leg or took off someone's shoe. The spectators permitted her to do whatever she wished. When, after several minutes, the girl made her way gradually out of the room, she was thoroughly marked with dirt from the floor.

Suddenly the crouched running figure of a man burst into the dimly lit room and rushed toward the far wall. Spectators quickly backed away to open a space, but he stopped short, charged at another group of watchers, then darted back to the center and slammed a cinder block that he was carrying loudly to the floor. Several times he repeated the sequence of running toward various sections of the audience, making them flinch, if possible, or move out of the way, and then returning to the pools of light to crash the heavy block down. Then, as abruptly as he had entered, he shouldered his way through the crowd and was gone.

In a moment the now-familiar bagpipe record was heard again, and the uniformed girl entered to sweep away the nails and to clean the central area. As she was finishing, two long cloth-wrapped wooden battens were carried in by a man the audience had not seen before and set on the floor at the feet of the spectators who lined the longer walls. At about the same time, two of the men who had previously performed carried in large rectangular frames covered with cardboard. Each frame measured approximately three feet by five feet. The performers, working on opposite sides of the room, held the rectangles directly in front of a group of spectators, pressed them back against the wall, and then moved on several feet to repeat the procedure. (One of the men later described how the blade of a knife had been thrust suddenly through his panel by someone in the audience. The blade made a four-inch slash and disappeared.) When the complete perimeter of the playing space had been covered, the panels were carried off, and shorter cloth-wrapped battens carried on.

Four performers (the previous three men and the girl in the middy blouse) began to unroll the cloth from the battens. They were standing so that the space between the wooden poles was rectangular—roughly that which had been occupied earlier by the long table. As the cloth unrolled, walls rose: when the performers were holding the battens over their heads, an enclosure or ceiling-less room had been formed by the four walls of white muslin. All of the hanging lights were inside the newly created room. They cast shadows on the cloth. As a slow, sentimental fox-trot began to play, the lower fixtures with their conical shades were switched off, leaving the three small blue bulbs that hung seven or eight feet above the floor as the only illumination. A man dressed in a suit and a girl in a pink street-length dress and pink shoes danced into the dim blue light of the room. Holding each other close, the couple moved easily through the spectators and into the cloth enclosure. The audience could not see them. There was only the soft sound of the music. When the spectators tried to look under or between the curtains to watch the dancers, the cloth was pulled from their hands, the openings closed. Only another performer (carrying a broomstick) was allowed to enter. For a minute or so the hidden fox-trot continued. Then the couple emerged from the curtains, and, oblivious of the audience, danced slowly back to the "offstage" room. When they were gone, the music stopped, and the lower, brighter lights were switched on again—again cast-

Walls: Panels are pushed against the spectators.

ing vague shadows on the sheeting. Someone (Claes Oldenburg) within the enclosure began to poke a round stick at the spectators, the cloth being pressed suddenly and insistently out. Primarily on the long sides where the watchers had little chance to escape, the wood prodded them. Then, abruptly, the attacks stopped; the cloth walls were rolled up again and carried off.

Again the uniformed girl adjusted the hanging lights. This time she inverted the conical shades, placing them in pails so that they were directed upward. Again the room was transformed: now the walls and ceiling were brightly illuminated, and the spectators looked down into the pails filled with light. For a moment the central space was empty of performers. Then the record player blared out the energetic "National Emblem March." Two men quickly carried stepladders in and set them up. They were followed swiftly by other performers carrying large objects made of stuffed cloth and daubed in rows with spots of paint. Climbing the ladders, they hung the objects with pressure clothespins from lines that formed an irregular web near the ceiling. Back and forth the performers went, getting stuffed pieces, looking for a vacant spot for hanging, shifting the ladders, clambering up and attaching

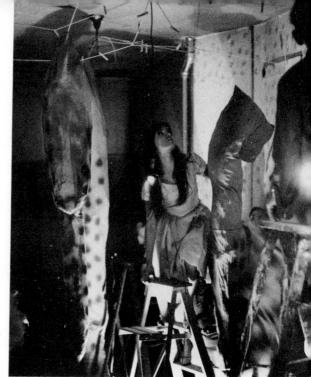

Ceiling: Stuffed "buildings" are hung upside down (Pat Oldenburg).

the objects. Almost everyone who had been involved so far and a newcomer or so were now active. Behind the activity, the march music played loudly. When the cloth objects hung, they resembled buildings with their bases toward the ceiling and their roofs toward the ground. The spots of paint were windows. Rapidly the hanging inverted city grew. Most of the lumpy buildings were three or four feet tall, some were almost as tall as a person, and one (was it the Empire State Building?) reached to the floor. When the supply of stuffed pieces had been exhausted, the performers did not return to the presentation space. Fewer and fewer people were active. The last piece was hung, the ladders carried off, the record stopped. The Happening was over. Around the walls of the room, the audience still stood under the stalactite city. For several minutes they waited; began to shift about, talk; gradually they emptied out into the warm spring night.

In the middle of one of the performances, a group of about fifteen doctors in a "mystery club" had walked out, handing their one-dollar contributions to a man connected with the Happening who was standing by the door. As he was given each bill, the man ripped it up. Weeks afterward Oldenburg was still finding small bits of torn money in the store.

GAYETY / *the script*

NOTE: *This is a preliminary working draft of a script for* Gayety. *One of several contained in Oldenburg's book of the production, it was modified during rehearsal.*

OVERTURE

The overture occurs in the corridor. A subway landscape has there been constructed using many chairs boxes newspapers and smoke. The spectators must pass thru the overture to reach the main space.

The main space is laid out like a map of Chicago such as one sees at the Museum of Science and Industry. There is a center stage (the Loop) a bit north of the center of the area. Bouras welding shop is the south steel works, Gary etc. Two sinks back to back on the right are the lake, and also function as the home and the exhibit of stoves (such as in the Edison building opp from the Art Institute). There is a graveyard for weather (place where noise is made). A blackboard for messages (maps, drawings, menus), stations and areas for action around the spectators seats which are set up to resemble right angular streets (a diagonal to the loop-stage—Milwaukee or Archer ave. f.ex.). At the southwest side is a large stuffed airplane either hanging above (as in the Mus of Sc and Ind) or drooping to the floor.

The happening is for me a personal composition out of elements at hand. It is not a question of chance or random effects.

In Gayety I want to create a civic report on the community of
234

Chicago, in the way I see it. After the overture there are six "combinations" of events, persons, articles, sounds—all the elements of experience in representative situation, either plain or enigmatic, demonstrating such categories as weather, climate, geography, education, culture, poetry, homelife, crime, products, food, traffic, heroes, art, entertainment, and so on. This is like the civic projects one did in sixth grade or I think of O Henrys or anyone elses municipal report, sociological studies etc. but that mine is poetic/satiric/symbolic. The enigmatic portions may be taken to be the situation of the spirit in the community, often these have a violent turn.

The relation of the incidents is fortuitous as is the case in real life. Imagine a map where all that goes on in the city can be seen from above at once, such as the fire charts of the fire dept or the multiplicity simultaneity of the taxi or police radios. A city is overlay upon overlay of incident. Unfortunately I am limited to typicalities, but the spectator may imagine the numbers.

The piece closes with a Finale, an apotheosis, in the form of a destruction which always seems appropriate in which the forces of the community are released functionlessly in relieving chaos.

Map of the City

Dantean panorama (diorama)   Parody on civic spectacle

The title gayety comes from the gayety burlesk and has no specific meaning in relation to the events. The Woopedah clip was found on a bus, paper of a Catholic Indian settlement in South Dakota.

I. Combination One: WAVES, MAPS, SPONGES

1. A girl comes in with a bucket and a sponge and colored chalks. Goes to blackboard, cleans it, starts drawing maps of Chicago.

2. Two women dressed in aprons clear tables and wash dishes

in the sink. The sound of dishes. Waves in lake. They hum like sirens. (weather)

3. Ten or twelve plastic bags filled with colored plastic sponges, desirable and buyable in the light on the loopstage are placed on the loopstage (products). Among them placed a man covered with newspaper (perhaps wet) tied up with laundrycord. He is trying to free himself.

4. From time to time the sound of coughing from under the loopstage.

II. *Combination Two:* EGGS, MEAT, THUNDER, SAND, DOUGH

1. In darkness a projector begins to project live some products in action: an egg blistering and frying, cigarettes slide out of a package, a piece of fine red meat.

2. After some moments of articles-projection, a man in a silver helmet, oversize white asbestos gloves, white fin-feet and in long underwear putteed calves mounts stage, reads rather quietly a poem made out of Chicago street names.

3. A heavybuilt man (butcher) in smock or coveralls, mounts a ladder over the grave with a box of junk, painted red and yellow and dumps it into the grave (lake Calumet) Garbage-Butcher man. Then another, and so on. Much noise. Weather-Thunder.

4. The tied figure on loopstage is taken off into an open area and unwrapped (found by a passerby). Thanks very much. Dusts self.

5. A bed slides in with a man in it and also filled with Sand (park district). The man in pajamas gets out of the bed takes out of it a shovel and shovels the sand out of the bed. By his bedside is a radio a very small white radio or tied to his arm with a band, which plays softly.

6. The poet in the helmet has a heckler (censor), a housewife

who shouts to him to shut up, to keep it down, when she is not baking and manipulating dough on the table in front of her. She climbs on a chair to shout.

III. Combination Three: POWDER, MUD, CANDLES, TRAFFIC,
MOON OVER LAKE

1. The poet removes his helmet, fins, gloves. He dresses in a shabby suit whose pockets are filled with talcum and which is dusty white. When he pats his pockets the talcum rises out of it. He mounts the white stage (of GraecoRoman) culture and patting his pockets. He maneuvers around, bundles of newspaper (new buildings), planning & unfolds papers from his pockets. Falls down, raises dust. Mumbles.

2. At the other end of the map, crime and massacre. The butcher-garbage man now starts throwing very fast gobs of mud, red yellow and black which spatter and hit hard the wall.

3. In front of the butcher-garbageman-gangster, coming out when he can and there is no fire, a clown, his hands full of cheap candles covered with colored balloons, with a mirror and shaving cream. Who sets up the candles on the table lights them and then shaves, while avoiding the thrown mud on the one side and only now and then popping a balloon by coming too close to the fire (Bing Crosby).

4. Three figures in burlap bags enter onto loopstage tie the bags shut and wriggle and wrestle. From the ceiling down comes bags stuffed with paper unclear ancient forms (turds amoebas, beginning of life) and coiled red sausages. The whole mixing. This is traffic.

5. Figure of a singer in a nice dress. She turns on the moon. She is like the singer in Xian Science church on Sunday but also the singer in Ohenry ballroom (band singer). She has a tape recorder which makes pneumatic sounds. She stirs a tambourine. She has a mike. The words she sings . .

IV. *Combination Four:* ICE, BUTTER, WATER, ORANGES, SKATES

1. A film is shown of a girl in a fur coat and carrying a package running and falling in the wide field of Washington Park ringed with chimneys. Little Eva. Three min. about. May be repeated. Memory. History.

2. Two men in aprons writing the daily special, taking turns on the bulletin board. First rule it carefully, put an item on, in big letters, like Ham and Eggs 75 cents. Erasure. The other sets it on. While one works the other butters bread and applies drawn pieces of meat. He has a big pile of them. Cuts it. Stirs a smoking pot.

3. A man nails up the four corners of the loopstage sticks and ties onto the sticks a christmas tree light strand so that the loop is ringed (with L). He steps inside, bringing with him a small table, a chair, a pitcher full of water a glass to drink it out of and a typewriter. He takes off his shirt breathes deeply several times, sits down and types and drinks water, gets up breathes and so on. Author, convict, murderer, intellectual, narcissus.

4. A girl sets up a still life of oranges. She is dressed in smock smeared with orange, has an orange paintfilled pot with an orange brush. She paints oranges, squeezing them out of shape cutting them eating them, they fall. She gets paint over herself and the oranges. In her hair. She smashes one with her fist. Rearranges them. Art.

5. A burly guy in his shirtsleeves knocks the dishes off the Kitchen table, puts down his cigarette on the sink and bending over the table chops it up. A girl with iceskates on and a moustache sits watching still.

V. *Combination Five:* FEET, HEARTS, BUCKETS, NUTS AND BOLTS

1. Woman in the kitchen cleans it up after the hatcheting, puts the bottles of beer in a neat row by sink. Her girl wipes off the moustache in the mirror and combs her hair. She takes

off the skates and washes her feet in the shower. Mama scrubs the floor with a brush and wipes it with a mop.

2. A girl enters in red costume with two halves of hearts in red oilcloth on sticks as illustrated and with a collection of feathers and other favors pinned on her costume. With a record player and three records which she sets up on table next to loopstage. She dances with the two halfhearts and throws favors at the audience. Entertainment.

3. Spectacle of education: men beat girls, girls beat men. Climbs and terrors. Newspapers, flashlights, buckets, in semidarkness on the south side.

4. The citizen out for a walk with his paper. Reads it drops it, ties it and stuffs it wherever he can. Ties it to his legs, stuffs his pockets. Finds things in the graveyard, collects it. Self-absorbed.

VI. *Combination Six:* JACKETS

1. Another girl follows the first, she with her three records. The first removes her paraphernalia. Dances with stuffed suitjackets which she takes down from a hanging position.

Finales: CHAIRS, SPARKS

1. Through windows opened to subway outside, chairs are handed in to men standing on ladders, about a hundred chairs which fill the room. Also panes of glass which are some dropped in the handling chairs and glass. Evacuation of school. Fire.

2. A huge plane of stuffed cloth is let down and wrestled with by several persons. Pressed against spectators and maneuvered threateningly.

3. Welding light in Gary sparks and pops. Great crashes from welding room.

NOTE: *The following is a sample of the final script that, with certain changes inserted, was posted "backstage" so that the performers could refer to it. Each "combination" was divided into the four sections shown here. In certain combinations there was no "residual action."*

Combination V: FINGERS

RISING ACTION

47. Projection five: fingers (bananas) *In stillness. In darkness.* 1 min.   0
48. Martha enters kitchen and cleans it up. *Sink lights on.*   1
49. Mary wipes off moustache. Combs hair. Washes feet in shower. Starts covering herself w. aluminum foil.
50. Harry enters. Empties umbrella, looks in grave and walks. *Front lights on.*   2
51. Pat enters with hearts. *Center light on. Puts on record, high volume. Same record put on by Johann at Volume set #2.*   2½
52. Len Fraser cuts ham. *Turns on Muzak music. Blackboard light on.*   3
53. Buggy and coffin collide, Dan, Peter, Norman, Kurt, David 1.   3½

FULL ACTION   6½ Min.

FALLING ACTION

54. *All lights out in rapid succession except Mary's extra kitchen light.* Mary remains seated on floor wrapped in foil.   10
    Record player off by Pat.
    Record off backstage by Johann.

RESIDUAL ACTION

55. Mary remains seated absolutely still through combination VI.

GAYETY / *the production*

LATE IN 1962, immediately after an exhibition of his plaster and stuffed canvas food sculptures at the Green Gallery in New York, Claes Oldenburg went to Winnetka to repair one of his pieces for a collector. At that time he decided to do a Happening in Chicago, his hometown. He searched for a large, empty space in a "proletarian" neighborhood, and compiled a list of possibilities from the Yellow Pages of the telephone directory: Atomic Halls, Chopin Cultural Center, Puerto Rican Social Center, Natural Knights Hall, Polish Falcons, Society of Danube Swabians, and Wonderland were included. Since he is particularly fond of the Division Street neighborhood that Nelson Algren described in *Man with a Golden Arm*, he looked at several places in that area. When he finally found a suitable space for the Happening—Lexington Hall on the South Side campus of the University of Chicago—he was disappointed that it was part of an academic community. But the old, wooden, frame structure, which had been a bakery and a gymnasium before its present limited use by the art department, was generally ignored by the university. And the university was not sponsoring the performance, nor had they given official permission for the use of the hall.

It was very cold. Snow blanketed the city, and the cast had difficulty getting to the four or five rehearsals that were scattered throughout the week preceding the performances. Work began slowly. The performers were unfamiliar with Happenings and unsure of what was expected of them. Several ideas were tried out and discarded: a group of girls did a striptease under open-mesh bags of brown cloth; words on cards were used to cue columns of performers with the people in each column reciting one letter and all letters sounded at once. Other things were found during the formal parts of rehearsal or the periods of waiting: a girl tried to learn a piece on the piano, repeating one passage over and over;

241

a little girl drew horses on the blackboard to amuse herself. An important change was required by the university, which had discovered the use being made of the hall. During the full rehearsal that preceded the actual performance, a motorcycle was used, but skid marks and oil stains marred the building, necessitating its removal from the "cast."

There was considerable publicity for the Happening. It was mentioned frequently in the newspapers, posters were placed around the university, and Oldenburg was interviewed on the local FM station. The Feigen Gallery, where Oldenburg exhibited, handled reservations and arranged a special screening of a film of the Happenings he had done the previous year in New York. But an announcement sent through the mails perhaps mystified more people than it informed. Although it included the vital information such as time, place and information about reservations and was headed "RAY THEATER GUN" (Ray Gun Theater), it was essentially a list. Under the caption "Our Want and Need List" were such items as "Soap and tooth paste," "Army blankets for twin size beds," and "Boys' socks, sizes 7-12." Oldenburg had found a discarded copy of a small newspaper or newsletter published by the Immaculate Conception Mission School for Indian children in Stephen, South Dakota. The list was taken from the paper. Some people apparently thought that the performance would consist of the items or that they should bring an item from the list to the performance, but it was intended only to indicate his interest in objects.

Gayety was presented on the 8th, 9th, and 10th of February, 1963. In 20-below temperatures the spectators made their way through the snow to Lexington Hall and pushed into the small vestibule. One hundred and fifty reservations had been taken for each performance, and the dimly lit space was soon crowded. Programs were available. At the top of the single sheet, the title, *Gayety*, was marked with an asterisk, and a footnote indicated that it was the "Name of a burlesk theater in Chicago." A subtitle read: "Composition for Persons, Objects, and Events," and after the heading of date, time and place were the words:

> A Map of Chicago
> 1. Overture
> 2. Six Combinations
> 3. Finale

Following the names of the performers was the statement that the performance would last "about an hour." Still not knowing what to expect, the people stood and waited long past the scheduled "curtain" time of 8:30.

Oldenburg was intentionally making the spectators wait. He went from performer to performer, asking how they felt and whether or not they had all of their props. He checked the apparatus. Finally, he walked to the vestibule and told the spectators to follow him. The crowd moved into a high-ceilinged hallway with a row of doors at one side and windows piercing both wooden walls about eight feet above the floor. At each performance a different arrangement of seventy-five solid oak chairs was made in the corridor. On the first evening, the chairs were scattered about randomly, so that the spectators had to push their way through. At the second performance, the chairs were lined neatly against one wall of the hallway, and identical copies of a newspaper were placed on each one. On the third evening, the chairs were arranged in a mazelike pattern through which the people passed.

The spectators entered a huge rectangular room. About twenty feet above the floor, heavy wooden rafters crossed the space and supports angled upward to the slanting roof. Double rows of windows lined all four walls: the taller upper windows, near the rafters, permitting a view of the cold night sky; the lower ones, eight feet above the floor, looking out on a hallway that surrounded the main room on all four sides (and through part of which the spectators had just passed). At floor level, the rectangular space had been made almost square, however, by eight-foot-high walls that divided off the ends of the room. Illuminated by a single hanging reflector bulb, a low wooden platform about one and one-half feet high and eight feet square occupied the center of the room. Contour chairs of white and coral molded plastic were grouped around the platform, leaving an open space between them and all four walls.

Behind the temporary wall at one end hung a huge American flag, and, off to one side, a brightly colored beach umbrella could be seen above the wall. Signs reading "NORTH," "GRAVE," and "MOON" had been attached to the wall itself, and a rectangular mirror hung in the center. Directly in front of the "GRAVE" sign was an eight-foot ladder and, at the foot of the ladder, an open rectangular construction, the walls of which were made of sawhorses covered with canvas. To one side of the ladder and near the "MOON" sign, a large crescent shape hung from the rafters. The crescent was merely an outline made of short pieces of wood nailed together. Two cross braces strengthened it, and Christmas-tree bulbs were spaced along the perimeter.

Near the corner where the temporary wall met the tall outer wall of the hall (actually only the pipe which supported the temporary panels at the top met the main wall, forming a wide opening through which performers would enter and exit) was a small platform on which a floor-model microphone, an electric fan, and a small plastic slot machine had been placed. A cluster of long balloons was attached to the composition-board panels that lined half of the wall. At the center of the wall, two sinks jutted into the room, and a hose rose from one of them: hanging from cords, it looped once in the air and dangled its open end about nine feet above the floor. Above the sinks, which were piled high with dishes, was another rectangular mirror. In the corner, where the side wall met the other temporary wall, was another small platform with a lectern and bundles of newspapers on it. Above the platform, a sign reading "GOD" had been placed. It, like the other signs, had been lettered in black spray paint.

Near the platform stood a baby carriage, a black rectangular mass of cardboard boxes towering six feet above it. Another construction, this one composed entirely of cardboard boxes that had been tied together and painted black, lay at the opposite end of the temporary wall. Against the wall between the constructions was a large three-foot-high platform with a row of chairs and some wooden boxes on it.

Centered in front of the fourth wall was a large classroom blackboard. Directly over it was the single word "EATS." Propped against the wall to the left of the blackboard was a tall ladder with its lower rungs covered with a large sheet of heavy paper. A long piece of wood slanted against the ladder, various pieces of cloth hanging from it. "WEST" appeared in large black letters on the wall near the ladder. On the opposite side of the blackboard, a pot of colorful artificial flowers stood in a graceful metal stand near a sign reading "SUNSET."

Small tables and various wooden chairs were scattered throughout the room. Near one corner of the central stand was a trash can with a peaked top. In addition to the crescent-shaped "moon," various things hung from the ceiling. Directly over the platform was another wooden outline; this one, edged with Christmas-tree bulbs that blinked on and off, resembled a pair of lips. Two long sausage shapes and a huge, bulbous, eighteen-foot-long construction of painted canvas hung near the rafters. (Stuffed with kraft paper, the construction was supposed to resemble an airplane. Floppy "wings" drooped like long ears at either side.) A bunch of men's jackets covered with bluish plastic bags also hung above the central platform. Near the corner in which the newspapers were piled, a hanging sheet, flattened by battens at the top and bottom, was pulled back at an angle. Various reflector bulbs hung throughout the room, but only the light above the central platform and the blinking outline of the lips were on.

Oldenburg was standing on the center platform, directing the spectators to the seats. He was dressed in a long, white, cloth work coat such as those worn by mechanics and butchers. Several people recognized him and called greetings. He did not answer. The chairs which faced the platform were soon filled, but many of the seats had been turned in other directions. Anyone sitting in them would face away from the center (where the audience expected the performance to take place), perhaps looking directly into the faces of other spectators. Few people wanted to sit in these chairs, but Oldenburg, speaking in a direct, humorless, businesslike way, ordered them to do so. They obeyed. Finally all the chairs on the main floor were filled, and the remaining spectators, many of them still angry from the long wait in the vestibule, were directed onto the large platform at the "South" end of the room. Some found chairs there; most of them stood. When everyone was in place, Oldenburg stepped off the central platform, and the lights went out. Only the Christmas-tree bulbs of various colors which outlined the large hanging lips blinked slowly on and off (as they would throughout the performance). The waiting, entrance, and seating of the audience had comprised what was referred to in the program as the "overture."

The image of a frying egg was projected on the hanging slanted cloth. (A large opaque projector located behind and above the "North" wall had been equipped with a hot plate so that a real egg could actually be fried in its projection chamber. Some of the spectators, not knowing what to expect and facing away from the screen, may not have noticed the projection, but the standees on the platform were facing both the screen and the projector, the image being visible from both sides of the cloth.) After thirty seconds, coughing was heard. Those near the center soon realized that it was coming from underneath the central stand. The projector was turned off, and the image of the frying egg disappeared.

A light went on over the blackboard, and an eight-year-old girl stepped into view wearing on her head an inflated rubber horse's head that had been painted silver. She walked purposefully to the board and began to draw horses. In various colors, the outline of a horse was repeated over and over. There were large horses and small horses. Sometimes one would be drawn inside the other. The loud coughing still continued sporadically.

A hanging bulb illuminated the sinks at the opposite side of the room, and a girl wearing a sleeveless smock moved into the light. (A man stationed on a platform behind the "North" wall, his head visible to the spectators, controlled the lights. He turned them on and off on an exact time schedule. Usually the performers, using the light as a cue, would walk into the area after he had illuminated it, and if they happened to move in before the scheduled time, the visibility of their actions was still controlled by "the operator.") There were perhaps seventy-five dishes in the sinks. The girl began to shift them back and forth. At times they clattered loudly; at other times only a steady tinkle could be heard.

The area in the center of the operator's wall was lighted. A girl with long hair, wearing a frilly yellow party dress that left her arms and shoulders bare, turned on the Christmas-tree bulbs that edged the hanging, crescent-shaped framework and stepped into the light with a bucket and a small pile of oilcloth. She dipped triangular oilcloth pennants into wet plaster in the bucket and hung them with clothespins on a line stretched parallel to the wall. As she worked, the plaster dripped down on her and spattered the floor of the area.

A fourth light, the one directly over the central platform, was turned on. A man crossed to the stand, his arms full of plastic bags containing variously colored synthetic sponges. He began to arrange the bags on the platform, perhaps grouping them rigidly in one corner or making linear patterns. (The particular arrangements were left to the performer and varied each night.)

From behind the "North" wall, a piano was heard. After a few

Combination One: Girl hangs plaster-dipped pennants on a line (Barbara Dickerson).

simple bars, it stopped abruptly and started again from the beginning of the piece.

Six separate things were now taking place in the room. Coughing came from under the central platform. The young girl drew horses, occasionally erasing them with a wet sponge taken from a nearby bucket. One girl moved dishes back and forth in the sink; another hung plaster-dipped pennants from a line. From "offstage" the same passage was repeated over and over on the piano. A man was arranging packages of colored sponges on the central platform. When he finished, he returned to the place from which he had entered, stepped briefly behind the wall against which the spectators stood, and reentered, dragging a man wrapped in newspaper and tied with twine. He pushed the body up on the central platform and walked away. Occasionally the wrapped figure twitched and wriggled as if trying to free itself. The hollow platform echoed when he thumped it, and, from under it, the coughing continued.

Throughout the performance the two mirrors, one above the sinks and the other centered in the "North" wall, reflected activities in the room. Because of the scattered locations of the various actions and the random seating of the audience, spectators were constantly standing up, turning, and twisting (From where he watched, Oldenburg thought the standing people looked like buildings in the "city.") Although they were a little farther from most of the action, the portion of the audience that was standing had much less difficulty following the simultaneous activities.

Sometimes the spectators would snatch bags of sponges from the platform, and at the second performance an impromptu "battle" began with the colored sponges being thrown back and forth around the room.

Six minutes after the piano began to play, the light over the blackboard was switched off. The little girl wearing the inflated horse's head disappeared behind the operator's wall. At fifteen-second intervals, the lights went off over the sink, the white pennants (which were now growing rigid as the plaster set), and over the central platform. On her way out, the girl in the yellow dress disconnected the lights of the hanging moon. The man who had brought in the paper-wrapped body now dragged it to a space near the standing spectators. As the last light went off, the piano stopped, and a man squirmed out from under the central platform and quickly walked off.

On the hanging projection screen, the image of buttered toast appeared. As the spectators watched, the butter slowly melted. By the dim light of a flashlight, the man who had dragged the newspaper-covered body off was carefully unwrapping it. Even those who could not see the body as it lay on the floor could hear the quiet rustle of the papers as they were stripped away. In the huge space of the hall, the flashlight, the projector, and the hanging lips were the only lights. Then, after a minute, the buttered toast abruptly faded away.

The central light went on. A tall, thin man with a red beard walked slowly in from behind the temporary wall where the projector was located. He wore white coveralls, heavy white asbestos gloves, and carried a portfolio from which the ends of thin white boards protruded. On his head was an old army helmet that had been painted white. Rubber swim flippers on his feet slapped the floor at every step. Gripping the trash can that stood near the central platform, he lifted it onto the stage under the light. The can had been painted white; patches of red, blue, and yellow gave it a mottled appearance. The man opened his portfolio, took out one of the long white strips of wood, closed the folder, and held the wood up as if he were reading something written on it. His lips moved, but there was no sound. (Oldenburg had asked him to recite the names of Chicago streets, but, feeling unable to do this, he substituted Shakespearean sonnets. The spectators, of course, did not know the difference.) Then he dropped the stick into the trash can, set the slanting doors in the peaked top of the can swinging back and forth, flapped his flippers rapidly against the resonant floor of the platform, and opened his portfolio to repeat the sequence. Even without the heavy gloves the portfolio of small boards would have been difficult to handle. The pieces of wood frequently slipped out and fell, forcing the man to bend and pick them up before he could continue.

At the same time, a dark, solidly built man in a white smock had entered with a large bag. Reaching over the sawhorses draped with canvas that made a rectangular enclosure near the hanging row of rigid white pennants, he began to pick up beer cans, bottles, glass and various objects and put them in the sack. When the bag was full, he climbed the ladder and, with a sudden loud crash of glass and metal, poured the contents back onto the enclosed space. Then he climbed down and repeated the operation.

A light went on behind the ladder leaning against the "West" wall, its lower rungs covered with a large piece of paper. The shadow of a man could be seen on the paper as he climbed the ladder from the back. To the right stood another man, his back to the audience, slowly playing "My Country 'Tis of Thee" on a trombone. After a short passage, he would stop abruptly and start

Combination Two: Helmeted man in white on center stage. Girl climbs paper-covered ladder. Trombone plays (John Cawelti, Ellen Sellenraad, Kurt Hayl).

over. A girl wearing a polka-dot dress began to climb the ladder. Various tools—saw, hammer, drill, screwdriver—hung on cords from her waist, making it difficult to climb. At each step, she had to kick through the paper in order to put her foot on a rung.

The area directly in front of the platform on which some of the spectators were standing was illuminated. Nearby, the man was still unwrapping the paper-covered body. Another man, dressed in pale striped pajamas, pushed a cot covered with a heavy bolster into the light. Taking a small radio from the cot, he plugged it in, switched it on, and got into bed. The radio played quietly.

Then the light near the "North" wall went on, and a girl carried in a large mass of dough, slammed it down on a small table, and began to knead it.

For six minutes these five actions continued simultaneously. The bearded man on the platform opened and closed his portfolio, dropped the sticks, and picked them up, silently mouthed words, set the angled lid of the trash can swinging, and flapped his flippers against the floor. From time to time, the girl kneading dough stopped, climbed on a chair, and screamed at the man on the platform: "Shut up." Her voice was piercing, her tone nasty. "Can't you keep quiet?" Over and over, the second man filled his sack, climbed the ladder and sent an explosion of objects crashing into the white-walled construction. The pajama-clad man tried different stations on the radio. Then he got up and threw back the bolster, revealing the cot filled with sand. Taking a shovel from under the covering, he began to shovel the sand onto the floor. He got back in bed but repeatedly got up to adjust the radio or shovel more sand. Slowly, the tool-decorated girl climbed the ladder. Ten feet above the floor, a long wooden pole, hung with various items of clothing, was fastened to one of the uprights with a single nail. She pulled at the short end of the pole, and the lower end gradually swung up until it was parallel to the floor. With effort, the girl was able to tie it in place. The long piece of wood jutted out, laden with hanging cloth. Over and over, the trombone repeated part of "My Country 'Tis of Thee."

The light over the bed went out, and the man in pajamas pushed it out of sight again. At thirty-second intervals, the people climbing the ladders left, the man on the platform lifted the trash can off and flapped slowly away as the lights went out, and the girl carried the dough away. The trombone stopped. Again the room was dark except for the slowly blinking lips over the central platform.

Several cigarette butts were flashed on the screen. Their ashes swirled and shifted silently. (A fan inside the projector was causing the movement.) Nothing else happened for one minute. Then the image disappeared.

A man walked to the small platform in one corner where bales of newspaper were piled. He switched on a small light over a lectern, then picked up one of the bales and dropped it onto the resonant flooring of the platform. A cloud of white powder swirled up. He moved another bundle of papers, and more white dust rose and drifted in the dim light. (Twenty-five pounds of talcum powder had been donated to the Happening.)

The girl in the yellow dress who had hung the pennants turned on a record player in the corner between the sinks and the ladder. A chorus was heard singing "Onward, Christian Soldiers." Then she lit the moon again, turned on a fan on the small platform in that corner, and began to sing quietly into the microphone along with the record. In her hands, which were behind her back, she had rubber toys that emitted high-pitched squeals as she pressed and released them.

Almost immediately, the light over the blackboard at the opposite side of the room went on. A Negro girl with close-cropped hair sat in a chair reading a newspaper. From time to time, she put the paper over her face or laughed a shrill, quavering laugh. Nearby, two girls were making grotesque faces at each other. They would stop frequently, suddenly covering their faces with their hands. Occasionally one of them would turn, point, and say, "Look over there!" She was not pointing to anything in particular, but the spectators would turn and look.

Only fifteen seconds after the girls were illuminated, the light went on at the end of the room where the pennants had been hung. A rotund man carried in a table and a box of plumber's candles. Inflated balloons of various colors had been attached to the front of his shirt. Setting the table down, he lit the candles one by one, dripped hot wax on the table, and set the candles in the wax so that, when he was finished, twelve candles stood in four rows.

The man who, moments before, had climbed the ladder now moved to almost the same spot with a pail of wet, gray modeling clay. He scooped out a handful of the clay, squeezed it quickly into a ball, and threw it at the pot of artificial flowers that stood just to the right of the blackboard. The projectile passed over the man arranging the candles and splattered against the wall behind the flowers close to the sign which read "SUNSET." Again the man formed a ball of clay and threw it at the flowers. Occasionally he hit them.

A minute and a half after the girl had turned on the record, the light was switched on over the central platform. Three men completely encased in burlap bags made their awkward way onto the stand and began to wrestle, the constantly changing brown masses tumbling over each other. The two red, eighteen-foot-long sausage shapes that hung near the rafters were lowered. Erratically, they dipped and were pulled up again, jerking and swinging above the wrestlers.

At the table filled with candles, the man wearing balloons had set up a mirror, covered his face with lather, and was attempting to shave. As he bent over the candles, the balloons would explode one by one. Above and behind him, the balls of clay flew toward the flowers and splattered against the wall. (The clay frequently embedded itself in the soft composition board, and, since the wall was not cleaned after the earlier performances, it developed a rich mottled texture.) On either side of the blackboard, the two girls continued to make distorted grimaces at each other, suddenly hiding behind their hands. "Look over there!" The third girl sat reading, laughing erratically, covering her face with the paper. On the opposite side of the room, the girl in the frilly yellow dress stood singing "Onward, Christian Soldiers" along with the record, her soft voice amplified over the loudspeaker. The toys behind her back squealed shrilly, and the fan whirred rhythmically from side to side. When the record ended, she started it again. From time to time there would be a loud thump from the corner where the man was rearranging the bales of newspapers, and spectators would turn to see another cloud of white powder rising into the already misty air. In the center of the space, the three brown forms wrestled with each other, and the long, stuffed, red shapes dipped and swung above them.

All the balloons were broken, but the man had succeeded in shaving himself by the time the lights went out. The man with the papers switched off his light, the singer turned off the record, fan, and moon, and all the performers exited, taking their props with them.

Melting ice cubes were projected on the screen by the opaque projector, but a motion picture was also projected on the same screen at the same time. The film showed two teen-agers necking on a couch. There were frequent close-ups of lips, cheeks, kissing. (Originally, Oldenburg had planned to follow one minute of the melting ice with a three-minute film of a girl running, falling, jumping, and rolling in the snow of Washington Park, but the film was lost in the mail. After viewing a lot of footage supplied by a film society at the university, he selected a substitute that was repetitious and essentially physical.) After a minute, the competing image of melting ice cubes went off, and the movie continued to run.

The light over the blackboard went on. The man who had just shaved while leaning across the candles and the man who had thrown the balls of clay at the flowers stepped into the light carrying buckets, jars of paint, and loaves of bread and placed their materials on a table. One carefully wrote a menu item in colored chalk on the board. Perhaps it said, "ham and eggs." The other wiped it out with a sponge from one of the buckets and replaced it with words of his own: "liver and onions" or "mashed potatoes." While one wrote, the other crumbled bread into a bucket and stirred it.

To the left of the platform where the spectators were standing, another light went on. The girl who had shifted the dishes back and forth during the first group of actions set up an easel, a canvas, and arranged oranges into a still-life composition. She began to make a painting of the oranges, but constantly stopped to cut the oranges into sections and rearrange the grouping.

The center light went on, and the man who had arranged the sponges earlier lifted a small table onto the platform and placed a typewriter and a pitcher of water on it. Taking off his shirt, he stood in front of the typewriter and typed slowly and nervously. (During rehearsal he had asked what he should type. Oldenburg said, "Pretend you are writing a ransom note of Bobby Franks," then told the story of how, when he was a newspaper reporter in Chicago, he had gone twice to the bridge in Jackson Park where Leopold and Loeb had thrown the ransom typewriter into the water. Clarence Darrow had promised to reappear at that point

Combination Four: Two men alternately write menu items on the blackboard (George Kokines, Harry Bouras).

on a certain date every year, and the man from Detroit with whom he had made the pact came every year to see if Darrow's spirit would rise from the water. During the performances, the man typed "I have just killed my Grandmother" over and over, but of course the spectators could not read it.) From time to time, the shirtless man poured himself a glass of water, drank it, and returned to the typing.

About thirty seconds after the center light went on—the lights in this segment had been switched on at half-minute intervals—a twelve-year-old girl wearing a patterned sweater, slacks, and ice skates, walked slowly to a white table at the left of the sinks and turned a light on over it. Looking into the mirror over the sinks, she quickly drew a mustache on herself, then sat down looking at the table.

A minute later, the man who had shifted the paper bales walked in quickly and began to smash the table with a small sledge hammer. Over his shirt he wore the top part of a baseball uniform with the words "Immaculate Conception" across the chest. The girl did not move as the table was broken into small pieces.

At the blackboard, the two men were still alternately writing menu items, stirring bread into the pail of water, and wiping out what the other had written. Now they were using watercolor paint and brushes or they merely decorated the board with various patterns of colored chalk, made richer by incomplete erasures and the blurring of the water. At times they pushed each other and clowned for the crowd. (They were both well-known in Chicago as artists.) The girl at the easel continued to paint a still life of the oranges. At the opposite side of the room, the young girl wearing ice skates watched the destruction of the table, and, on the platform in the center, the shirtless man alternately poked at the typewriter and drank water. Above all this, the movie of the young lovers was still being projected. (Plans had been to repeat the short film again, but, since its loss, the longer film would continue throughout the action.)

Again at half-minute intervals, the man with the sledge hammer walked away after piling the pieces of the shattered table out of sight, the two men left the blackboard carrying the buckets and bread, the painter picked up the easel and oranges and left, and the man on the central platform put his shirt back on, set the table to one side, and exited with the typewriter. As each area was vacated, the lights went off except for the light over the young girl in ice skates who still sat in the chair.

Now the projection screen showed the image of fingers. While the fingers changed simple positions, folding and turning over, the girl began to unlace her skates. After one minute, the projector went off, the light went on over the sinks, and the girl who had previously kneaded the dough entered and switched on a vacuum cleaner. The hose had been attached to the exhaust, and she used it to blow white powder from the sinks. It rose in clouds, drifting through the bright areas of light.

The young girl had finished unlacing her skates. She took them off, walked to the mirror, wiped off the mustache she had drawn earlier, and combed her hair. Then she turned on one of the faucets in the sink. Water flowed from the hose that circled and hung in the air. The girl stood and watched the thin stream of water fall nine feet and clatter and splash into a metal washtub. (She was supposed to wash her feet, but she refused to do so.)

As the light was switched on where, forty minutes earlier, the pennants had been hung, the man who had worn the balloons entered in a raincoat and carrying an umbrella. Rubber toys tied under each shoe squealed at every step. When he started to raise the umbrella, balls of crumpled newspaper fell from it. Slowly he walked back and forth, the toys squeaking.

A girl entered and started a record player near the central platform just as the hanging light in the center went on. The record, played at the loudest possible volume, was a popular rock-and-roll vocal called, "Tell Him," and the same recording was now broadcast over the loudspeaker. But the two records were not synchronized: at each moment, two different parts of the same song were heard. The girl disappeared for a moment and returned with two six-foot wooden poles to each of which was attached a stuffed hemisphere of shiny red cloth. Together, the two sections would have formed a heart. As she held one pole in each hand, the red sections stood out at either side of her like rounded wings. Her long, red, taffeta dress, slit up the side, had neither sleeves nor back. She wore gold slippers, a corsage at her waist, earrings, teased hair, and mink eyelashes. She carried a paper bag, which she set to one side, and in her mouth was a large heart-shaped sucker. To the blaring record—"I know something about love . . ."— she began to dance, swaying the red shapes about her, momentarily disappearing behind them, dragging them gracefully behind her on the platform.

To one side, a man the audience had not seen before turned on a small transistor radio and exited. A table to the left of the blackboard had been fitted with a welded metal spit, and when the light over the board went on, the man returned carrying a ham, placed it on the spit, and began to carve it.

Suddenly, although no special area light had been turned on, the two constructions that had remained at either side of the standing segment of the audience—the baby carriage piled with black cardboard boxes and the long rectangular structure of boxes—were smashed together directly in front of the spectators. One man was pushing the baby carriage, and four men, two on either side, carried the other construction like a battering ram. After the collision, both structures backed up and then came forward to crash again.

Again all units of a "combination" were in action. At one side the vacuum cleaner was roaring, blowing white dust into the air, and the young girl who had removed her skates sat on the floor pressing pieces of aluminum foil around her body until she began to resemble a large metal doll. On another side, the man in a rain-coat walked back and forth with squeaking toys tied under his shoes, putting his umbrella up and down, dropping small objects, and bending to retrieve them. On the third side, a ham was being carved and a small radio played quietly. On the fourth side, the two black constructions repeatedly rammed into each other until finally the boxes worked loose or the cords broke and the structures collapsed. And on the center platform, in the glaring, powder-filled light, the girl in the low-cut red dress danced to the blaring rock-and-roll song that was heard simultaneously from two sources. Sometimes she swayed in the center of the heart formed by the red cloth attached to the poles. Sometimes she laid the poles down and danced alone or, taking candy hearts from the bag she had carried on, kissed them and threw them to the spectators. When the record finished, she started it again, and behind the control wall, the same thing happened to the record playing over the loudspeaker.

Six and a half minutes after the first collision of the constructions, all of the area lights went out almost simultaneously except

Combination Five: The girl in red dances on central platform (Pat Oldenburg).

a small bulb near where the young girl sat, carefully covering her-self with aluminum foil. As they had done before, the performers exited in the semidarkness.

The head of a hammer was seen on the projection screen. Slowly it moved back and forth. The young girl finished encasing herself in aluminum foil and sat motionless.

As the five preceding projections had done, this one went off after one minute. The light above the central platform went on. The Negro girl who had sat reading a newspaper earlier entered carrying two boxes. She wore six starched men's shirts, and the layers of white cloth gave her body a bulky appearance. Her legs were bare, and on her feet were black, high-heeled pumps. She set the boxes down and put a record on the record player. Instead of music, sound effects were heard: sirens, animal noises, locomotives. The rope supporting the hanging bunch of men's jackets covered with transparent plastic ran through a pulley fastened to the rafters and down to the central platform where it had been se-cured. The girl unfastened the rope and lowered the jackets until they were two or three feet above the platform. She pushed them back and forth in a wide, swinging arc. She raised and lowered them. Then she fastened the rope again and gracefully moved the two boxes about the rectangular wooden stand. The boxes, painted in the same manner the trash can had been, were white mottled with red, yellow, and blue. About the size of drawers—they were not very tall—the top of one was lined with ties, the top of the other with socks, painted in the same manner as the boxes.

To the right of the standing spectators, five men and a girl, the beams of flashlights shining from their back pockets, were group-ing together in the semidarkness. One of them began to climb across the others as they bent to form a human bridge.

The light went on at the opposite side of the room where the rigid pennants still hung. A man and a girl arranged plates, silver-ware, beer cans, and other objects on a table and sat down opposite each other. The man was the same one who had thrown the clay at the flowers. The girl had danced and distributed candy hearts during the previous set of actions, but she had quickly changed into a simple dress and let her hair down. Some of the objects on the table were "food" made from rubber, straw, broken bottles, and the performers pretended to eat. Then they began to argue, yelling and gesticulating at each other without making a sound.

The noise of objects substituted for the sounds of voices. The man switched on an electric drill. The girl bit into a rubber pork chop, and the toy emitted a high-pitched squeal.

The hanging bulb over the sinks was lit. The man who had shoveled sand from the bed walked in carrying a child's tricycle to which plastic bags filled with variously colored paint had been attached. Crossing to a white panel mounted to the left of the sinks, he pressed the tricycle against it, trapping one of the bags between the board and the metal and finally breaking the bag. Paint splattered over the panel, the tricycle, and the floor. The man turned the tricycle and tried to break another bag. To the right, the girl who had just used the vacuum cleaner began to clean the sink.

In the center of the room, the girl in the bulky white shirts raised and lowered the bunched jackets, swung them back and forth, and shifted the tie and sock boxes. At one side of her, the man and the girl argued in pantomime, the electric drill whining as it bit into the table. (During the second performance, the man crashed

Combination Six: Girl on central platform lowers jackets. Man with tricycle breaks paint-filled bags (Ted Dickerson, Toni Robinson, Martha Ansara).

to the floor. The leg of his chair had been almost sawed through by a spectator who, perhaps misled by the announcement that had listed tools and by the desire to "participate," had brought a saw to the first performance.) Across from them, flashlight beams swung randomly in the darkness as the huddled people crawled over each other. The sinks were being cleaned, and nearby several colors stained the panel as succeeding bags of paint were broken. When all the plastic containers had burst, the man hung the paint-splattered tricycle in the center of the board.

As the other "combinations" had, this series of actions lasted ten minutes from the time the projection went on until the final light went out. Over an hour had passed since the Happening began. The area lights went out in rapid succession, leaving only a small bulb burning near the foil-wrapped girl who still sat motionless on the floor.

A bright light went on in the corner to the right of the standing spectators. A big, powerful man in white overalls, whom the audience had not seen before, set a pot full of earth on a table and struck it with a large sledge hammer, shattering the container with a loud thud and scattering dirt and pottery in all directions. Immediately, fluorescent lights hanging below the rafters were turned on for the first time. In contrast to the yellowish incandescent bulbs, white light now filled the entire hall.

On the opposite side, there was another noise as the man who had been controlling the lights poured a large bag of books over the wall and onto the floor. (At the first performance, he spontaneously yelled, "Merry Christmas!" with his Dutch accent. Oldenburg asked him not to do it again, but he changed his mind after the second performance, and the shouting was heard again on the third night.)

The windows set eight feet above the floor in the "West" wall behind the blackboard were opened from the outside. (At the last performance, one of the large brittle panes broke with a crash.) Ladders were set up, and the heavy oak chairs that had been in the hall when the spectators entered began to be handed through the windows and piled up around the audience. With three men working in the hallway and three in the main room, the chairs passed in quickly.

Behind the low wall against which some of the spectators stood, an arc welder was switched on. Its loud buzz and crackle could be heard and the brilliant flashing light seen above the wall. At the same time, the long fluorescent lights above the spectators began to flicker and blink. (It was at this point that the motorcycle had been used during rehearsal. Roaring through the hallways, it was able to pass completely around the large central room, and the spectators would have been able to follow its progress by its sound and the moving light of its headlight seen through the high windows. As it was, the confusion apparently was contagious. At the third performance, several young children excitedly broke the mirrors hanging on the walls.)

The large, stuffed construction was suddenly lowered from the rafters. Several performers supported it, and the soft mountains of cloth flopped and swayed as the people moved under it. (Plans had been to drop the "airplane" on the spectators, but after a "live" test during rehearsal, the procedure was changed.)

Two performers (one of them was Oldenburg) walked to the central platform and began to toss handfuls of dried lima beans over the audience. They struck the spectators and rattled onto the floor. Then the two reached under the platform, pulled out several bundles of folded muslin, and, holding one end, threw them out over the seated spectators. The cloth, its movement intermittently illuminated and "frozen" by the blinking lights, unfolded in the air, falling over the heads of the watching people. Soon the entire seated section of the audience was covered. The huge stuffed airplane was thrown onto a group of spectators. When Oldenburg walked off the platform, the lights ceased their blinking, the movement of the chairs stopped, and the arc welder was turned off. The Happening was over, but some of the spectators still struggled to get out from under the muslin.

AUTOBODYS / *the script*

Poem One

    0 Lloyd drives in from NE
Maneuvers
Stops center facing south
Sits

1–5 Pat enters from NW
Walks to trunk
Opens trunk
Takes out milk bottles

Milk bottles out, Lloyd drives forward
Stops
Sits

Pat leaves field

Bottles isolated

———————

Lloyd backs up to bottles
Pat returns with bucket
Uncaps bottles
Empties milk in bucket
Opens trunk
Puts empty bottles in trunk

Pat walks off field
Spills milk as she walks

Lloyd drives forward
Makes clockwise circle in reverse *twice*
Stops center, facing south
Parks middle south edge on *diagonal* (SE)
Gets out of car
Locks doors on both sides
Walks to center
Returns to car
Opens trunk
Breaks glass in trunk
Closes trunk

Walks off field following milk path (NW)
Smears milk with his shoes

5 Concrete Mixer enters from center north
Drives to point marked on field
Stops
Turns on drum

Jim and Tom enter from NE with hoses and brushes
Wash Concrete Mixer tires both sides of truck

---

6 Drum stops
Jim and Tom continue to wash to end of poem

Pat enters from NW

Walks over field to Lloyd's car
Lights traffic flares
Places flares in semicircle around back of car

Johnny drives in sound truck from north beside CM
Maneuvers, placing sound truck Mercedes close to side of
    CM
Stops
Turns on sound track
Sound track remains on for *five* min. One past end of poem

7   Lloyd enters from NE
Walks to car
Unlocks car
Leans in and turns on radio (or phonograph)
Locks car
Walks back and off NE

---

10   POEM ONE END

Poem Two

APPROX. MIN.

Sound track plays one min. after end of Poem One

0   When track ends Santos enters field on motorbike from NE
Circles field slowly twice
Maneuvers to stop "S" center (leaves room for Dejon)
    facing south
Kick down
Guns motor
Sits motionless

2–10   Dejon drives on field from NW to N center
Stops car
Fires flashbulbs in car
Works out of car without opening doors over back
Fires flashbulbs
Lies down all sides car

Presses against car
Fires flashbulbs under car
etc.

3-9   Ken and Richard enter field from NW
With ice cakes on dollys and creeper
Lift Santos off motorbike
Lay Santos on creeper
Shove Santos on creeper into field

Santos rigid in bike position
Bike continues to run

Ken and Richard shove ice dollys into field
Ice remains to end of *all* poems, melting
Ken and Richard return to NW for sheet of clear plastic
    and laundry cord
Walk to Lloyd's car
Tie Lloyd's car in plastic

Return from time to time to shove dollys or Santos

---

9   Carwash Mannekin brought in by Tony from NE
Mannekin brought to SE corner of Concrete Mixer and
    turned on by Tony
Tony returns to NE entrance

Ken and Richard, finishing tying up Lloyd's car, replace
    Santos on motorbike
Ken and Richard leave by NW

Santos kick up
Rides off NE

Ken and Richard off field, *taking creeper with them*

10 Dejon drives off field to SW corner
Parks car
Locks car

Dejon waits by car

POEM TWO END

Poem Three

20

APPROX. MIN.

0 Johnny drives Mercedes sound truck forward
Sound track, for ten minutes

———————

* From all directions players appear.
NE — Lloyd, Jim, Santos
NW — Ken, Richard, Pat
SE — Lori
SW — Dejon, Rolf, Judy, Nancy
Walk slowly in individual patterns
Indifferent to one another
Diagram of path and tempo in imagination of each one
Effect of scattered particles.   Autobodys

———————

1 Charlie drives station wagon from SE into center through
pedestrians
Slowly with little starts and stops and little honks
Debby inside
Debby moves around showing herself and parts of herself

Charlie leaves car (joins pedestrians)

* Pedestrians positions at beginning of poem:

Debby opens doors
Pedestrians converge on station wagon

_____

Pedestrians press close to station wagon
Take out seats
Walk through station wagon
All slowly
Join mass to station wagon mass

_____

5   Johnny gets out of Mercedes sound truck and starts to push
       it from behind
   Tom enters from NE
   Tom pushes sound truck from front against Johnny
   Continues to end of poem

_____

Pedestrians resume form of scattered particles
Debby closes doors
Locks doors
Turns on radio (controls station & loudness)
Smokes much
Moves around, as before

Debby honks horn (1st time)
Pedestrians fall to ground motionless
Debby honks horn (2nd time)
Pedestrians change lying positions
Debby honks horn (3rd time)
Pedestrians get up. Resume scattered form

Debby honks horn (4th time)
Pedestrians converge on locked station wagon
Rock wagon. From side and from front and back

Debby honks horn (5th time)
Pedestrians leave field (return to entrances)

8 Tony enters from NE with bucket of blue suds and yellow
     sponge
   Walks to wagon and washes it, part by part
   Debby still inside

10 Tony pushes station wagon covered with suds (Debby in-
     side) off field diagonal to E middle
   Tony leaves NE with bucket and sponge

POEM THREE END

Poem Four

30

APPROX. MIN.

0 Dejon on field from SW pushing Rolf as whitebag Santa in
     wheelchair

From NW, Howell on field in Dauphine, radio on
Dauphine aimed at Dejon
Dejon sidesteps
Aimed again. Continuing

Rolf: business
Dejon: business   to end of poem
(Jim: business)

---

1 Richard drives Microbus on field from NE, carrying tires,
     tubes, & Pat
   Turns so that back faces center (diagonal, SW)
   Pat presses out tubes
   Richard unlatches truck and tubes spring out
   Richard gets back in driver seat
   Drives Microbus forward
   Stops

Pat unloads white and red tires on silver ground
Richard drives Microbus forward again
Stops
Pat jumps off

Richard drives Microbus to NE section
Parks
Richard off NE

Pat builds nativity scene at NW corner of Cement Mixer

---

5   Lloyd drives Willys in from SW
Parks in SE area perpendicular to Charlie's station wagon
Leaves car. Off SW

Judy and Nancy from SW with muslin bandages
Bind up Willys
Sponge Willys with red
Climb on top Willys

Judy: business
Nancy: business
Remain on car until end of all poems

---

6   Cement Mixer drum starts turning
Turns until covered in Poem Five

---

10   Pat leaves field (cues end) NW

Dejon leaves field SW

Rolf is left tied near W edge (south section) until end of all
   poems

Jim parks Dauphine with radio on, diagonal to W edge
(north section)
Jim leaves NW

POEM FOUR END

Poem Five

40

APPROX. MIN.

0 Ken and Richard on field from NW with black plastic sheets
Give sheets to Judy and Nancy on top of Willys

Judy and Nancy unfold sheets

———————

Ken and Richard return to NW
Get aluminum ladders, one tall, one short
Place ladder next to Concrete Mixer

———————

2 Concrete Mixer (drum turning) advances slightly toward
center
Ken and Richard move ladders

———————

Lori skates in (candy bar and business. bike?)

———————

Tom and Jim turn water on in hose and wash asphalt of field
Keep it wet and glistening

———————

Ken and Richard to Judy and Nancy to get unfolded plastic
sheets
Take to Concrete Mixer
Cover Mixer, using ladders (and poles)

Mixer drum stops on being covered
Cords thrown over and plastic tied on

_____

6   Daggett drives black Cadillac convertible from SE corner,
      behind parked cars, up W. lane, behind parked cars
      and on field via NW
Into center
Tom and Jim clear path for Cadillac

_____

Spectators asked to turn on car radios

Daggett leaves car. Motor running. leaves SW
Bobby leaves car. Off NE

_____

10 Spectators asked to turn off car radios (by Claes)

_____

Jim's Dauphine remains playing radio

_____

Judy and Nancy off SE

Debby out of wagon and off SE

_____

Lori pushes bound Rolf off SW
Walks to Concrete Mixer
Climbs up on fender
Climbs down from fender
Off NW

POEM FIVE END

AUTOBODYS / *the production*

CLAES OLDENBURG PRESENTED *Gayety* in Chicago in February of 1963. In April of the same year, he created a Happening which he called *Stars* for the Washington Gallery of Modern Art. When he moved to Venice, California, a few months later, he decided to complete a transcontinental trilogy by doing a Happening in Los Angeles. It would be called *Autobodys* and would be based upon that basic element of Californian life: the automobile. The concept was already clear in his mind when, on November 22, 1963, President Kennedy was assassinated. Certain ideas were intensified by the television images of slowly moving black automobiles in the funeral procession.

Even before finding the parking lot which he knew he would need in order to present the Happening, Oldenburg did some "sketching." He drove his old Chevrolet to a parking area near the shore in Venice and stopped it in various spots, "composing" it with the edges of the rectangular lot in somewhat the same way a line in a painting is composed in relationship to the edges of the canvas. He drove at various speeds. He backed the car around in circles. Sometimes he got out of the car and lay down on the asphalt surface.

A parking lot behind the American Institute of Aeronautics and Astronautics in Los Angeles was rented, and performances were scheduled for Monday and Tuesday evenings, the 9th and 10th of December, 1963. Since the lot would only be available for rehearsal on the Sunday afternoon before the first performance, another location had to be found for preliminary work. Allowing the usual week for preparation, the first meeting of participants was held at the Venice parking area where Oldenburg had done his "sketching." It was evening. He experimented with the cars moving at various speeds with their headlights on and with people, illuminated by the headlights, walking across the open space of

272

the lot. But, as it often does in Venice, a heavy fog rolled in from the Pacific and brought an end to the work.

The second and third rehearsals were held on a third-floor parking lot on Wilshire Boulevard in Los Angeles. During the first meeting there, Oldenburg was concerned not only with "auditioning" prospective performers but with "auditioning" automobiles as well. Only white (or near-white) and black cars would be used. He was concerned with body style, age, size and general effect. (Originally he had intended to list the wheeled "performers" along with the human members of the cast.) He had the people walk around, through and over his old Chevrolet. He had everyone drive around the lot in their cars until a jam formed. Horns honked enthusiastically. When the police arrived to investigate the noise, they found Oldenburg standing in the middle of the lot directing the traffic.

Oldenburg spent the days driving around Los Angeles looking for things that would be right for the Happening. One day he saw a large mannequin of a man in a white uniform whose flapping right arm waved passing motorists in to have their cars washed. On enquiring if he could rent the figure, he was sent to a man near Venice who made the mannequins. The photograph on the advertising circular showed a long line of mannequins available for rental. The mannequin-maker conducted Oldenburg to a garage behind his house, and the door was unlocked. There stood a single figure: white trousers, white shirt, black bow tie—and a female head with blond, bobbed hair. The man offered to change the shirt to something more feminine, but Oldenburg wanted it just the way it was. In leasing it, he had to sign a guarantee that he would take it inside if it rained and that he would not let juveniles tamper with it.

Another day he left his studio in Venice and saw twenty huge, white concrete-mixer trucks lined up outside. He had thought of using a white garbage truck in the Happening, but now he changed his mind. When they learned that the presentation would be covered by the press, the company agreed to send a truck and driver to each performance.

Even at the last moment, changes were made. When Oldenburg went to buy ice for the first performance, the salesman asked him whether he wanted cakes or cubes. He had not previously considered using ice cubes, but now he thought he could find some way to include them. In addition to the cakes of ice, he bought one hundred pounds of cubes. As the salesman carried them out, he tripped, spilling the cubes into the street. They glittered in the light of passing headlights and snapped through the air as tires passed over them. Oldenburg felt as if he were watching a preview of the Happening.

The Monday evening of the first performance was cool and quite windy. The spectators drove to the American Institute of Aeronautics and Astronautics on Beverly Boulevard and turned into an unpaved alley at the side of the large flat-roofed building. When they arrived at the parking lot in the rear, they were met by one of the four people who were directing the parking. Especially with the scattered early arrivals, the "attendants" sometimes motioned the cars forward and back or asked them to turn their lights off and then on again in what, it soon became apparent, was non-functional activity. The visitors' automobiles were carefully positioned side by side to form the perimeter of a rectangle about fifteen cars long and nine cars wide with openings at each corner. They faced each other across the empty central space. Those arriving later were formed into a second row behind the others.

Programs were distributed. Five parts (called merely "Part One," "Part Two," etc.) were listed, preceded by "Parking" and followed by "Unparking." The names of twenty "players" were arranged alphabetically. It was stated that "the composition continues without a break about an hour," and thanks was given to the Blue Diamond Company for the concrete mixer.

The lot was surfaced in black asphalt. Two white lines ran parallel to the sides, and shorter lines slanted across them to indicate individual parking spaces. The white patterns—looking like the skeletons of fish—are common in large parking areas. In the center of the north side of the rectangle, the huge, white concrete-mixer truck loomed above the private cars, while behind it, perhaps a hundred yards farther north, the large windows of the institute glowed brightly. To the south, somewhat farther away across an open field dominated by an oil well, was a drive-in movie theatre, its screen set at such an angle that the film could be seen from the parking lot where the Happening was taking place. All around the lot, the lights of Los Angeles could be seen, yet, because it was some distance from a main street, the area had an intimate, isolated quality.

The permanent lights that lit the area for night parking were turned off. Some of the spectators had gotten out of their cars (as Oldenburg had intended), but most of them—even those in the back seats—remained seated. A tall man in a long white coat and a blue hat (Claes Oldenburg), one of those who had directed the parking, began to walk around the rectangle of automobiles, asking the drivers to turn on their engines and their lights. Car by car, the headlights switched on, illuminating the central area. Motors roared into action and settled into a steady hum. After a few minutes (Oldenburg was checking with the performers in the "offstage" areas at each corner of the rectangle), the man in the white coat walked to the north end and stood talking with a man in a black suit.

A white, four-door Plymouth sedan drove slowly out from the northwest corner of the rectangle. Pieces of black paper had been fastened on the rear and side windows, partially obscuring the view. The driver, who was the only occupant, drove backward and forward as if trying to park in a very exact spot. Finally the car stopped in a central position at the south end of the space, with its trunk pointing toward the northwest corner.

After a moment, a girl in a black sweater, tight white slacks and high-heeled shoes walked slowly in from that corner and crossed straight to the Plymouth. Very deliberately, she opened the trunk and took out five full milk bottles capped with black tape (the white liquid was actually water-soluble paint) and set them carefully on the asphalt. The Plymouth moved forward several feet and stood with the motor running, wisps of white fumes curling out from its exhaust and being whipped away by the wind. Without hurrying, the girl walked back to the corner from which she had appeared and returned carrying a brand-new silver bucket. Again crossing to the bottles, she emptied them one by one into the pail. Then she carried the empty bottles to the Plymouth, raised the lid of the trunk, put the bottles in and closed the trunk. As she carried the bucket back to the place from which she had started, the liquid spilled out at each step and left a glistening white trail behind her.

The Plymouth started to move again. After maneuvering into position, it made two slow clockwise circles in reverse, then stopped in approximately the same place it had been before. The man who had been driving got out, moved around the car, locking all four doors, and walked off into the same direction the girl had gone.

At about that moment, the man in the white coat who had asked the spectators to turn on their headlights and motors walked to a spot directly in front of the concrete mixer and motioned it forward. The huge machine had only gone four feet when he signaled it to stop. He had it brought forward another foot. Then he called up to the driver to start the drum, and the huge cylinder began to turn quietly.

The driver of the Plymouth had not walked very far when he stopped as if he had forgotten something, returned to the car, and opened the trunk. Leaning in, he smashed some glass with a hammer. Then he closed the trunk and walked off along the white trail left by the girl, rubbing at the liquid with his shoes as he went.

When the glass was smashed in the trunk of the Plymouth, two men entered from the northeast corner of the rectangle, carrying buckets. Using large hand brushes they scrubbed the wheels of the concrete-mixer truck while the large drum turned above them. About one minute after it had started, the man in the white coat called for the drum to be switched off. The men with the brushes continued washing, soapy water running over the dark asphalt.

The girl entered again and walked once more to the Plymouth. She was carrying twelve traffic flares which she lit one at a time and placed in a semicircle around the rear of the car. They burned brightly with a cold pink light.

While the girl was lighting the flares, the driver of a small black Mercedes, which had been parked just to the west of the concrete mixer, moved it forward so that it was close to the large truck and jutted out a few feet farther into the space within the rectangle. The side windows of the car were covered with silver paper, and on the roof was a loudspeaker. A tape recording composed of several brief dramatic passages of music was broadcast. Maximum volume was used, but the wind sometimes carried the sound away. (The recording had been made from the sound tracks of old movies as they played on television. Most of the short segments were taken from *Made for Each Other* while others included unintelligible fragments of dialogue from a Mickey Rooney film. The tape formed a loop that would repeat automatically when it was completed.

Poem One: Girl lights flares. View is toward the American Institute of Aeronautics and Astronautics. Mercedes and concrete-mixer truck are in background. Plymouth is at right (Pat Oldenburg).

The driver of the Plymouth returned to his car, unlocked the door, turned on a transistor radio inside, locked the door again and walked off. When the girl finished lighting the flares, she also exited. Dramatic crescendos and "climax" music were still coming from the loudspeaker of the Mercedes, and those nearby could hear the radio inside the Plymouth. Five minutes after it began, the tape was switched off.

A motorcycle entered from the northeast corner and traveled very slowly around the rectangle in a clockwise direction. After making two circuits, the driver, who wore white pants, a white canvas jacket, and a white crash helmet, stopped in the center facing south, put down the kick stand, and sat motionless, the motor roaring. (Once while the motorcycle was "onstage," a motorcycle also appeared on the screen of the drive-in movie to the south.)

A blond girl drove a white Jaguar convertible with its top down into the performance area. Moving to a point behind the motorcycle, she maneuvered her car violently forward and backward, starting and stopping suddenly. Then she parked it and squirmed out feetfirst over the trunk. She was wearing a loose white blouse, white slacks and low black boots, and she carried a small camera with a flash attachment. As she crawled out of and around the Jaguar, she would occasionally fire off a flashbulb or, reaching inside the car, ring a bell with a bright, clear sound.

About a minute after the white Jaguar had driven in, two men in black plastic raincoats walked into the area from the same entrance at the northwest corner, each of them pulling a cake of ice on a dolly. One of the men carried a "creeper" or small, padded wooden frame with casters that service station attendants use to get under automobiles easily. They crossed to the motionless white figure on the motorcycle, lifted the rigid man off his machine, and placed him on his back on the creeper. Then they shoved it, rolling the creeper and its human cargo—still in a seated position but lying on his back—ten or fifteen feet away.

The two men in black raincoats began to push the dollies with the melting cakes of ice randomly about the space. Each would shove the dolly, walk until he caught up with it, and then shove it again. At the same time the blond girl continued to move about the white Jaguar, intermittently firing flashbulbs and ringing the bell.

The two men walked to the northwest corner of the playing area, returned with a large sheet of semitransparent plastic and some laundry line, and began to cover the white Plymouth that stood with its doors locked and a radio playing inside at the south side of the space. The reddish-white flares still burned brightly in a semicircle around the rear of the car, gradually turning to a gray ash that was blown away. The stiff wind made their job difficult, but finally the men tied the billowing plastic in place over the automobile.

From the northeast corner, the tall white car-wash mannequin with a woman's head on the white-uniformed body of a service station attendant was wheeled in and positioned to the east of the

Poem Two: Motorcycle rider on creeper. Girl with camera by Jaguar. Plastic-covered Plymouth in background (Santos Zuniga, Dejon Greene).

concrete mixer. The battery was switched on and the right forearm began to flap back and forth.

The two men in black lifted the still-rigid figure of the motorcyclist and placed him back on his machine, the motor of which was still running. He came to life, raised the stand, and drove slowly around the rectangle, exiting at the southwest corner. As he drove off, one of the men in black picked up the creeper, and the both left the area. The blond girl got into the Jaguar, drove it to the corner where the motorcycle had just gone out, parked the car, locked it, and walked off.

A moment after the motorcyclist disappeared, the black Mercedes that was parked beside the concrete mixer pulled forward ten or fifteen feet. Now the tiny car was clearly separated from the huge truck. The continuous tape that had been broadcast earlier was turned on and again the collage of dramatic music from motion-picture sound tracks was heard over the loudspeaker.

Performers entered from all four corners of the rectangle. Some the spectators had seen before: there were the two men in black raincoats, the girl in white slacks and black sweater, the blond girl in white. Others had not appeared previously. All were dressed in white, black or a combination of the two colors. Each at his own rate, they walked randomly about the area, crossing and recrossing the space independently of each other.

A black Buick station wagon drove in from the southeast corner. It moved slowly through the walking people, stopping and starting, honking occasionally at the performers who paid no attention to it, and stopped somewhat west of the center of the space. The man who was driving got out, plugged in a heavy electric cord that lay on the asphalt, and joined the walkers. A cold white fluorescent light went on inside the station wagon. A girl in black slacks and a white jersey sweater could be seen moving about, smoking elaborately, briefly reading a newspaper, making impish faces at the spectators. (Oldenburg had wanted to dress her in a white rabbit costume with long ears, but could not rent the outfit in time.) After a while (when she felt it was the proper moment), she opened all of the doors. The walking performers moved toward the wagon and gathered around it. Groping around inside, they began to pull out three or four ice cubes at a time, scattering them in all directions. Soon the area nearby was covered with cubes of ice that shone with the reflected light of the spectators' headlights.

When the performers converged on the station wagon, the driver of the Mercedes got out and began to push it forward and then back a few feet at a time. The music could still be heard from its loudspeaker.

The girl in the station wagon closed the doors, and the other performers again dispersed into their random pattern of walking, some of them kicking the cubes of ice as they went. Again the whole area was filled with scattered people moving in various directions. The radio of the station wagon was turned on and off several times, its sound welling up suddenly and quickly dying away. Illuminated by the fluorescent light, the girl inside energetically puffed a cigarette, filling the rectangular volume of the Buick with smoke. She honked the horn: the walking people fell to the ground and lay still. Perhaps half a minute later, she honked

Poem Three: Performers fall among scattered ice cubes.

it again: the people changed position, twisting around and turning over. She honked the horn a third time: the performers got up
and resumed their independent walking. The fourth time she blew
the horn, the scattered people again closed in on the station
wagon. They began to rock it—first from side to side and then
from back to front. The girl blew the horn a fifth time, and the
performers walked away, exiting at the corners from which they
had entered.

A man wearing a black plastic fedora and one of the black
plastic raincoats appeared from the northeast entrance carrying
a bucket. He crossed to the black station wagon and began to
wash it with a large sponge. The water was blue. First he washed
the fenders, then the windows. The fluorescent light inside shone
through the bluish suds as they ran slowly down to form glistening pools on the asphalt. When he had finished washing the win-

dows, the man disconnected the fluorescent light and pushed the Buick off as the girl inside steered.

A whitish Volkswagen pickup truck appeared from the northeast. In the open body of the truck, which was piled full, was the girl in the black sweater and tight white slacks who had carried the "milk" and lit the flares early in the Happening. The truck stopped near the concrete mixer and the mannequin. Suddenly the sides and the back of the truck fell down (a switch in the cab had released them), and inner tubes sprang out and rolled in all directions. Tires wrapped in white, blue and red plastic tape and tumbleweeds, which were immediately caught by the wind, fell to the asphalt. The girl finished unloading the truck. She lifted down a five-foot-square rubber mat, two tall rectangular mirrors hinged back to back to form an inverted V, a metal sign used by the city on road construction projects, various smaller items and whatever inner tubes and wrapped tires had not fallen out when the sides were dropped. The truck drove off.

A shiny chromium wheelchair was pushed in from the southwest corner by a man in a dark golf cap. In the chair sat another man, a roll of white cloth tied on top of his bandaged head and white muslin rolls held in his cloth-covered hands and placed on top of his feet. The man in the golf cap untied the roll on the other's head, and the seated man snapped his head forward. The cloth, one end of which encased his head, fell to the ground and unrolled. He threw the cloth in his hands out to the side, and it unrolled in the air. He kicked his feet and sent the white rolls that were attached to them spinning out across the black asphalt. His head, hands and feet had been inserted into tubes of muslin eighteen feet long and now the tubes lay reaching out around him in five directions. The man in the golf cap began to straighten them out and arrange them so that they lay parallel to the white lines painted on the parking lot. As soon as he was finished, the man in the wheelchair stood up and walked away, destroying the arrangement. The wind flapped the long white streamers. When he stopped and lay down, the other man rushed to align them again.

The girl with the pile of materials laid out the silver-colored rubber mat. Then she arranged the other items on or near it. The mirrors stood in the middle. Inner tubes and wrapped tires were placed one by one. When the sign was set upright, a light in it began to blink: "Careful! Thank you," the sign read. The girl occasionally interrupted her construction project to plug or unplug a small, loud electric siren which she alternated with a tiny electric light that lay on the asphalt. She also decorated some of the items with a spray can of artificial Christmas "snow" and, using individual stencils, spray-painted six-inch letters on the tubes, tires and mirror. (Directions were to paint only three intentionally confusing pairs of words: "gas war," "free glass," and "three gals.")

The plastic-wrapped Plymouth and the white Jaguar were still within the rectangle. The large white concrete mixer and the black Mercedes with the loudspeaker on its roof had been moved out from the north side. To the east stood the tall mannequin mechanically gesturing with its right arm, while farther toward the center the girl worked on her construction. The chrome wheelchair, the ice on the two dollies and the scattered ice cubes reflected the light from the surrounding automobiles.

Poem Four: Building the construction (Pat Oldenburg).

Julian Wasser

A girl wearing a black coat with a fur collar pushed a wire shopping cart onto the south side of the rectangle. She was followed by a man driving a small, black four-door Dauphine. The girl took a white oilcloth rectangle from the cart, set it down, laid out place settings with silverware and metal pizza plates, added slices of bread and pushed the cart a short distance away to repeat the process. As soon as she left, the Dauphine, which had been slowly moving around the activities in the performance area, drove over the "picnic," crushing it. Each time the girl completed an arrangement, the black Dauphine drove over it.

A Willys station wagon appeared at the northeast and threaded its way carefully through the confusion to the west side, where the driver parked it and walked away. Two girls dressed entirely in white, one with a white band around her hair and the other with a white kerchief over her head, brought out a long piece of

Poem Four: The cloth tubes attached to the man from the wheelchair are arranged parallel to white lines. Willys station wagon, concrete mixer, Dauphine, mannequin, and construction in background (Rolf Nelson, Tom Etherton).

Julia

muslin sheeting and wrapped it over, around, and under the station wagon. When the boxlike body of the Willys was draped with the cloth, the girls walked off for a moment and returned with a circular mirror, long corrugated aluminum sheets and stainless-steel rectangles. The shiny aluminum was twisted against the station wagon and the bent pieces left lying on the asphalt. The girls went off again and came back with one of the brand-new metal pails and two pies with thick meringue topping. Using sponges, they splotched the cloth wrapping with rose-colored paint. Then they climbed up on the flat roof of the station wagon where they ate the pies, used the mirror and stainless-steel rectangles to reflect each other's images and those of surrounding activities, and waved rather mechanically to the spectators (Oldenburg told them to wave as if they were on a Rose Bowl float).

Four separate activities were now going on within the rectangle of automobiles. At the north the girl was arranging the tires, tubes and tumbleweed on the square mat and alternating a loud siren with a small electric light. Nearby the two girls in white had climbed on top of the Willys station wagon. In the south and east of the space, the small black Dauphine continued to drive over the pizza-plate "picnic" settings as soon as they were completed. And in the center and west the man with long streamers trailing from his head, hands, and feet intermittently lay still while the man in the golf cap carefully arranged the strips of cloth parallel to the white lines of the parking lot; then he got up and walked around, destroying all of the work of the other.

The concrete mixer was moved four or five feet farther forward, and the drum was turned on. A few minutes later, the girl had finished her construction. She lit three flares, placed them around it and walked off. The drum stopped turning. The driver of the Dauphine parked it, turned the radio on, locked the doors, raised the hood and walked away. The "bandaged" man returned to the wheelchair and was tied into it with the long white strips by the man in the golf cap. A connection was made, and thirty-five Christmas-tree lights that were hung on the back of the wheelchair lit up.

The two men in black raincoats, who had removed the rigid motorcyclist from his machine in an earlier part of the Happening, carried aluminum ladders, large black plastic sheets and laundry line to the concrete mixer and began to wrap it with the help of

Julian

Poem Five: The two girls on the wrapped Willys can be seen above the construction. In foreground are two crushed "picnics." Concrete mixer and man washing asphalt, center. Girl on roller skates and mannequin, right (Tom Etherton, Laurie Weber).

the man in the white coat. As they worked, the wind billowed the plastic.

A blond girl on roller skates entered from the southeast corner. She wore black tights and a simple white dress that left her arms and shoulders bare. She skated slowly, tentatively and without expression about the space, eating candy.

The driver of the Mercedes was using number stencils and spray paint to make signs indicating amounts of money. "$1078," $455," "$2459," they might read. Sometimes he sprayed the numbers directly on the asphalt. Sometimes he used cardboard and propped the signs against the car.

The man in the golf cap began wetting the asphalt with water from a long hose. As he moved around the rectangle of cars, he asked the spectators to turn on their radios, and some of them complied.

A long black 1964 Cadillac convertible rolled slowly in from the southeast corner and stopped in the center. In the rear seat was a girl in a black crepe evening dress. The Mercedes pulled forward to a spot about twenty feet away and the man who was riding in it stepped out and held the rear door open. The girl got out of the Cadillac, took a few steps toward the Mercedes and curtsied. She walked a few more steps and slowly turned around. During her stately, detached passage to the other car she paused every few feet to curtsy, bow or turn around. She entered the Mercedes, the door was closed behind her, and the car moved off at the same corner from which the Cadillac had entered. The man with the hose, the two girls on top of the station wagon, and the blond girl on roller skates had all disappeared. The driver of the Cadillac got out, closed the door, and walked off, leaving the engine running.

When the permanent lights of the parking lot were switched on, indicating the end of the performance, the rectangle contained six automobiles: the Plymouth wrapped in plastic, the white Jaguar, the Willys station wagon wrapped in cloth, the Mercedes, the Dauphine with its hood up, and the Cadillac. The white concrete mixer had been covered with black plastic sheets. The cluster of tires, tubes, mirrors and sign was illuminated by flares. The man wrapped in white cloth sat motionless in the wheelchair decorated with glowing Christmas-tree lights. Throughout the area the asphalt glistened from the hosing it had received and from the water of the melting ice.

On the evening of the second performance, the wind, which had caused some difficulty in wrapping the automobiles and concrete mixer, had stopped. It was very cold and still. But things did not go as smoothly as they had the first night. Among other things, the Cadillac did not arrive. Instead, the girl in the black evening gown walked in carrying a four-foot ice-cream bar made of painted vinyl and foam rubber and left it in the center before getting into the Mercedes.

When the Happening ended, two or three cars were stalled because of the drain on their batteries and one car boiled over. The "unparking" section listed in the program was not directed.

Julian

Poem Five: Girl in evening gown crosses from the Cadillac, right, to the Mercedes, center (Laurie Weber, John Weber, Bobbie Neiman).

The spectators competed for places in the line of traffic and moved away just as they would have done from a baseball game or a drive-in movie.